The Library as Place in California

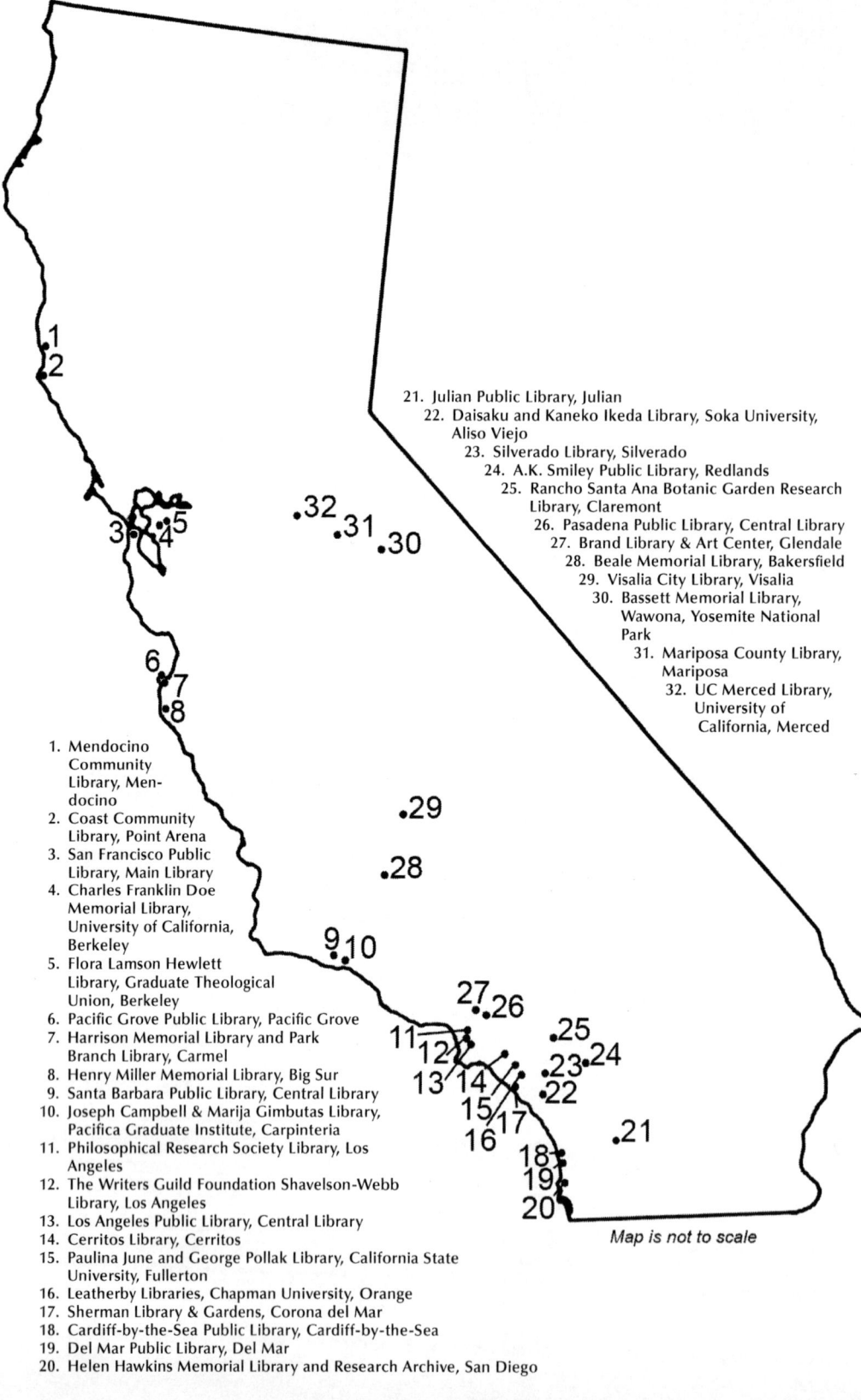

The Library as Place in California

Stacy Shotsberger Russo

McFarland & Company, Inc., Publishers
Jefferson, North Carolina, and London

Frontispiece: The libraries included in this book.

Photographs by William Russo.

LIBRARY OF CONGRESS CATALOGUING-IN-PUBLICATION DATA

Russo, Stacy Shotsberger, 1970–
The library as place in California / Stacy Shotsberger Russo.
  p.   cm.
Includes bibliographical references and index.

ISBN 978-0-7864-3194-6
softcover : 50# alkaline paper ∞

1. Libraries — California.
2. Library buildings — California.
I. Title.
Z733.C2R87 2008   027.0794 — dc22   2007050425

British Library cataloguing data are available

©2008 Stacy Shotsberger Russo. All rights reserved

No part of this book may be reproduced or transmitted in any form or by any means, electronic or mechanical, including photocopying or recording, or by any information storage and retrieval system, without permission in writing from the publisher.

On the cover: The reference wing at the A. K. Smiley Public Library (photo by William Russo); background texture ©2008 PhotoDisc

Manufactured in the United States of America

McFarland & Company, Inc., Publishers
Box 611, Jefferson, North Carolina 28640
www.mcfarlandpub.com

For my parents
Rena and Dave Shotsberger

A deep human need exists for associations with significant places.
— E. Relph in *Place and Placelessness*

Acknowledgments

Shortly after beginning this book, I realized, once again, that I am a member of a great profession. The library directors, librarians, and library staff of each library included on the following pages responded, often enthusiastically, to my inquiries and provided exceptional assistance. My requests for photography within the interior of the buildings were met with similar enthusiasm. I was particularly impressed by the librarians at the busier libraries who came to work early or stayed late to allow my husband to take photographs without impacting the library users. It was clear that everyone included within this book shares a passion for their profession and for the libraries where they are employed. I would like to individually acknowledge those who graciously offered their time and assistance: Blair Whittington and Alyssa Resnick (Brand Library & Art Center); Karen Pedersen (The Writers Guild Foundation Shavelson-Webb Library); Stanley Strauss (Cerritos Library); Charlene Baldwin (Leatherby Libraries, Chapman University); Maryann Hight (Daisaku and Kaneko Ikeda Library, Soka University); Dr. William O. Hendricks (Sherman Library & Gardens); Janice Jones and Diana Lamb (A.K. Smiley Public Library); Wynne Weiss (San Diego County Library Headquarters); Gretchen Schmidt (Del Mar Public Library, San Diego County Library); Jon F. Noland (Julian Public Library, San Diego County Library); Patty Lindberg (Rancho Santa Ana Botanic Garden Research Library); Faith Niles (Cardiff-by-the-Sea Public Library, San Diego County Library); Anne Connor (Los Angeles Public Library, Central Library); Dan McLaughlin (Pasadena Public Library, Central Library); Ruth Loc (Silverado Library); Nila Stearns (Beale Memorial Library); Mike Drake (Visalia City Library); Virginia Blackburn (Bassett Memorial Library); Jacqueline M. Dodd Meriam (Mariposa County Library); Sara Davidson and Bruce Miller (Merced Library); Richard Buchen (Joseph Campbell & Marija Gimbutas Library, Pacifica Graduate Institute); Denise Sallee (Henry Meade Williams Local History Room, Carmel); Carol L. Keator and Jace Turner (Santa Barbara Public Library); Magnus Toren and Keely Richter (Henry Miller Memorial Library); Ellen Gill Pastore and Jean Chapin (Pacific Grove Public Library); Robert Benedetto, Clay Edward Dixon, Lucinda Glenn, and Caryl Woulfe (Flora Lamson Hewlett Library, Graduate Theological Union); Imani Abalos and Isabel Stirling (Doe Memorial Library, University of California

Berkeley Library); Karen Strauss (San Francisco Public Library, Main Library); Daniel Driver (Mendocino Community Library); Maja D'Aoust (Philosophical Research Society); Sarah Williams (Helen Hawkins Memorial Library and Research Archive and the Women's History Museum and Educational Center); Terra Black, Sue Halderman, and Alice Woodward (Coast Community Library); and Sharon Perry (University Archives and Special Collections, The Paulina June and George Pollak Library, California State University, Fullerton).

I would also like to thank the following individuals: Laurie Putnam, my former professor at San Jose State University School of Library and Information Science, who provided recommendations and guidance during the early stages of this project and my brother David Shotsberger who had the excellent idea to structure my book by geographical region. A special thanks is also due to Kelly Donovan of the Faculty Development Center of California State University, Fullerton, who so kindly and efficiently created a map for the book.

I would like to extend my thanks to California State University, Fullerton, for awarding me a Junior Faculty Research Grant, which was funded through the Auxiliary Services Corporation. This grant generously supported several research trips to libraries throughout California.

Above all, I am most fortunate for my husband and friend, Billy Russo, who traveled with me to photograph each library and who provided much support and encouragement during the long hours this project demanded.

Table of Contents

Acknowledgments vii

Preface 1

Introduction 5

A Note on the Libraries Included 13

Part I. San Diego and the Inland Empire

1. A.K. Smiley Public Library   17
2. Del Mar Public Library   25
3. Cardiff-by-the-Sea Public Library   31
4. Julian Public Library   36
5. Helen Hawkins Memorial Library and Research Archive, Women's History Museum and Educational Center   42

Part II. Orange County

6. Sherman Library & Gardens   49
7. Leatherby Libraries, Chapman University   57
8. Daisaku and Kaneko Ikeda Library, Soka University   66
9. Silverado Library   72
10. Paulina June and George Pollak Library, California State University, Fullerton   78

Part III. Los Angeles County

11. Brand Library & Art Center   91
12. Cerritos Library   97
13. Central Library of the Pasadena Public Library   106
14. The Writers Guild Foundation Shavelson-Webb Library   113

15. Central Library of the Los Angeles Public Library   119
16. Philosophical Research Society Library   129
17. Rancho Santa Ana Botanic Garden Research Library   134

Part IV. Santa Barbara County

18. Joseph Campbell & Marija Gimbutas Library, Pacifica Graduate Institute   143
19. Central Library of the Santa Barbara Public Library   150

Part V. Central Valley and Mariposa County

20. Beale Memorial Library   157
21. Visalia City Library   164
22. Mariposa County Library   168
23. Bassett Memorial Library   174
24. UC Merced Library   180

Part VI. Monterey County

25. Henry Miller Memorial Library   191
26. Harrison Memorial Library and Park Branch Library   199
27. Pacific Grove Public Library   207

Part VII. San Francisco Bay Area

28. Charles Franklin Doe Memorial Library and Gardner Stacks, University of California, Berkeley   215
29. Flora Lamson Hewlett Library, Graduate Theological Union   223
30. Main Library of the San Francisco Public Library   230

Part VIII. Northern California Coast

31. Mendocino Community Library   241
32. Coast Community Library   247

Index   253

Preface

This book is the result of my personal love affair with libraries and California. I met libraries before I met California and I can possibly trace my first significant encounter to a moment in 1970s Pennsylvania. The day sticks out in my mind and I remember parts of it vividly, although I was still a small child. I drove with my aunt to drop my cousin off at Penn State University. While sitting in the truck, my aunt said to me, "There is the university library." I peered out the window, saw the building, and was immediately intrigued by what may have been going on inside. I have other memories of the public library my mom would faithfully take me to in Mechanicsburg, Pennsylvania, but the university library memory is the most profound from that period of my life.

In 1981, we moved to Southern California. My mom immediately sought out the Fullerton Public Library, where she became a regular patron. She would not only go to the main building, but she would also walk and drive to the library's bookmobile to experience this wonderful library-on-wheels. In fact, her friendship with the bookmobile librarian continues to this day. Although they now live across the country from each other, my mom and the librarian continue to correspond through letters.

While attending high school in Fullerton, California, I thought of myself as a social and political rebel. I was amazed to find that the school library had several books on anarchist thought, which I checked out and carried around with me as much for reading material as for shock value. I remember receiving a notice that my copy of *The Black Flag of Anarchy* was overdue, but what astonished me most was that no one at the library seemed taken aback by my reading habits, no one wanted to investigate me when I came to return the book, and no one inquired about my mental stability. The library was definitely a special place.

One of the most wonderful feelings I have experienced occurred when I was an undergraduate student at UC Berkeley and I first walked into the large reading room of Doe Memorial Library. I have no doubt that memories of the room will remain with me for the rest of my life. I would sit for hours with my legs curled up in one of the oversized, wooden chairs. I believe spending time in this room and gazing up at the marvelous arched ceiling introduced me to the magic of the academic world more than any other building on campus could. It was also within the stacks at Berkeley that I was initiated into the sheer pleasure of browsing. I would gaze at the reserved graduate student study carrels with awe and can still conjure up the musty perfumes of all those beloved tomes.

My stories of libraries could go on and on. Some may find these stories silly or may simply not understand the meaning or depth, but I suspect, if you picked up this book, we may share similar experiences.

It was not until many years after Penn State and Berkeley that I began to seriously consider why libraries are unlike any other buildings to me. Others who I discussed my ideas with, before they materialized into this project, often nodded in agreement. I ultimately believe that libraries have a unique sense of place, which is what led to the first thoughts behind this book.

Having lived in both Southern and Northern California and driven up and down the state countless times has also planted within me a strong bond with the state that I liken to a love affair. Although many Californians see a vast difference between the northern and southern regions, something that causes some resentment, I don't experience it and I have always felt torn between the magic of both. When those who live in less-crowded and less-expensive states try to coax me to move there with promises of a large home and more savings in the bank, I find it hard to imagine leaving. California has a sense of place that draws me in and asks me to never leave.

What California means to me is hard to define, yet I do not believe all things need definitions to make them real, especially those of a mystical nature. A recent post I read in an online discussion group, however, spoke to me directly about one significant aspect of the state. A woman in another part of the United States was commenting on the horrible persecution a young man was experiencing due to his sexual orientation. She said that his options were to remain where he was and suffer or to move to California. I am certain she did not truly believe the solution was this easy, but her use of California was poignant. All places have their problems and one need not look far to find them here or anywhere, but I think California is still a place unparalleled in that it welcomes the seekers, the travelers, the dreamers, and those who do not fit in anywhere else.

What you will find on the pages that follow is not a directory of libraries or an objective, scientific study, but a work that is more creative, although it may one day lead me to more research-oriented shores. It is also important to note that I did not set out to find fault with the libraries I visited and provide a critique of what was lacking or poorly executed. I was concerned with what the libraries offered individuals and the community, what was unique, and what they did well. Finally, you will not encounter discussions of virtual libraries or library Web sites, even though I am an Internet fiend and believe online environments can create their own unique spaces.

This project is about the physicality of libraries, of the experiences of walking and sitting within them, and the road trips I embarked on to meet them in the flesh. As I wrote the chapters for the individual libraries, I allowed what struck me about the histories, communities, and exterior and interior spaces of the buildings to dictate the structures of the chapters. It is for this reason that the chapters do not all follow the same format, nor do they all have the same headings. Each library, I believe, has its own story to tell and its own sense of place.

Introduction

California's libraries are as diverse as the California landscape. This is evident when comparing the grandeur of the Doe Memorial Library at UC Berkeley to the significantly more humble Julian Public Library to the specialized Henry Miller Memorial Library, nestled in the splendor of the Big Sur wilderness and pure in its sole devotion to the controversial writer. It is as difficult to classify California's libraries as it is to define its citizenry. One should not exert much effort on such endeavors, however, because Californians tends to embrace their free spirit along with their diversity. Their libraries are an extension of an eclectic California philosophy.

One conclusion that can be drawn from a tour of California is that its libraries, both individually and collectively, evoke the concept of "library as place." The libraries that were selected for this book represent much more than physical structures, as do most libraries. They are places that reflect the communities they serve and the particular missions they set out to pursue. They contain the histories, stories, and experiences of those who visit. They provide a sense of place for groups, families, and individuals on a solitary discovery. The chapters that follow provide a tour of California's libraries to demonstrate the magic and uniqueness of the state's library buildings. Before beginning the tour, a further discussion of libraries and the concept of place is warranted.

THE MYSTERY OF LIBRARIES

During Ray Bradbury's (n.d.) speech upon receipt of the National Book Foundation Medal for Distinguished Contribution to American Letters, he recalls his experience of a library:

> As a boy of ten years I could imagine nothing finer than running to the library on a windy October night, pushed by the cold wind and traveling with autumn leaves to arrive at the wonderful place, the library, where I would stand for a moment in the wide open door and call into the deeps: "Are you there?"

In response, he would hear the "silent voices" of such literary giants as Dickens and Hawthorne reply that they were most certainly there waiting for him. Bradbury's experience is not unlike Lombardi's (2000) recollection of various libraries, including the New York Public Library and the Library of Congress: "Each one is in my imagination as a physical place with its own personality that tells me what sources I can expect to find within its walls."

A study (Kracker and Pollio, 2003) of undergraduates' memories of libraries revealed similar experiences. One student in the survey responded, "Some of my first library experiences are happy childhood memories. I always felt comforted when I was there.... The library was a warm refuge" (p. 1113). Another student recalled, "When I think about my experiences with the library fond memories appear" (p. 1113). What is startling about many of the undergraduates' memories is the vividness of the details. Memories of libraries are also found in Weise (2004), when she states, "libraries as places have been 'like home' to me" (p. 6). These reflections on libraries speak to something greater than the pieces that make up the whole.

Within library buildings there are numerous components, including the collections, computer workstations, reference services, the patrons and library staff, individual and group study areas, and exhibits. The library is home to a potentially infinite number of activities. Unique and stimulating discoveries are made by scholars browsing the stacks or searching in journal databases. Others experience themselves as part of a community in libraries. One's community may be that of the university, city, or small town. All of these elements considered together constitute the library as place, yet there is something mysterious about libraries that is almost beyond explanation.

Gorman (2000) acknowledges the mystery in libraries when he writes that people "need the library as a place because we are human beings" (p. 45). He further explains, "They are places that embody learning, culture, and other important secular values and manifestations of the common good, and there is a need arising from our common humanity to visit such places" (p. 45). Writing on the recent opening of three public libraries in the California communities of Belmont, Hercules, and San Mateo, King (2006) states, "No government building has the presence of a good library.... Libraries exist to unfurl dreams, offering access to knowledge and entertainment and everything in between. They symbolize the ideal that all citizens have a right to be informed" (p. B1). Those who frequent libraries are aware of the sense of place they experience upon walking in the doors. They also, as demonstrated earlier, may have vivid memories of their experiences of libraries. These memories add to both personal and cultural histories. Godkin (1980) finds, "The places in a person's world are more than entities which provide the physical stage for life's drama. Some are profound centers of meanings and symbols of experience. As such, they lie at the core of human existence" (p. 73).

Understanding the importance of place is significant, because it tells something about a culture's values and the human need, on both communal and solitary grounds, for the experience of place. According to Buttimer (1980), "People's sense of both personal and cultural identity is intimately bound up with place identity.... People have not only intellectual, imaginary, and symbolic conceptions of place, but also personal and social associations with place-based networks of interaction and affiliation" (p. 167). The fact that libraries often create a satisfactory relationship between an individual, his or her community, and an experience of place, seriously puts into question the demise of libraries, as is often predicted in this technological age, but instead points to the continuing vitality of the library as a physical structure.

This is not to say that libraries will remain the same. Anyone who has read or contributed to the ongoing conversation of the fate of libraries in the digital age knows that libraries have changed and will continue to change. They will erect virtual spaces to live alongside physical spaces. The expertise of the reference librarian is still needed, and perhaps more than ever, to help patrons navigate the Internet and determine the authority and credibility of materials within an increasingly expanding and sometimes chaotic online environment. Large numbers of materials continue to only be available or preferred in print form. These are some of the significant factors behind the steady need for libraries, but the concept of library as place is the encompassing force that has turned libraries into cultural institutions and, I believe, continues to make them indispensable today.

Relph (1976) finds a person's "authentic and unselfconscious sense of place" as both "important and necessary" for the betterment of society. He finds, "An authentic sense of place is above all that of being inside and belonging to *your* place both as an individual and as a member of a community, and to know this without reflecting upon it" (p. 65). Libraries provide this bridge between the individual and the community, across economic, religious, philosophic, gender, and ethnic lines, better than any other place in the modern world. Libraries further fit Relph's understanding of place when he writes, "People are their place and a place is its people.... In this context places are 'public'— they are created and known through common experiences and involvement in common symbols and meanings" (p. 34). It is from these "common experiences" that libraries construct a communal understanding of place where all are welcome.

According to Demas and Scherer (2002), "despite long-standing predictions of their demise and current reports of 'deserted libraries,' people are using America's libraries — virtual and physical — more than ever" (p. 65). A recent study (Antell and Engel, 2006) on the use of library space by faculty and doctoral students at the University of Oklahoma reports: "Unexpectedly, younger scholars value the physical library's 'conduciveness to scholarship' more than older scholars" (p. 553). Furthermore, "younger scholars overwhelmingly report spending the most time in the library, making both more visits and longer visits than older scholars" (p. 553). A study by Shill and Tonner (2004) examined academic library construction projects between 1995 and 2002. Responses from 182 of 357 libraries confirmed 80 percent of the libraries experienced greater facility usage. The median usage increase was 37.4 percent, but 25.6 percent experienced increases over 100 percent. Another study (Engel and Antell, 2004) of faculty spaces in academic libraries for the 2002–2003 academic year reported similar findings. The study found that 48 percent of the institutions surveyed had waiting lists for library faculty spaces. Engel and Antell also reported on a similar finding by the Association of Research Libraries that concluded more than 70 percent of responding libraries had fully occupied faculty spaces. The way faculty understand and define their library space is also interesting. One interviewed faculty member in the 2004 Engel and Antell study defined her space as "sacred space." Another described his as "intellectually freeing" (p. 12). It is no doubt, considering the connections people feel with their library spaces, that libraries remain popular places.

During an October 2004 tour of Chapman University's new Leatherby Libraries, located in Orange County, California, Charlene M. Baldwin, dean of the libraries, commented on the continuing importance of the library as place (personal communication, October 30, 2004). Speaking to the continuing draw of libraries, she stated that if a library is built, people will come. The number of visitors to the Leatherby Libraries has proven Baldwin to be correct in her assessment.

Humans and Place

Beyond the focused examination of library as place, it is important to understand where this investigation fits into the larger discussion. How human beings experience the places they frequent is a topic of interdisciplinary inquiry that has been building momentum for decades. Architecture, literature, psychology, and religion are just some of the disciplines engaged in the dialogue.

Bachelard's (1994) *The Poetics of Space* is an early example. Bachelard's work, an exploration across the boundaries of architecture, philosophy, and literature, is a study of the experience of intimate places. He writes, "Space that has been seized upon by the imagination cannot remain indifferent space subject to the measures and estimates of the surveyor. It has been lived in, not in its positivity, but with all the partiality of the imagination" (p. xxxvi). His understanding is in agreement with Lombardi's (2000) statement that the libraries from his past continue to live within his imagination. For Bachelard, "all really inhabited space bears the essence of the notion of home" (p. 5). Physical structures take on greater meaning once people dwell within them.

Understanding the significance of place is also a matter of great inquiry amongst poets. Neruda's (2003) poem titled "House," for example, gives the human-made structure an eternal quality that lives beyond the life of the speaker and, paradoxically, the time of humans: "Maybe this is the house where I lived / when I did not exist, when the earth did not exist, / when everything was moon or stone or shadow, / when the motionless light had yet to rise" (p. 934). Neruda's lines infuse mystery into what would ordinarily be a lifeless structure. His understanding is not unlike Whitman (1973) who wrote in "A Song for Occupations," a section of his classic long poem, *Leaves of Grass*: "All architecture is what you do to it when you look upon it; / Did you think it was in the white or gray stone? or the / lines of the arches and cornices?" (p. 102). Thomas Moore, who primarily writes in the fields of spirituality and psychology, would understand the work of the poets.

In Moore's *Re-enchantment of Everyday Life* (1996), he devotes a chapter to what he calls "the Particularity of Place." According to Moore, "Sometimes the spirit lies in the history of a place." This is similar to Day's (2004) assessment of what happens when a building has been used for generations: "The place becomes imprinted by a spirit" (p. 178). Moore's understanding that places are more than physical structures leads him to call on those who wish to live in an "enchanted world" to "honor the particular qualities that make a place unique, or at least take them as a starting point for imagination" (p. 147). Moore's writing ties him to Visser's (2000) conclusions in *The Geometry of Love: Space, Time, Mystery, and Meaning in an Ordinary Church*.

Visser's work, which can be classified as a meeting point between travel literature, architecture, history, and religion, is ultimately an examination of the "church as place" with honed attention on one Roman church. She writes, "Meaning is intentional: this building has been made in order to communicate with the people in it" (p. 14). Visser even goes beyond this point to explain that "the building 'refers' to things beyond itself" (p. 14). She compares the place of church with theater, but one could easily apply the following definition to libraries, especially if a library is understood as the building that houses the memory of individuals, communities, and cultures: "Memory, in a church, is not only individual, but also collective: the building is a meeting house for a group of people who agree with each other in certain important respects" (p. 12). Areas of agreement, regarding a library, could be the preservation of materials, the belief in providing open access to materials, the respect for intellectual inquiry, or the simple love of books and information. "A church," Visser explains, "reminds us of what we have known" (p. 12). Libraries, as places of preservation, perform this function as well.

Further understanding of the connection between the nature of place in churches and libraries can be reached through a reading of Merkel (1999). Although Merkel's focus is on the relationship between spaces and people on a college campus, her study has interesting findings that can be applied elsewhere. Investigating the intriguing aspect of the folklore of space, Merkel points out that one of the ways "people shape their space" is through the performance of "ritualized activities that occur in these places" (p. 418). Similar to the structure of many church services, those who use libraries often perform their functions in a ritualized way. Library rituals may include browsing the stacks in a favorite section or sitting at a terminal to search the online catalog.

Touching on the mystery of place, Tuan (1977) comments, "We may say that deeply-loved places are not necessarily visible, either to ourselves or to others" (p. 178). Tuan is not suggesting that a "deeply-loved place" is not physically present, but that what evokes the spirit of a place is often not tangible. It exists more in the realm of emotions. He states the following, which ties into Merkel:

> the "feel" of a place takes longer to acquire. It is made up of experiences, mostly fleeting and undramatic, repeated day after day and over the span of years. It is a unique blend of sights, sounds, and smells, a unique harmony of natural and artificial rhythms.... The feel of a place is registered in one's muscles and bones [p. 183–84].

In Tuan, as in Merkel, ritualized activities bond the individual to a place.

Another important work to consider is Downing's (2000) *Remembrance and the Design of Place*. Downing examines the aspects of architectural design and place. She is particularly concerned with the methodologies that go into design and how humans remember significant places. According to Downing, "We all retain memories of places. They identify who we are as individuals. At the same time, they tie us to networks of people, culture, and society" (p. 3). Her investigation began with interviews of 150 architects and student designers. From the results, she noticed the reappearance of certain places that she grouped as "domains of place experience" (p. 22). Taking Downing's domains under consideration, it becomes quite evident how the library satisfies more than one domain. Examples of the domains include: (a) places of self that evoke "discovery, reflection, and realization"; (b) sensate places where the body "moves, sees, touches, smells, hears, and responds"; (c) places of desire such as a staircase that suggests "the comings and goings"; (d) places of comfort, such as an "overstuffed chair"; and (e) gregarious places, including "student unions, baseball games, and theaters" where people hope "to be surrounded by others" and "to commune" (p. 32–43). What is interesting about Downing's study is that a library does not necessarily fit into any one domain. The library has the ability to house several domains within one location, making them, what Downing calls, "fluid domains." Due to the library's ability to satisfy multiple human needs for place, it is no wonder that people continue to find a need for visiting one.

A theory to also consider is that of "third places." Oldenburg's (1989) highly entertaining and thought-provoking *The Great Good Place* examines the significance of what he calls third places. Unlike home or work places, Oldenburg sees the need for third places, which exist as "neutral ground." One is not required to meet any expectations to visit a third place, such as might be demanded at work. A third place provides the opportunity to meet or simply see other community members, making such places essential for the deterrence of isolationism. Examples Oldenburg provides include cafes, coffee shops, bars, community centers, and other "hangouts." Libraries may be added to the list. He writes:

> There must be places where individuals may come and go as they please, in which none are required to play host, and in which all feel at home and comfortable. If there is no neutral ground in the neighborhoods where people live, association outside the home will be impoverished. Many, perhaps most, neighbors will never meet, to say nothing of associate, for there is no place for them to do so. When neutral ground is available it makes possible far more informal, even intimate, relations among people than could be entertained in the home [p. 22–23].

Libraries fit this description exceptionally well, especially when considering how one's financial situation does not preclude entry. Oldenburg importantly points out that "third places exist on neutral ground and serve to level their guests to a condition of social equality" (p. 42). All are free to "come and go as they please" in libraries, which may include simply reading amongst others or involving oneself in a book discussion group or other community event.

Conclusion

> Casey (1993) states:
>
> We get a more positive sense of the insurrectional power of place when we reflect on the familiar phrase "spirit of place," *genius loci*. Like the con-generic terms *soul* and *feeling*, *spirit*, signifies that which refuses to submit to dichotomizing. To get into the spirit of a place is to enter into what makes that place such a special spot, into what is concentrated there like a fully saturated color [p. 314].

The pages that follow investigate this notion of the "spirit of place" through a "sight-seeing" tour of select California's libraries. Such an inquiry provides insight into one of the mysterious dimensions of human experience: the experience of place. From the stimulating, intellectual world of UC Berkeley to the humble one-room library in Silverado Canyon and into the cities, beaches, valleys, mountains, and parks, the tour of California's libraries will now begin.

References

Antell, K., and D. Engel. "Conduciveness to Scholarship: The Essence of Academic Library as Place." *College and Research Libraries* 67 (2006): 536–60.

Bachelard, G. *The Poetics of Space: The Classic Look at How We Experience Intimate Places.* Trans. M. Jolas. Boston: Beacon, 1994. (Original work published 1958.)

Bradbury, R. "Upon Being Informed that I Am the Recipient of the National Book Foundation Medal for Distinguished Contribution to American Letters." n.d. www.raybradbury.com/awards_response.html (retrieved November 22, 2004).

Buttimer, A. "Home, Reach, and the Sense of Place." In *The Human Experience of Space and Place*, ed. A. Buttimer and D. Seamon. New York: St. Martin's, 1980.

Casey, E. *Getting Back into Place: Toward a Renewed Understanding of the Place-World.* Bloomington: Indiana University Press, 1993.

Day, C. *Places of the Soul: Architecture and Environmental Design as a Healing Art.* Oxford: Architectural Press, 2004.

Demas, S., and J. A. Scherer. "Esprit de Place: Maintaining and Designing Library Buildings to Provide Transcendent Spaces." *American Libraries* 33, no. 4 (2002): 65–68.

Downing, F. *Remembrance and the Design of Place.* College Station: Texas A&M University Press, 2000.

Engel, D., and K. Antell. "The Life of the Mind: A Study of Faculty Spaces in Academic Libraries." *College and Research Libraries* 65 (2004): 8–26.

Godkin, M. A. "Identity and Place: Clinical Applications Based on Notions of Rootedness and Uprootedness." In *The Human Experience of Space and Place*, ed. A. Buttimer and D. Seamon. New York: St. Martin's, 1980.

Gorman, M. *Our Enduring Values: Librarianship in the 21st Century.* Chicago: American Library Association, 2000.

King, J. "3 New Icons of Community Pride: Libraries Designed to Reflect Civic Priorities in Belmont, Hercules and San Mateo." *San Francisco Chronicle*, December 17, 2006.

Kracker, J., and H. R. Pollio. "The Experience of Libraries across Time: Thematic Analysis of Undergraduate Recollections of Library Experience." *Journal of the American Society for Information Science and Technology* 54 (2003): 1104–16.

Lombardi, J. V. "Academic Libraries in a Digital Age." *D-Lib Magazine* 6, no. 10 (2000). www.dlib.org (retrieved November 22, 2004).

Merkel, C. "Folkloristics of Educational Spaces: Material Lore in Classrooms with and Without Walls." *Library Trends* 47 (1999): 417–38.

Moore, T. *The Re-enchantment of Everyday Life.* New York: HarperCollins, 1996.

Neruda, P. "House." In *The Poetry of Pablo Neruda*, ed. I. Stavans and trans. G. Soto, 934. New York: Farrar, Straus and Giroux, 2003. (Original work published 1959–1961.)

Oldenburg, R. *The Great Good Place: Cafes, Coffee Shops, Community Centers, Beauty Parlors, General Stores, Bars, Hangouts and How They Get You through the Day.* New York: Paragon House, 1989.

Relph, E. *Place and Placelessness.* London: Pion Limited, 1976.

Shill, H., and S. Tonner. "Does the Building Still Matter? Usage Patterns in New, Expanded, and Renovated Libraries, 1995–2002." *College and Research Libraries* 65 (2004): 123–50.

Tuan, Y. *Space and Place: The Perspective of Experience.* Minneapolis: University of Minnesota, 1977.

Visser, M. *The Geometry of Love: Space, Time, Mystery, and Meaning in an Ordinary Church.* New York: North Point, 2000.

Weise, F. "Being There: The Library as Place." *Journal of Medical Library Association* 92, no. 1 (2004): 6–13.

Whitman, W. *Leaves of Grass.* In *The Portable Walt Whitman,* ed. M. V. Doren, 30–187. New York: Viking, 1973. (Original work published 1855.)

A Note on the Libraries Included

While writing my book, I was often asked by colleagues and others how I was selecting which libraries to include. This was no easy process, since California is rich in libraries. There are enough libraries worthy of inclusion to fill numerous volumes, but difficult decisions had to be made based on time, travel, and the size of the book. One primary goal was to include as many regions of the state as possible, but some areas remain for future discoveries. Several of the libraries I included were ones that I had used myself, visited in the past, discovered during a conference, or was already aware of through the professional literature. Others were recommended by friends and colleagues. Finally, several I located through independent Internet research and use of the *American Library Directory* (R.R. Bowker, 59th ed.). This book is not meant to be a representation of the best libraries in the state or any such ranking, yet one unifying element that connects each library that I chose is a unique sense of place that became apparent to me during my visits.

Part I

San Diego and the Inland Empire

1

A.K. Smiley Public Library

LIBRARY DATA

Address: 125 W. Vine Street, Redlands, CA 92373
Phone: (909) 798-7565
Web site: www.akspl.org
Square Feet: 64,636
Circulation: 263,946 (2004/2005)
Collection: 132,278 books; 38,124 documents; 3,497 microfilm reels; 2,436 audio; 1,971 video; 309 periodicals (2004/2005)
Source for above: *California Library Statistics 2006* (California State Library, Library Development Services Bureau)

Redlands is located in an area of Southern California called the Inland Empire. The city is approximately 65 miles east of Los Angeles. Articles appearing in the *Los Angeles Times* from the early years of the 20th century demonstrate an interest and appreciation for the city. An article from 1905 describes Redlands as a community that is "celebrated the world over for its climate and scenery, these two elements attracting persons of wealth from the four corners of the earth" ("San Bernardino County, Twice as Big as Massachusetts"). Twelve years later, another article commented on its growth through a glowing report on its agricultural development:

> Thirty years ago the horseshoe of hills around Redlands was covered with sagebrush, the stamping grounds of coyotes, but today the hills are green with thousands of acres of orange and other fruit trees. Below them in the valley are the level fields of alfalfa and of grain, the rule being fruit trees on the hills and slopes, and farming in the valley ["San Bernardino County's Most Prosperous Year," 1917].

Writing much later in 1951, Hinckley described Redlands as "the last stopping place before reaching the mountains or deserts" (p. 11). Hinckley continued, "To the north the Cajon Pass leads through the San Bernardino mountains to the Mojave Desert, and to the east the San Gorgonio Pass leads to the Colorado Desert" (p. 11). The explosion of development throughout much of Southern California over the last several decades may have changed Redlands from being "the last stopping place" to *one* of the last stopping places, yet Hinckley's description demonstrates the history of a city that is located in a region of the state that continues, in present day, to retain some sparseness.

Agriculture, climate, and placement are not the only attributes that have made Redlands a place of interest to many. Hinckley, for example, commented on the impact of the A.K. Smiley Public Library: "The distinctive and unique architecture of the building has added greatly to the attractive appearance of our city, and even greater has been the cultural effect" (p. 83). The articles mentioned above from the *Los Angeles Times* both mention the library. It is described in 1905 as "one of the best on the Coast" ("San Bernardino County, Twice as Big"). Listing the library as one of the city's attributes, the 1917 article simply concluded: "The A.K. Smiley library has more than 30,000 volumes" ("San Bernardino County's Most Prosperous Year").

Before it was even built, the library put Redlands on the map. An 1897 article in the *Los Angeles Times* reported: "The structure will be a mammoth affair, and will be designed in the mission style of architecture. It will be thoroughly modern, lighted by electricity and heated by steam" ("Plans for the Smiley Library Building Completed"). Offering the prediction that the library will cost approximately $60,000 to build, the library is envisioned to be "one of the finest library buildings west of Denver" ("Plans for"). Modern-day visitors to the library, partaking of the wondrous interior and exterior spaces of the building, may find this lofty prediction fulfilled.

History of the Library

Andrew Carnegie visited Redlands in 1892 and again in 1910. During his second visit, he toured the Smiley Library. Carnegie stated, "This is the first time it has ever been my privilege to sign the visitors' book of a library which I had not founded, and it gives me the greatest pleasure" (Nelson, 1963, p. 241). Carnegie described the library as a "magnificent structure" (p. 241).

Writing on the early days of the library, Irshay (1988) stated "that the library from the very first was a success and popular among all ages. There were always crowds at the shelves during all hours of the day and evening" (p. 51). One individual, Alfred Smiley, was the primary force behind the origin of the library. He was later joined considerably in his efforts by his twin brother, Albert K. Smiley.

In 1891, several Redlands citizens, including Alfred Smiley, were focused on securing a public library for the city. The initial library, which was dedicated on February 22, 1894, was located in a Y.M.C.A building. There was almost an immediate need to secure a larger and more permanent structure ("The History," n.d.). This led to discussions, throughout 1896, between the Smiley brothers:

> Alfred's desire for a library building coincided with Albert's wish to provide a downtown park for the enjoyment of Redlands citizens. By

March of 1897, Albert K. Smiley had purchased sixteen acres of downtown land to build Redlands its new library building ["The History," n.d.].

The vision for the library was realized at the dedication of the building and a surrounding park (Smiley Park) on April 29, 1898.

The library, which was designed by T. R. Griffith in the mission style, retains its original space, along with four additions in 1906, 1920, 1926, and 1930, as well as a 1990 expansion (A.K. Smiley Public Library, 2003–2004). Newspaper articles from 1929–1930 speak to the popularity and growing collection that resulted in the need for the 1930 addition. "More stack room" was cited as the reason behind the call for more space in a November 1929 article ("Redlands Library"). In April 1930, the *Los Angeles Times* reported, "The monthly reports of Miss Innis, the librarian, show a steady and astounding growth in all departments. More volumes are being issued to card holders each month, the number of card holders being greater than ever before" ("Smiley Library"). The article further mentioned how "crowded conditions are apparent to any one who will look." In July 1930, the *Los Angeles Times* reported on the library once again to announce an astounding 100 percent increase in the circulation of books with 70 percent of the Redlands population being library card holders ("Redlands Folks"). Over 20 years later, in July 1952, another article in the *Times* discussed the library's 58th annual report that demonstrated a continuing increase in circulation, despite television and radio, and the reading room "filled with newspapers from across the country" being "more popular than ever" ("Library Use").

The library continues today to be a central location for services and community events, as illustrated in the 2003–2004 annual report, the library's 109th such report. Once one sees the library in the distance, with its striking exterior that was recently restored to its original red color, it becomes quite apparent why people would want to spend time in such a magnificent structure. The library sits on the grounds of a large area that includes a memorial shrine and museum for Abraham Lincoln and the Redlands Bowl across the street, a small version of the Hollywood Bowl that holds live, outdoor concerts in warmer weather. Visitors to the library will want to dedicate several hours to tour the historic building and walk the grounds.

Front Lawn

A lush grass lawn with several trees is located immediately in front of the main library entrance. Visitors may sit on one of the two benches located on the lawn. This area provides a rather quiet setting, with occasional traffic heading toward or away from the historic downtown area. Bells from the First Presbyterian Church, a short walk from the library, chime every hour. Viewing the library from a position on the lawn is ideal. The red exterior is dramatic, yet warm and inviting. A Moorish-style tower that was removed in 1936, but rebuilt in 1999, greatly complements the structure (A.K. Smiley Public Library, 2003–2004). The tower matches the rest of the structure with its red exterior.

A statue at the far corner of the lawn, near the intersection of Vine and Eureka, pays tribute to the Smiley brothers. The Smiley Memorial Statue, created by artist Linda Hundevadt Pew and dedicated on March 17, 1991, shows the two brothers with the following caption: "This memorial is placed in deep appreciation of Albert K. and Alfred H. Smiley and also their brother Daniel. These men of noble character and generosity are examples of the best of mankind."

Entrance

When approaching the main entrance, located on the north side of the library, one will notice a circular flower bed with pansies. In addition to the statue tribute, pansies are planted in the library flower beds each year in honor of the twin brothers. Pansies are used, because the brothers share a birthday with St. Patrick, whose favorite flower was a pansy.

The main entrance includes an impressive double archway that allows one to first walk through to the original 1898 library. The small area is an engaging space with art reproductions displayed on the walls, hardwood floors, and a curious sandstone devil carved into an interior arch that faces the circulation desk. During a visit to the library in December 2005, I noted that fresh roses were in a vase on the reader services desk, a few feet to the right of the entrance. A grandfather clock, also found close by, chimes every quarter-hour.

Commenting on the entrance, the most recent annual report reads: "The patron is given several directions from which to choose, acting almost as fingers branching out from the main foyer" (A.K. Smiley Public Library, 2003–2004). This description accurately portrays the openness of the area, inviting visitors to immediately see the different rooms they may wander into.

Reference Wing

To the left of the entranceway, is the expansive Reference Wing, which resembles a grand hall. The wing is comprised of both the original 1898 building and a 1907 expansion that includes the Dr. Meredith Beaver Lounge in the far corner. This area is similar in size and appearance to the main hall of the Pasadena Public Library's Central Library. The Redlands Reference Wing and the main hall in Pasadena both provide a striking area that takes the form of a traditional, large reading room, providing ample seating in spaces that are expansive, yet warm and inviting. Besides the expected seating at tables arranged throughout the room, the Reference Wing also includes a charming feature: an old fireplace built along one of the walls with bench-style seating for two.

The Reference Wing at the A.K. Smiley Public Library resembles a grand hall from earlier years.

Scott Conservatory

The conservatory is arguably one of the most appealing rooms in the library, especially for those looking for a space to curl up with a good book or newspaper. Located just off from the main entrance, the conservatory, which was part of the 1990 expansion, is a reading room with two round tables. Each table is surrounded by four cushioned wicker chairs. Three oriental rugs and two wooden bookcases with periodicals add to the charm. Windows look out to a courtyard garden.

Children's Room

The Children's Room, located next to the Scott Conservatory and accessible from the Reference Wing, is first reached through a narrow walkway of hardwood flooring. This unique entranceway sets the Children's Room off from the rest of the library and gives one the impression that a unique space is about to be entered. Besides creating an entranceway, the walkway doubles as a gallery of signed Norman Rockwell lithographs that depict scenes from Mark Twain's *Tom Sawyer*.

A peaceful space at the A.K. Smiley Public Library in Redlands features wicker furniture and views of the surrounding gardens.

A small aquarium is located on the right and visible immediately upon entering the Children's Room. Not only does the narrow walkway fit perfectly with the theme of entering a children's space, but small windows on both sides of the room also illustrate that this is an area used by smaller people. Stained glass on the windows include depictions of scenes from famous children's books.

Since the Children's Room is surrounded by gardens on both sides, the room is quite enchanting with views of these outdoor spaces. On one side is the garden courtyard that is also visible from windows in the conservatory. The other side provides views of the Children's Garden. Windows along the back of the room look out to the Lincoln Shrine with views of the lawn between the library and the shrine. The Children's Room, therefore, is a space surrounded by nature on three of four sides.

COMPUTER CENTER AND STACKS

To the right of the entranceway, behind the readers services desk, is an Internet room called the North Wing Computer Center. This room, established in March 2003, is described as "extremely popular" in the library's most recent annual report (A.K. Smiley Public Library, 2003–2004, p. 25). Another fireplace, similar to the one in the Reference Wing, is here, providing bench-style seating. A long table with computers sits surrounded by several works of art, including plaster reliefs of angels with musical instruments, a replica of the *Venus of the Vatican* statue, and an additional replica of the ancient Greek *Venus de Milo* statue. This room demonstrates how libraries can effectively merge modern technology with classical or traditional features to create an interesting space.

Next to the computer room is the Stack Wing, the needed expansion of 1930 that was written about considerably in the previously mentioned *Los Angeles Times* articles. The need for inviting areas, even within the stacks, is not lost here. A lounge area, located in one of the far corners of the wing, includes four wicker chairs and a small table on an oriental rug.

LINCOLN SHRINE

As mentioned earlier, the library shares its space with a park and the Lincoln Shrine. One can walk around to the back of the library to reach the small park that leads to the Lincoln Shrine, or exit the library through one of the garden courtyards. The shrine must be discussed before concluding this chapter, since it is very much a part of the library. In fact, the annual report and promotional materials about the library include information about the shrine.

The shrine, established in 1932 and designed by architect Elmer Grey, was a gift to the City of Redlands by philanthropists Robert and Alma Watchorn. Features of the shrine include "the famous Carrara marble bust of Lincoln by the noted sculptor George Grey Barnard as well as distinctive allegorical murals painted by prominent illustrator Dean Cornwell" (Lincoln Memorial Shrine, 2004). A brochure available at the library circulation desk describes the shrine "as a research center for scholars, students and all who are interested in Abraham Lincoln and the American Civil War" (A.K. Smiley Public Library, n.d.). It is further described in the brochure as "the only museum, archives, and library dedicated to President Abraham Lincoln west of the Mississippi River."

A wealth of material may be found at the shrine, including thousands of volumes on Lincoln and the Civil War; a manuscript collection with letters and documents from Lincoln, his family, and cabinet members; rare pamphlets; an extensive collection of clippings from newspapers and magazines; photographs; diaries; and other museum display items (Lincoln Memorial Shrine, 2004). It is quite easy to see why a visit to the A.K. Smiley Public Library should also include a walk through the park to the shrine, further pointing to the need for a long visit to Redlands to experience such a distinctive place.

REFERENCES

A.K. Smiley Public Library. Brochure, n.d. (Available at the A.K. Smiley Public Library circulation desk.)
_____. "The History of the Library." n.d. www.akspl.org/history/index.html (retrieved November 28, 2005).
_____. *The One Hundred and Ninth Annual Report of the A.K. Smiley Public Library Redlands, California*. 2003–2004. www.akspl.org/annual.pdf (retrieved November 28, 2005).
California State Library. Library Development Services Bureau. *California Library Statistics 2006*. www.library.ca.gov/assets/acrobat/StatsPub06.pdf (retrieved December 23, 2006).
Hinckley, E. P. *On the Banks of the Zanja: The Story of Redlands*. Claremont, CA: Saunders Press, 1951.
Irshay, P. C. *The Pride and Glory of the Town: The Story of the A.K. Smiley Public Library*. Redlands, CA: City of Redlands, 1988.
"Library Use Gains Shown Despite TV." *Los Angeles Times*, July 11, 1952.
Lincoln Memorial Shrine. "Shrine History." 2004. www.lincolnshrine.org (retrieved January 8, 2006).
Nelson, L. E. *Only One Redlands: Changing Patterns in a Southern California Town*. Redlands, CA: Redlands Community Music Association, 1963.
"Plans for the Smiley Library Building Completed." *Los Angeles Times*, August 8, 1897.
"Redlands Folks Studious." *Los Angeles Times*, July 9, 1930.
"Redlands Library Notes Great Growth." *Los Angeles Times*, November 10, 1929.
"San Bernardino County's Most Prosperous Year." *Los Angeles Times*, January 1, 1917.
"San Bernardino County, Twice as Big as Massachusetts." *Los Angeles Times*, January 1, 1905.
"Smiley Library Promised Gift," *Los Angeles Times*, April 20, 1930.

2

Del Mar Public Library

Library Data

Address: 1309 Camino del Mar, Del Mar, CA 92014
Phone: (858) 755-8869
Web site: www.sdcl.org
Square Feet: 4,700
Circulation: 82,560 (2004/2005)
Collection: 28,490 total all materials (2004/2005)
Source for above: "Community Profile, Del Mar," August 2005 (publication of the San Diego County Library)

Del Mar, Spanish for "of the sea," is a beachside community located in northern San Diego County. Historic route 101 becomes Camino del Mar when it runs through the center of the city. Del Mar, which was settled in 1884, has the flavor of a small town. A walking map freely available to visitors describes the city as "a village by the sea." Specialty shops, cafes, and restaurants line Camino del Mar. Hiking trails, bird watching, surfing, and biking are all readily available to residents and visitors. Located within the heart of the community at the intersection of Camino del Mar and 13th Street is the Del Mar Public Library, a branch of the San Diego County Library.

Library History

The Del Mar Public Library has one of the most unusual histories of all the libraries included in this book. The first location of the library, in 1914, was in the home of the librarian. Between 1924 and the 1950s, the library moved to various locations along 15th Street, including at least one other residence. In 1957, the total square footage of the library, at a location on Camino del Mar, was just 273 feet. Twenty years later, the library was moved to a 2,400-foot modular trailer, where it remained for almost another two decades. It was not until 1993 that the library found a more permanent home ("Community Profile," 2005).

The story of the Del Mar Public Library is connected with the history of another Del Mar building: the Church of St. James. In 1914, the Catholic Diocese

The Del Mar Public Library building was a Catholic Church, two restaurants, and a company's headquarters before its conversion to a library.

of San Diego established the church, designed by John Austin, at 1309 Camino del Mar. Interestingly, this was the same year that the library was established in the librarian's home ("Community Profile," 2005). It would not be until nearly 80 years later that the story of the church and the library would intertwine.

St. James Church, a Craftsman-style building, continued to function as a Catholic Church for over half a century. Several celebrities worshiped at the church, including Jimmy Durante, Desi Arnaz, Pat O'Brien, and Bing Crosby ("A History," n.d.). When the San Diego diocese purchased larger property in nearby Solana Beach, services were no longer held at St. James.

After the closure of the church, the building became the Albatross Restaurant and later a Mexican restaurant called Pancho's. The building's fate was not to end with the restaurant industry; it was then converted into a company's headquarters ("A History," n.d.). Eventually the building was sold to the city in the early 1990s. It was at this time that the library found its home within the walls of the former Catholic Church–Mexican restaurant–office building. The Del Mar City Council purchased the building in 1993 with the intent of housing the library at this location (Friends of the Del Mar Library, n.d.). The library was dedicated in 1996 ("A History," n.d.).

LIBRARY WALL

Surrounding the library is a striking mixed-media mural wall designed by Pat Welsh, artist and children's book author, in collaboration with Betsy Schulz, muralist and graphic artist ("A History," n.d.). Although the wall was formerly a four-foot-tall plain, gray concrete structure measuring 92 feet long, much creativity and work was put into transforming the wall into a piece of community art that changed the overall appearance of the library. The mural on the wall was dedicated on June 7, 2003 (Friends of the Del Mar Library, n.d.). The wall has become a true symbol for the library and the community it serves. Bookmarkers available for purchase at the library are designed with graphic depictions of a section of the wall on one side and information on the history of the wall on the other. A brochure available at the library includes a photograph of various community members working on the wall during its initial creation.

Depicted on the wall are rocks, ocean waves, sky, land, and plants and animals common to the region. A document published by the Friends of the Del Mar Library (n.d.) provides details on the story behind the wall:

> The wall mural was constructed using brick, terra cotta tile, black rocks, and rusty "found" objects. Many neighbors brought special objects, such as rocks; fossils; railroad spikes; horseshoes to remind us of when horses from the race track ran on the beach for exercise; pieces of dishes dug up in gardens from the old Del Mar Hotel; and a piece of the Berlin Wall. One boy would go to the beach each day to find white rocks and bricks to place on the wall. Local artists and volunteers sculpted more than thirty birds, animals, fish and Torrey Pines. Every piece on the wall has a special memory for someone. It truly was a "village" that made a special wall.

Further information about the wall is available in a children's book for sale at the library and select bookstores. The book, *The Magic Mural and How it Got Built: A Fable for Children of All Ages*, published in 2005 by the Friends of the Del Mar Library, was written and illustrated by Pat Welsh with photographs by Betsy Schulz, the creative forces behind the wall. Welsh offers a photo gallery that documents the creation of the wall, including many photographs of community members and children working side-by-side, on her Web site (www.patwelsh.com/gallery.html). In addition, a television documentary titled "It Takes a Village ... To Raise a Wall," produced by Nicole Holliday and Tracy Phillips through Del Mar T.V. Foundation, may be viewed in a room at the library. The continuing significance of the wall to the community illustrates how a public art project at a library can integrally connect citizens with the building.

Entrance

A signpost on the street at the corner of 13th Street and Camino del Mar reads "Historic Route 101." Several large trees located on Camino del Mar provide a natural canopy for the library, when viewed from across the street. A side entrance to the library, located off of 13th Street, has an outside display case immediately to the left of the doors. Inside this glass-covered case are postings of library and community information. After passing through the entrance, the reference desk is located directly in front. A small computer lab is off to the right. Similar to the Julian Public Library, the library is primarily one large room with some alcoves, furniture and art to divide the building into different spaces.

Terrace

To the left of the reference desk is a small space devoted to periodicals and reference. A door from this area opens to one of the great features of the library: a terrace that doubles as an outdoor reading room. The terrace, which opened in October 1996, provides a wonderful space for users with several wood benches and chairs for seating. Having an outdoor reading room at this library is especially nice, since the building is located just a few blocks from the beach. Those who partake of this space will enjoy ocean breezes while watching others walk down Camino del Mar.

Children's Room

A ramp leads to the Children's Room. Two walls within the room are composed of collages of small tiles painted by children. Tiles are also used as a trim to other areas of this space. Librarian, Gretchen Schmidt, explained that the tiles were part of a fundraiser for the Friends of Del Mar Library. Schmidt also provided an interesting bit of history of the Children's Room. In the old St. James Church, the rectory was located where the Children's Room is today (personal correspondence, December 17, 2005).

Alcoves

Two alcoves that provide special spaces within the interior include one near the front of the library and another near the center. A small alcove in the front with windows looking out toward Camino del Mar houses "Del Mar Voices," the oral history project of the Del Mar Historical Society. Also found here is the Friends of the Library book sale. Two chairs and a television for viewing Del Mar community videos are also available. According to Schmidt, this room was where babies used to be baptized when the building was a church (personal correspondence, December 17, 2005).

The second alcove, a gift of the Del Mar Farmers Market, has room for more guests. A table provides seating for seven. One must make a step up to get to this space. Schmidt explained that this area was formerly the altar in the church (personal correspondence, December 17, 2005).

FINAL THOUGHTS

Most of the remainder of the interior is filled with book stacks, intermingled with places for visitors to read and study. The library is a charming and inviting building with a rich and interesting history. It is also a decidedly community space with a central location in a scenic beachside village.

A terrace at the Del Mar Public Library in San Diego County provides a unique outdoor reading room with ocean breezes.

REFERENCES

"Community Profile, Del Mar Branch." Publication of the San Diego County Library, August 2005. (Provided by the Del Mar Public Library.)
"A History of the Del Mar Library." n.d. (Provided by Gretchen Schmidt of the Del Mar Public Library.)
Friends of the Del Mar Library. Brochure, n.d. (Available at the Del Mar Public Library.)

3

Cardiff-by-the-Sea Public Library

LIBRARY DATA

Address: 2081 Newcastle Avenue, Cardiff-by-the-Sea, CA 92007
Phone: (760) 753-4027
Web site: www.sdcl.org
Square Feet: 5,977
Circulation: 132,448 (2004/2005)
Collection: 24,682 total all materials (2004/2005)

Source for above: "Community Profile, Cardiff-by-the-Sea Branch," August 2005 (publication of the San Diego County Library)

Cardiff-by-the-Sea, another San Diego County beachside city, is located a few miles north of Del Mar near Solana Beach. The city was first settled in 1880 by S. Hector Mackinnon, a farmer and inventor from Scotland. Over 30 years later in 1911, a gentleman named Frank Cullen bought part of Mackinnon's coastal ranch. Cullen named the area Cardiff-by-the-Sea and his wife, who originated from Cardiff, England, changed the names of the avenues from Spanish to English names ("Community Profile," 2005). The public library, located at 2081 Newcastle Avenue, sits across the street from the Cardiff Town Center, which includes Yogi's Bar & Restaurant and the Seaside Market with outdoor seating. The hilly streets of Liverpool or Birmingham will lead one to Newcastle.

Cardiff-by-the-Sea is a relatively quiet place with a population of just 17,900 ("Community Profile," 2005). One can easily walk to the beach from the library. Special collections at the library, including one devoted to surfing, demonstrate the influence of the beach lifestyle. In fact, *Surfer* and *Surfer's Journal* were prominently displayed on the periodical shelves during a visit to the library in December 2005.

A woman who noticed me taking notes and my husband photographing the building from outside stopped to speak to us. When I explained I was writing a book about libraries in California, she responded, "We're very proud of our library." An exploration of the spaces within the small building, as well as information on the variety of community programs offered, made it quite evident why the library has a sense of place.

Library History

The Cardiff-by-the-Sea branch of the San Diego County Library System has a history of much temporality, until it found its more permanent address in 1984. The library first opened on March 18, 1914. It was housed at the S.M. Holbrook Store at San Elijo and Chesterfield. For the next nearly 50 years, the library found its home in a general store, an insurance company, and other locations. In 1961, it was moved to a building on Newcastle. The establishment of the Friends of the Cardiff-by-the-Sea Library in 1984 created a strong advocacy group for both keeping the library open and securing a larger building. It was in 1984 that the library moved to its present location where Liverpool and Newcastle intersect. In 2000, a new facility was built, which opened on March 22, 2003 ("Community Profile," 2005).

The planning and opening of the new facility received some positive press. The magazine *San Diego Home Garden Lifestyles* featured plans for the library in the May 2001 issue, describing the proposed building as "a friendly new neighbor" ("Books-by-the-Sea," p. 20). An article in the *San Diego Union-Tribune* by Littlefield appeared a few days before the new building opened (March 20, 2003). Littlefield titled this solely optimistic piece "A Convergence of Light and Color: Comfy New Cardiff Library Ready to Open." After the opening, Littlefield wrote another positive article (March 28, 2003). Interest in the library did not stop with the opening. In November 2005, for example, another article appeared in the *San Diego Union-Tribune* describing a postcard display at the building (Daniels).

The recently opened new building, designed by Manuel Oncina Architects, features a copper roof. It is an environmentally friendly building, also referred to as a "green building," that was constructed from recycled materials. Some of the natural and recyclable materials used in the construction include cork-lined flooring and cotton insulation (Littlefield, March 20, 2003). Rocks provide decoration around the building.

Community Events

Numerous events held at the library give insight into the eclectic interests of the neighborhood. The community room provides space for events within the library, yet it is set off from the rest of the building. Visitors may enter the room through a door in the corner of the library or a door that leads to the outside.

A series titled the First Wednesday Program, sponsored by the Friends of the Cardiff-by-the-Sea Library is described as an opportunity to meet authors, musicians, and performers from the community. Held the first Wednesday of each month, this series has included a talk by a columnist for the *San Diego Reader*, evenings of jazz and Celtic music, a dance performance of ancient and modern cultural dances of Hawaii and Tahiti, Spanish and Latin American guitar music, and a poetry competition featuring the Full Moon Poets of the local 101 Artists' Colony.

Book Nook & Exterior

What is perhaps most striking when first viewing the library is the amount of exterior space covered by green-tinted glass. The side of the building that provides an entrance from the parking lot is nearly entirely enrobed in glass. According to Littlefield (March 28, 2003), Oncina felt that "no search for enlightenment would be complete without — well, light." According to the architect, "The natural light will bathe deep inside the building and actually save a lot of electrical power.... It would be hard to find a dark spot in the building." One need not even enter the building to see how this is true.

Regardless if one enters the building from the parking lot or the side of the library positioned at the intersection of Liverpool and Newcastle, it is simply an inviting structure. Three benches are available for seating outside the building. The Book Nook, a small room that is accessible from the street, houses the Friends' book sale. While visiting the library on a Saturday morning, some sale books were arranged on carts outside in the sunshine. The ability to peruse books outdoors in the midst of ocean breezes only adds to the allure before even venturing inside.

Reading and Computer Workstation Areas

Near the periodicals and new books shelf is an illuminated reading area with floor-to-ceiling windows. This prime area, that is truly bathed in natural light, provides cushioned seats with small chair-side tables for several visitors. One can also gaze out of the windows to Newcastle Avenue.

The library provides two computer workstation areas. The most visible one upon entering the library is located off from the reference desk near the center of the building. The eight computer stations here are designed with privacy in mind. The workstations, although all attached, sit at angles from each other with short walls between each work area. Another computer area located in a corner nook is the dimmest place in the library, yet it still has some natural lighting.

Other Interior Spaces

The Children's Room is another nooklike space. Less windows in this space make it cozy. Tiny, inventively designed lights are suspended on cords here, similar to lights that may be found in a modern coffeehouse. Not far from the Children's

A reading area in the Cardiff-by-the-Sea Public Library in San Diego County provides comfortable window seating.

Room are four study niches located along the wall and close to the mixed media and book stacks. These spaces provide for individual study in a location that is more hidden than others.

In addition to specific spaces, the library also provides unique collections and displays, which only add to the diversity of the interior. Spanish books, described by Faith Niles, branch operations manager, as an increasing collection, mirror other efforts the library has employed to reach out to Spanish-speaking residents, such as a Thursday night lecture series on various topics (personal correspondence, December 17, 2005). Reflecting the uniqueness of the building, there is also an eco-green architecture collection.

A "theme table," located not far from the reference desk and entrance, is used as an outlet for promoting specific parts of the collection. Near the theme table is a glass-enclosed display case that includes a complete collection of all the Beatrix Potter characters. This case is next to another that showcased an exhibit of ceramic pieces by artists Robin Neff and Bobbie Bradford in December 2005. Although the library is considerably smaller than others included in this book, it is quite evident that much can be done with little room, including the creation of a sense of place.

REFERENCES

"Books-by-the-Sea." *San Diego Home Garden Lifestyles*, May 2001. www.friendscardifflibrary.org/new_library/magazine.htm (retrieved November 28, 2005).

"Community Profile, Cardiff-by-the-Sea Branch." Publication of the San Diego County Library, August 2005. (Provided by the Cardiff-by-the-Sea Library.)

Daniels, A. "Postcards on Display at Library Capture Glimpses of Cardiff's Past." *San Diego Union-Tribune,* November 19, 2005.

Littlefield, D. "Comfy New Cardiff Library Ready to Open." *San Diego Union-Tribune*, March 28, 2003.

_____. "A Convergence of Light and Color: Comfy New Cardiff Library Ready to Open." *San Diego Union-Tribune,* March 20, 2003.

4

Julian Public Library

LIBRARY DATA

Address: 1850 Highway 78, Julian, CA 92036
Phone: (760) 765-0370
Web site: www.sdcl.org
Square Feet: 9,700
Circulation: 37,960 (2004/2005)
Collection: 22,478 total all materials (2004/2005)
Source for above: "Community Profile, Julian Branch," August 2005 (publication of the San Diego County Library)

    A photograph taken from a California beach that hangs in a Southern California coastal restaurant provides the caption: "What should I do today? Ski or surf?" The photograph shows a sunny beach in the foreground and snow-covered mountains not too far in the distance. This speaks to the extreme differences in landscapes and climates that one can easily encounter within a few hours drive from almost anywhere in California. Sannwald (1991), writing for *Library Journal*, noted this difference when commenting on the various branches of the San Diego County Library. Initially noting that the libraries "look out at some of the nation's most spectacular scenery," he then clarified: "They are spread from the northern avocado orchards of Fallbrook, down south to Bonita (boasting more horses than people), and from the mountain village of Julian to the desert oasis of Borrego Springs" (p. 48).
    Although the words "San Diego" are typically associated with certain features of the region, including spectacular beaches, sunshine, and the county's famous zoo and animal park, Sannwald's discussion of the libraries points to the fact that much more may be found here. The county of San Diego spans far and not unlike many territories that make California a unique state, diverse landscapes, including mountains and beaches, are easily found within the county lines. The historic mining town of Julian, located approximately 50 miles inland from the coastal cities of Cardiff-by-the-Sea and Del Mar, speaks directly to the differences in landscape and temperature one can expect.
    Huddled between the northern end of the Cuyamaca mountain range and the southern slope of Volcan Mountain, Julian sits at an elevation of 4,500 feet,

enough to make the air considerably cooler than other parts of the county. Although the drive to Julian does not require the skill often associated with winding mountain roads, Highway 78 that leads one to the heart of the town does demand a certain mixture of resolve and dedication. The small town with its attractive and charming library will offer rewards for the drive.

History of Julian

The 2005 "Community Profile" provided by the Julian Public Library states that the town, with a current population under 5,000, "started as a mining town in 1869 when cattleman Fred Coleman found gold in a creek." Julian's gold rush period was rather short-lived, lasting "little more than a decade," but those who came for the riches remained to farm. "The finest crop proved to be apples, which are still grown in Julian, and the many delicacies made from them have become Julian's trademark tourist attraction" ("Community Profile," 2005). Visitors today will find signs advertising apple pie for sale in nearly every restaurant or bakery within the small downtown. The downtown area retains many original buildings. Newer structures are built with the historic theme in mind, creating a unique mountain community that is quite different from the San Diego just one hour to the west.

Like much of San Diego County, the terrain of Julian has been used by filmmakers over the years. According to Williams (2002), "San Diego, as early as 1898, was one of the premiere western locations for the motion picture industry" (p. 99). This was not only for the shorelines; San Diego was also a desired spot for filming, due to the landscapes found in areas like Julian. These areas were not chosen because of their likeness to California, but due to their un–California-like appearance. Williams further reports: "The northern and eastern areas of San Diego County have presented filmmakers sufficient open space to film movies with big budgets or small budgets in a variety of genres including science fiction, western, military, gangster, and horror movies" (p. 122). He most shrewdly observes, "It is the part of the county that is most often represented as somewhere else" (p. 122). Julian, Williams points out, was used for Texas in a Dean Martin comedy-western released in 1966.

Library History

Established in 1913, the Julian Public Library is one of the 11 original San Diego County branch libraries. It has been housed in several facilities, including the high school, various businesses, and even within the Julian Chamber of Commerce. For many years, beginning in 1971, the citizens of Julian were serviced by the library within a century-old one-room schoolhouse known as the Witch

The Julian Public Library is located in a mountain village in San Diego County.

Creek School Building ("Community Profile," 2005). It was described by Sannwald (1991) as a "charming, gabled library," which was "featured in movies, on magazine covers, and even wine labels." It became quite evident as the town grew, however, that a larger building was necessary.

On September 14, 2004, the new facility, built on the Julian High School campus yet sitting off from the high school in its own space, opened to the public. Simpson (2003), reporting in the *San Diego Union-Tribune*, described the agreement by the county and school district to jointly use the library as "an unusual but necessary arrangement," citing the lack of a junior high school library and small high school library as significant reasons. The old schoolhouse continues to be put to good use, in its new capacity as home to the Julian Historical Society (Lepper, 2004).

ENTRANCEWAY

Upon entering the library, guests will find themselves in a small lobby area that includes the Friends of the Julian Library Bookstore to the left. This space is set off dramatically from the rest of the library by a handsomely crafted interior gate that one must walk through to reach the main room. The gate is arguably one of the finest features of the entire interior space. Designed in multiple colors by local artist James Hubbell, the gate, made out of forged steel, bronze, and stained glass, is fluid, as opposed to geometric, in its overall composition. This creative treasure of the library not only intensifies the experience of movement from the lobby into the main room of the interior, but also provides a hint of the unique art to be found once inside.

MAIN ROOM

Aside from the friends bookstore, administrative offices, and a multipurpose room, the Julian Public Library is essentially one large room that has been cleverly divided into different spaces through the use of art and the organization of furniture. Walking through the library definitely proves that imagination and creativity place no limits on what can be accomplished in a single room. What is also noticeable is the lack of a crowded feeling. Although much is going on in this one room, it is obvious that attention was paid to the placement of furniture and library materials. One can easily walk about in this open space, yet also find a snug niche for reading.

Artwork throughout the library, provided by the Julian Arts Guild, succeeds in tying the whole room together. Paintings hang on the walls, while small sculptures rest on the top of lower bookshelves. It was interesting to note that some of the pieces were for sale, providing a welcome space to community artists that ultimately functions as a gallery.

After passing through the Hubbell gate, one will find the reference desk set off to the right at the head of the room and a bank of computer stations to the left in front of the reference desk. Reading tables built of a lighter shade of wood are also found in the main room. Anchored lights on the tables may be turned on and off by the library users, allowing guests to manipulate the lighting according to their own needs. Open book stacks fill much of the one side of the room.

Children's Space and Teen Zone

The children's space was created and set off from the rest of the main room with the usual elements one can expect, but a large mural is what ultimately gives this area its uniqueness. The mural is of a nature scene and includes various animals: raccoons, ducks, deer, birds, and squirrels.

The teen area is primarily made into a different space than the rest of the room with the use of furniture and library resources. Cushioned seats are arranged in a square formation in the middle of the area. Periodicals, selected specifically for a teen audience, 80 in all, line the shelves around the seats. Windows in the space provide views of the highway and trees. The location of this area is also key. Not only is it found in the far back area of the library, but two study rooms located on either side make the space into a type of alcove that seems slightly more hidden than other areas in the main room.

Community Events

The Julian Public Library is also a place for various community events. Librarian Jon Noland has arranged a series of programs titled Native American Heritage Month. This series, which received press in the local *Julian Journal*, recently featured an event with Dorsa O'Dell, wife of the late Scott O'Dell, author of the classic *Island of the Blue Dolphins* and other children's books (Zane, 2005). The 1st Ever Kirsten Dunst Film Festival, also created by Noland, is specifically targeted at teens. Held in the multipurpose room on Tuesday evenings, the festival includes a movie screening and pizza (J. Noland, personal correspondence, December 17, 2005).

Other events receiving local press include Noland's free basic computer class. An article titled "It's Never Too Late to Learn Computing at the Library" portrays the library as a welcoming place where all may seek instruction. This concept of the library is enhanced by a picture of 80-year-old Julian resident Laurea Burt, seated at a work station in the library, who has become "a successful computer user" (2005). A column titled "Library Happenings" found on the front page of the *Julian News* in December 2005 describes events as diverse as restoring sculptures of artist Albert Hubbell that were damaged in the devastating Cedar Fire that swept through the area in late 2003 and a two-part lecture series on the country of Turkey, provided by a resident and writer who has traveled extensively throughout the country.

These various community events, combined with an openness, art, and diverse spaces, all make the Julian Public Library a unique place. The charming building, located in a mountain village that seems far removed from San Diego County beaches and the bustling energy of Los Angeles, exemplifies the diversity of libraries, while it also illustrates the eclectic nature of California.

REFERENCES

"Community Profile, Julian Branch." Publication of the San Diego County Library, August 2005. (Provided by the Julian Public Library.)
"It's Never Too Late to Learn Computing at the Library." *Julian News*, December 14, 2005.
Lepper, R. "Historical Society Writes New Chapter for Old Library." *San Diego Union-Tribune*, December 29, 2004.
"Library Happenings." *Julian News*, December 14, 2005.
Sannwald, W. W. "When It Comes to Sights to Be Seen, Nothing Tops the Libraries of San Diego." *Library Journal* 116, no. 4 (1991): 48.
Simpson, M. "Julian Library to Meet Town's Needs: Public Facility to Serve Students." *San Diego Union-Tribune*, November 19, 2003.
Williams, G. L. "Filming San Diego: Hollywood's Backlot 1898–2002." *Journal of San Diego History* 48, no. 2 (2002): 98–148.
Zane, B. "Scott O'Dell: A Literary Tale." *Julian Journal* 5, no. 9 (2005): 2–3.

5

Helen Hawkins Memorial Library and Research Archive, Women's History Museum and Educational Center

Library Data

Address: 2323 Broadway, Suite 107, San Diego, CA 92102
Phone: (619) 233-7963
Web site: www.whmec.org
Square Feet: 2,000 (entire museum)
Circulation: Noncirculating collection
Collection: over 7,000 books and additional archival collections (2006)

Sources for above: S. Williams, personal correspondence, October 26, 2006, and the Women's History Museum and Educational Center Web site

The Helen Hawkins Memorial Library and Research Archive is housed within the small Women's History Museum and Educational Center (WHMEC). WHMEC is located in the historic San Diego Golden Hill neighborhood at the corner of Broadway and 23rd Street. One can easily walk to downtown San Diego from Golden Hill or take in views of the city's skyline while walking on the hilly sidewalks. The neighborhood is part of the Greater Golden Hill community, an area that displays homes of various architectural styles, including Victorian, Colonial Revival, Craftsman, and Farm House (City of San Diego, n.d.). The majority (34 percent) of the housing units in Greater Golden Hill were built before 1939 (San Diego Association of Governments, 2003). The historic nature of the community becomes evident from a brief walk. Across the street from the WHMEC is the 1908 Alfred C. Platt House. Also found on the corner of the next block up the hill is the rather extravagant 1896 Quartermass-Wilde House. WHMEC shares a space in the neighborhood's Art Union Building. The mostly purple building also houses ballet and art studios.

Museum and Library History

The history of the Women's History Museum and Educational Center is a landscape lined with numerous significant developments. Founded in 1983 by Mary B. Maschal, the nonprofit organization was initially the Women's History Reclamation Project (WHRP). The following year Maschal received a grant to conduct oral history interviews. She was also a dedicated collector and preserver of women's history. Maschal's home was filled with historic documents and ephemera (WHMEC, 2005b).

An open house for the community, which was coordinated to allow for a simultaneous celebration of the seventy-fifth anniversary of women being granted the right to vote, did not take place until 1995, over ten years after the founding of the organization. The open house was held in Maschal's home, which served equally at the time as the headquarters of WHRP and an exhibition space. The collection was moved the following year to the Art Union Building museum where it opened to the public in September 1996. In 2003, WHRP changed its name to WHMEC as a reflection of its larger goals (WHMEC, 2005b).

Over the years WHMEC has run various programs and exhibits in fulfillment of its mission "to educate and inspire present and future generations about the experiences and contributions of women by collecting, preserving and interpreting the evidence of that experience" (WHMEC, 2005b). Programs and events have included a 2000 Women's History Poetry Contest that opened along with an exhibit titled In Our Own Voice: Women's History through Women's Poetry; a traveling exhibit, Women Who Dare that was established in 2001; and the creation in 2005 of the permanent exhibit All Our Grandmothers.

Part of the history of WHMEC is the growing Helen Hawkins Memorial Library and Research Archive. The book collection is primarily comprised of books written by or about women, spanning various subject areas, such as women's history, sociology, women's studies, fiction, biography, and others. Special collections include the Alice Park Archive, a collection that "contains information and artifacts from the women's suffrage movement of the late–19th and early–20th centuries" (WHMEC, 2005a). Three other collections are the Lucy Killea Papers that document Killea's political career; the UN Conferences on the Status of Women collection; and the Neff-LeClair Collection, which is a collection of antique costumes dating back to the 18th century.

Entrance and Gift Shop

The entrance to the museum resembles a welcoming storefront with a single door. An artfully designed banner with the museum's name and the title of the permanent exhibit hangs over the doorway. The name of the museum is also printed on a large glass window that faces the sidewalk.

The Helen Hawkins Memorial Library and Research Archive is housed within the Women's History Museum and Educational Center in a building that also houses ballet and art studios.

Since the museum and the library essentially share the same space, it is important to write about the interior of the WHMEC as a whole. Once opening the door, visitors will find one room (not including the office and other spaces in the back) that provides exhibit areas, a small store, and a library. Immediately inside the museum and to the right is a gift shop that sells items that reflect the nature of the organization, such as jewelry, T-shirts, posters, note cards, and both used and new books.

Permanent Exhibits

All Our Grandmothers, one of the permanent exhibits, runs the length of one wall. The exhibit is in two phases with phase one focusing on Native and African American women and phase two focusing on Latin and Asian American women. In addition to photographs and other objects on display, there are four glass exhibit cases. A collection of items in one case is titled "Health and Home." Found here are many historic objects, including sewing supplies and health-related products.

Another case titled "Recreation and the Outdoors" contains ice skates and tennis rackets from the early to mid–20th century. A bird-watching journal and scrapbook of Ruth Nelson, dating from 1919 is also on display.

Along the back wall is the San Diego County Women's Hall of Fame. This area is decorated with framed photographs of many women. The mission of the hall of fame "is to acknowledge and honor women who have significantly contributed to the quality of life and who have made outstanding volunteer contributions in San Diego County" (WHMEC, 2005c). Five women are inducted into the hall of fame during annual ceremonies.

Located next to the library bookshelves is another permanent exhibit titled 85 Years of Women's Suffrage. Included here is an exhibit case with items such as suffrage pins and suffrage and antisuffrage postcards. A khaki outfit worn by a suffragist activist, which dates from the 1910s, is one of the interesting items on display.

Intermingled with some of the book collection, demonstrating further the interconnectedness between the library and museum, are pieces of art from the Muriel Fisher Doll Maker's Collection. Fisher was a local artist. Her creation of 12 dolls has been described as the "crowning achievement of her 'crone years'" by Many Hands Crafts Gallery, San Diego's oldest artist cooperative of which Fisher was a member for nearly 30 years (2005). Fisher's unique dolls are composed of materials including found objects, according to Sarah Williams, WHMEC executive director (personal correspondence, October 28, 2006). The handcrafted dolls, which are cleverly and beautifully designed, include Anais Nin, Gertrude Stein, May Sarton, Frida Kahlo, Toni Morrison, Georgia O'Keeffe, and others. Due to the placement of some of the dolls within the library's space, one may come upon them while browsing the shelves.

The center of the room provides space for changing exhibits. In October 2006, the area was filled with the temporary exhibit Making History, Making Zines. Visitors to the museum could examine and read a large display of self-published magazines, including many local zines. Two workshops sponsored by a group called Grrrl Zines a Go-Go were also held at the museum during the run of the exhibit. The workshops were designed to introduce attendees to the world of self-made publications.

LIBRARY SPACE

The library is located to the right of the entrance in its specially dedicated corner. A sign that reads "The Helen Hawkins Memorial Library and Research Archive" hangs above four rows of bookshelves. The majority of the shelf space is filled with books. One entire row, however, contains periodicals including a *Ms.* magazine collection and other periodicals that are in line with the mission of the museum, including *Spokeswoman*, *New Women*, and *Women & Employment*.

Limited seating on rather curious furniture that could be taken as part of the museum exhibit is available. One example is an older loveseat and small table located next to the bookshelves. Relaxing on this loveseat while perusing through materials from the collection provides visitors the experience of sitting simultaneously in a library, gift shop, and museum. The atmosphere of the sitting area perfectly captures the sense of place of the WHMEC, a facility that contains numerous discoveries of varying formats within a small space.

REFERENCES

City of San Diego. "Community Profiles: San Diego Community Profile; Greater Golden Hill." n.d. www.sandiego.gov/planning/community/profiles/greatergoldenhill/index.shtml (retrieved November 1, 2006).
Many Hands Crafts Gallery. "Many Hands Craft Gallery Presents a Special Homage to an Exceptional Woman in the Arts." *Many Hands Crafts Gallery Newsletter*, April 2005. www.manyhandscraftgallery.com/newsletter.htm (retrieved November 10, 2006).
San Diego Association of Governments. "Census 2000 Profile: Golden Hill Community Planning Area: City of San Diego." June 12, 2003. http://cart.sandag.org/profiles/cen00/sdcpa1408cen00.pdf (retrieved November 1, 2006).
Women's History Museum and Educational Center (WHMEC). "Our Collection." 2005a. www.whrp.net/libarch.html (retrieved October 3, 2006).
_____. "Our History and Timeline." 2005b. www.whrp.net/history.html (retrieved November 10, 2006).
_____. "San Diego County Women's Hall of Fame." 2005c. www.whrp.net/sd_hof.html (retrieved November 10, 2006).

Part II
Orange County

6

Sherman Library & Gardens

Library Data

Address: 2647 East Pacific Coast Highway, Corona del Mar, CA 92625
Phone: (949) 673-1880
Web site: www.slgardens.org
Square Feet: approximately 1,727
Circulation: Noncirculating collection
Collection: 25,000 books, pamphlets, and other printed items; over 2,000 reels of microfilm; several hundred thousand papers; various archival documents (2006)
Sources for above: J. Thrasher, personal correspondence, October 18, 2006, and the Sherman Library & Gardens Web site

Sherman Library & Gardens is located in Corona del Mar not far from a stunning section of the Southern California coastline. Corona del Mar sits between the cities of Newport Beach and Laguna Beach, communities known for their wealth and beauty, yet, they are also areas where one encounters the free-spirited nature and openness often found in California beach communities. The impeccably manicured library grounds are truly a feast for the senses and the intellect. Plant lovers and historians will feel at home here, as well as any weary traveler who seeks refuge in a place of tranquility often not found in the busy world. An article appearing in the *Los Angeles Times* over two decades ago describes the property appropriately as "an oasis of peace, beauty and history in an increasingly developed area" (Tripoli, 1983).

Building History

The research library started as a home, was later converted into office space, and eventually became a library (Sherman Library & Gardens, 2004). William Hendricks, director of the library, has worked at the building for 40 years. During his early years of employment, he worked alongside the founder. In fact, Hendricks has been the instrumental force behind the collection at the library. He acquisitioned the various collections, and continues to do so, receiving many materials through gifts and donations (personal correspondence, September 14, 2005).

The focus of the library is on the Pacific Southwest, an area defined as "California, Arizona, adjacent parts of Nevada, plus the area around the upper end of the Gulf of California" (Sherman Library & Gardens, n.d.). It is evident from a brochure about the library that its mission is intertwined with the Pacific Southwest territories it seeks to understand. "Once remote and difficult to reach," the brochure reads, "this region has evolved over the past century and a half into one of the world's most dynamic regions. One of the aims of the Library's holdings is to help explain this extraordinary transformation" (Sherman Library & Gardens, n.d.).

Information on the library Web site states that "first-time visitors to the Library are often struck by the charm and unusualness of the building" (Sherman Library & Gardens, 2004). According to Hendricks, the original small adobe house, that is currently an entranceway to the library and exhibit hall, was built by a couple around 1940 (personal correspondence, September 14, 2005). The couple purchased the lot for a mere $600. The property was later bought by Arnold Haskell in the 1950s upon his move from Brentwood, California, to Corona del Mar. The lot expanded over the years to a much larger property consisting of the research library, botanical gardens, gift shop, and cafe. A plaque immediately outside the library entrance reads:

> This beautiful cultural center was founded in 1966 by Arnold D. Haskell (1895–1977). Motivated by his love of history and horticulture, he conceived and developed Sherman Library and Gardens over an eight-year period. Through his generosity and personal effort, the purchase of this entire block and all construction were made possible. Sherman Library and Gardens is now a public charity and is maintained for the benefit of the general public.

BOTANICAL GARDENS

Both public entrances to the library, one on Pacific Coast Highway and the other on the back parking lot, require that visitors walk through a portion of the botanical gardens before reaching the library. Wide brick walkways wind throughout the gardens, providing a feeling of spaciousness and elegance. Flower beds and fountains complement the paths. The botanical collection features "more than 1,500 plants ranging from rare cacti and succulents of desert regions to exotic vegetation of tropical climates" (Sherman Library & Gardens, n.d.). So stunning are the grounds that those coming to do research may find themselves walking around the property before heading over to the library. It would be impossible to separate the experience of place of the garden from the library, since the two are intertwined and equally feed the senses.

A few of the many discoveries I made in the garden along the way to the library in September 2005 include: Flamingo Lily (Columbia), Sago Palm

Sherman Library & Gardens in Corona Del Mar is on a scenic and romantic stretch of the Pacific Coast Highway in Orange County, California.

(Southern Japan), Blue Mexican Fig, Red Ti (India to Polynesia), Bower Vine (Australia), Feather Duster Palm (New Zealand), Chinese Flame Tree, and Blue Ginger (Brazil). Also of note were many California native plants, a section of carnivorous plants, a cactus garden, orchids, and a rose garden. Some of the plants are housed within a tropical conservatory that also features a koi pond. When entering the conservatory, one cannot help but notice the change in temperature to a more warm and humid climate, especially when compared to the cool Pacific Ocean breeze outside.

On the other side of the conservatory, one will find the Discovery Garden of Touch and Smell. An inviting sign above this assortment of plants reads: "The Discovery Garden features plants whose principal appeal is not to the eye, as is the rest of the gardens, but rather to the sense of touch or the sense of smell. Please enjoy the many unusual textures and aromas of this area." Chocolate Basil Mint, Apple Mint, Purple Basil, Rose Geranium, Nutmeg Geranium, and Canary Island Sage are a few of the unusual plants that visitors will come across.

Research Library Entrance

After winding through the gardens, heading in the direction of the research library, guests will enter the cactus garden. This meticulously manicured area is also a place to pause. The entrance to the library is on the other side of this assortment of cacti. A large California pepper tree sits in front of the entrance. Lights draped within the branches of this wonderful tree must create a beautiful image in the dusk and evening hours.

Adobe

The old adobe is the first part of the library that guests enter. They must pass through this small structure to reach the collections. An awning over the adobe is covered by royal trumpet vine, demonstrating once more the interconnection between the garden and library. The inside of the adobe serves as an exhibit room.

In September 2005, an exhibit of black-and-white photographs by M. R. Johnson (1889–1949) was on display. Johnson was a former president of the Pacific Indemnity Company. His son donated about 300 of his father's photographs to the library (Sherman Library & Gardens, 2005). The photographs, all taken in the 1930s, celebrate the Western landscape, tying in very nicely with the library's collection of the historic Pacific Southwest. Sequoia National Park, Yosemite, Death Valley, and Mission San Juan Capistrano are some of the California locations captured in the images.

Also on display in this small room is an oak dining table that belonged to Moses H. Sherman. Haskell named the property after Sherman, an educator and

6. Sherman Library & Gardens 53

The entrance to the research library at the Sherman Library & Gardens is a small adobe house that was built around 1940.

California pioneer (Sherman Library & Gardens, n.d.). According to an informational card located within the glass covering of the table, several U.S. presidents sat at the table while visiting Sherman in California.

DRESSING ROOM

While providing a tour of the facility, Hendricks opened the door to a room just before the main library. He explained that the room serves as storage for newspaper clippings and as a dressing area for brides and grooms who are being married on the premises (personal correspondence, September 14, 2005).

HISTORIC READING ROOM

Before reaching the stacks, visitors will walk through an old reading room where some employees, including an archivist, currently work. Also within this room is an old card catalog. Hendricks pointed out that the library collection cannot be searched electronically at this time, but the card catalog continues to meet the needs of the researchers (personal correspondence, September 15, 2005). A short hall and a few stairs lead from this room to where the majority of the library's books are kept.

BOOK COLLECTION

The room most often used by visitors is small and charming. A reading table with several chairs is off to the right of the entrance. Other chairs are dispersed within the stacks. Several rows of shelves hold historic city directories. The directories tell a story about a city's history and development, through information on businesses and residents. One directory of Los Angeles dates from 1888; another of San Francisco is from 1886. Even smaller communities and cities in Arizona and Nevada are included. Hendricks mentioned that the directories are the most sought-after resources in the collection. He can never anticipate the number of users per day. On the day of my visit, he had received no researchers. The previous day, six individuals came to the library. Many who use the directories are investigators from environmental companies, researching soil pollution levels, who hope to discover what structure previously occupied a certain plot of land.

In addition to the city directories, the library has a collection of Southwest Blue Books dating back to the early 20th century. These books are described as "a society directory of names, addresses, telephone numbers, names of clubs, and their officers." One may also find club registers and marriage announcements.

Art that mirrors the collection is dispersed throughout the small room. On one wall hangs a series of watercolors of missions on Southern California Indian reservations. The paintings were created during the fall of 1953 and spring of 1954 by the late Dr. Horace Parker and his wife, Laverne. To the right of each watercolor is an explanatory note and a photograph taken 25 years later of the same mission captured in the 1950s watercolor.

A few impressionist paintings of California also hang on the walls within the stacks. Included in this collection are two 1924 paintings by Clarence Hinkle titled *Houses on Cliff, Laguna* and *Houses on Shore at Laguna*. Similar to the black-and-white photograph display in the adobe, all of the displayed art is in harmony with the scope of the library's collection.

ARCHIVAL COLLECTION

The archival collection is housed in a basement room, accessible down stairs not far from the entrance to the book collection. What the room lacks in beauty or space it makes up for in mystery and an abundance of intrigue. Compact shelving and all the boxes in this small area would be a delight to any historian who is studying the Pacific Southwest region. In fact, so much material lines the shelves and floor that I had to follow Hendricks down a narrow path that was the only available walking space. He pointed out how space continues to be a problem for the burgeoning collection.

Included within the archives are various historic maps of Corona del Mar and neighboring cities, as well as aerial photographs. One map dating from 1878 shows the Newport Beach Harbor area. Many shelves are lined with archival boxes full of the personal papers of various citizens. Hendricks pointed out the papers of William Michael Mathes, a retired University of San Francisco professor, those of Evaline Morrison, a former Los Angeles school teacher and columnist for the *Riverside Press Enterprise*, and the papers of Manuel Ruiz, a Los Angeles attorney. Company records for such firms as the Pacific Life Insurance Company and Colorado River Land Company are also here.

Hendricks delighted in pointing out some real treasures of the collection, such as an 1884 Spanish language newspaper from Phoenix that was decorated with gold dust lettering. Other interesting items include antique maps that show California as an island, various local newspapers dating back to different eras, and several large donations. One donation that lined numerous shelves was a three-generational family collection of California books and magazines.

Events and Changing Seasons

Although the historic collection of the library may lead one to conclude that the library is a stationary place, locked permanently in a time other than today, the Sherman Library & Gardens is very much a work in progress, just like an understanding of history is. The overflowing boxes within the basement archives demonstrate that a wealth of information is stored within the small structure. Casual visitors or those conducting research at the library will likely never reach the bottom of the collection, especially when considering that new donations continue to arrive. If this is not enough to compel visitors to return, the changing, seasonal colors of the botanical gardens outside the door of the library are sure to help.

In addition to the gardens and the historic resources, the facility hosts many events, including various gardening classes. Other events tie specifically to the local community and fall within the scope of the library collection. A lecture series for 2006 titled *Historic Newport Beach* is one such occasion that illustrates Sherman Library & Gardens as a place committed to learning about not only the larger Pacific Southwest, but the communities its local supporters call home.

REFERENCES

Sherman Library & Gardens. Brochure, n.d. (Available at the Sherman Library & Gardens.)
_____. *Education Program: Fall/Winter 2005/2006.* Brochure, 2005. (Available at the Sherman Library & Gardens.)
_____. "The Library." 2004. www.slgardens.org/the_library/default.asp (retrieved August 11, 2005).
Tripoli, S. "Sherman Gardens: A Cultural Oasis Amid Urban Scene." *Los Angeles Times*, October 30, 1983.

7

Leatherby Libraries, Chapman University

Library Data

Address: One University Drive, Orange, CA 92866
Phone: (714) 532-7756
Web site: www1.chapman.edu/library
Square Feet: 100,000
Circulation: 58,407 (2005/2006)
Collection: 220,759 books, bound journals and e-books; 1,731 print periodicals; 690,630 microfilm and microfiche; 10,294 audio visual items, 30,000 electronic periodicals
Sources for above: C. Baldwin, personal correspondence, September 17, 2005, and California Library Chapman University Leatherby Libraries 2004–2006 (yearly report)

It is possible to walk onto some college campuses and know immediately which building is likely the library. This is exactly the case with the Leatherby Libraries of Chapman University. The university campus has changed dramatically over the past few years with the construction of several large and spectacular buildings. In fact, someone who has been away from the campus since the late 1990s may return to the expanding grounds and be quite stunned by the growth. A new law school, business and economics hall, music hall, and interfaith center have been added in a relatively short time and construction is currently underway on the future home of the Dodge College of Film and Media Arts, which will be complete by the time this book is published. Even with all these new developments mixed in with the everlasting grandeur and tradition of the older buildings, the Leatherby Libraries sits at the heart of the campus and is arguably the most dynamic building. The concept behind the library is much like that of the ancient Library of Alexandria, described by Demas (2005) as a "temple of muses" that included "a research center, a museum, and a venue for celebrating the arts, inquiry, and scholarship" (p. 25).

Downtown Orange

It is not unusual to overhear the location of Chapman University described as "near the Orange Circle." This section of Orange, also known as Old Towne Orange, has a sense of place like many historic downtowns. Filled with numerous antique shops, cafes, an Irish pub, and some excellent eating establishments, the Orange Circle area provides an eclectic mix. One can choose to have breakfast at several locations, including the Cuban Felix Continental Café and the American-style Watson Drugstore. Later in the day, a walk down the sidewalk could lead to dinner at Rutabegorz, a restaurant in a 1915 building that is known for its near book-length menu and an abundance of vegetarian dishes, or the more elegant and upscale Citrus City Grille. Also found on Glassell, one of the main streets that runs into the heart of the community, is the Ugly Mug cafe which provides, unbelievably, a hair salon in the back room of the coffeehouse. Located just a few steps from this eclectic mix is the campus of Chapman University. Although the campus sits on the edge of the downtown area, it is very much a part of the local scene.

University History

Chapman University, founded in 1861, is one of the oldest private universities in California. Its history is marked with a series of name changes. The university traces its roots to Hesperian College in Woodland. It then merged with Los Angeles based California Christian College. In 1934, the name was changed yet again to Chapman College, after an Orange County benefactor. In 1954, the college moved to Orange County, where it has remained. A further name change came about in 1991 when "college" was replaced by "university" to reflect its granting of both bachelor's and master's degrees (Chapman University, 2004a).

Chapman's current location was originally the site of the old Orange Union High School. The high school buildings, found on the west side of the campus, were built in 1904 in the neoclassical tradition. Five of the buildings are listed on the National Register of Historic Places (Chapman University, 2004b). They now sit in the midst of a growing collection of expertly crafted modern buildings. The architectural changes over the years that have plagued some campuses, resulting in a group of unevenly styled buildings, has not occurred at Chapman. Although there are definitely buildings of various styles, the campus environment provides an elegant atmosphere that has somehow managed to avoid conflict by blending the old with the new very well. The Leatherby Libraries is a microcosm of the larger campus, demonstrating how several different colors and themes can result in an aesthetically pleasing mixture. The library cleverly does this through its unusual interior spaces, which are comprised of nine libraries within one building.

History of the Library

Before the Leatherby Libraries, the university had the Thurmond Clarke Memorial Library. This library, which opened in 1967, was the first free-standing

The Leatherby Libraries of Chapman University feature nine distinct libraries within one building, including the Sala and Aron Samueli Holocaust Memorial Library and the John and Donna Crean Library of Film and Television.

library for the institution (C. Baldwin, personal correspondence, September 20, 2005). It resembled many two-year and four-year college libraries built in the same era. The old 35,000 square foot library was arguably not a spectacular building, but an essential and functional one with several attractive spaces. It provided seating for 150, 18 computers, and shelving capacity for 200,000 volumes (Chapman University, n.d.). According to Charlene Baldwin, dean of the libraries, it was demolished in May 2003 to make room for the new library (personal correspondence, September 20, 2005).

The Leatherby Libraries, which opened in August 2004, provides seating for 700+ with over 100 computers. It also has shelving capacity for 300,000–500,000 volumes, significantly more than the old building. The library provides several other features that were not found previously, including a 24-hour study area, cafe, instruction room, and wireless access, as well as a stunning interior of various spaces (Chapman University, n.d.). Designed by the architectural firm AC Martin Partners, the building has 100,000 square feet spread out over five floors. Perhaps the most telling example of the splendor of the new building is the number of visits it receives. According to Baldwin, before its retirement, the old Thurmond Clarke Memorial Library had 179,000 visitors during its last year. Within just the first month of the new library, there have been 70,000 visitors (personal correspondence, October 30, 2004). The large number of visitors has continued. Tracing one year from August 30, 2004, to September 1, 2005, over 605,000 visitors came through the main entrance (C. Baldwin, personal correspondence, September 17, 2005).

EXTERIOR GROUNDS

The exterior perimeter of the Leatherby Libraries is an area comprised of white park benches, grass, trees, and several carved busts of famous individuals. Each bust sits on a raised platform of several feet. Included on the side of the library that faces Argyros Forum, a busy and large building that houses various student dining options, classrooms, an Albert Schweitzer exhibit, and the university gift shop, are busts of Presidents Washington and Lincoln and the filmmaker Cecil B. DeMille. The platform each bust sits on includes a plaque with a quote. Similar busts are found in front of Argyros Forum, as well as further down the sidewalk past the library. In fact, a significantly larger bust of Albert Schweitzer sits at the top of the stairs leading into Argyros Forum, making it very visible to those exiting the library. "Search and see if there is not some place where you may invest your humanity," reads the quote beneath Schweitzer.

In addition to the art and several places for seating, a large fountain is also located next to the library. Called the Gentle Spring Fountain, the arrangement of rocks within the fountain resembles a Zen-like structure. The fountain and other elements surrounding the exterior of the building create an enchanting and artistic atmosphere before one even enters the library.

Rotunda

Described as the "architectural icon" of the building, the rotunda provides different spaces on each floor for either solitary studying or group gatherings. The first floor of the rotunda remains open 24 hours a day Monday through Friday, allowing students access to the building when the rest of the library is closed. The 24-hour access policy, which is also found at Soka University in Aliso Viejo, California, truly provides a "home away from home" for those who take advantage of it.

The first floor includes a study commons with several tables and four computers. A highlight of the rotunda is a skylight located 62 feet above. Windows and the magnificent skylight allow for much natural lighting. Another feature of the first floor is a cafe that provides coffee and snacks. Demas (2005) discusses the growing phenomenon of having cafes inside academic libraries:

> Borrowing from bookstore and café culture, more libraries are including cafes inside of or adjacent to their service areas. When done thoughtfully as part of an overall strategy for library development and stewardship, cafes can be a positive element in creating a sense of place in a library [p. 34].

Not only does the library offer this cafe area, but a few paces from the rotunda is the adjacent Lewis Family Lounge with vending machines that sell soda, hot drinks, and snacks. The lounge, which is also open 24 hours, provides more seating and two group study rooms.

The impressiveness of the rotunda continues through the second and third floors. The second floor offers a reading room with lounge chairs near the windows. The third floor provides an aesthetically pleasing two-story reading room with tables and chairs and spectacular views of the campus.

Predictable Spaces

Spaces that occur for the same purpose and in the same location on each floor of a multistory library create not only a seamless interior, but a sense of comfort through predictability. This can be especially significant for students who are trying to navigate a large building. The Leatherby Libraries has several instances of spaces that are both predictable and functional.

The second and third floors, which house the majority of the libraries' collections, both have oval-shaped lobbies that provide the main entranceway to the floors via the elevators or stairs. These spaces offer several openings to different wings and reading rooms, allowing for a sense of openness. Also found on the second and third floors are copy alcoves in the same locations near the centers. Library users may easily find these spaces, since one may enter and exit the alcoves through openings on the left and right.

The Leatherby Libraries provide spaces of functionality and beauty across four floors and a basement.

Art

Shortly after the opening of the new building, Baldwin explained there was a goal to bring art into the library (personal correspondence, October 30, 2004). It is quite clear that this goal is being met. Art from the permanent collection and exhibitions may be found throughout the entire building.

Some of the most striking pieces from the permanent collection are granary ladders located around the perimeter of the second floor lobby. These eight ladders, crafted by the Lobi people of North Ghana and Southern Burkina Faso in the late 19th and early 20th centuries, are each carved from a single tree trunk. Ascending steps worked into each ladder provided access to the Lobi's dwellings.

Exhibitions of artists' works may also be found within the library. The artwork is not within gallery spaces, but hangs on the walls where students sit below or nearby to study. In December 2005, for example, an exhibit titled Retrospective of an Artist's Life Journey, which included watercolors and oils by Gloria Bradeson, hung in three areas on the second floor. Bradeson, a longtime resident of Newport Beach, a city located approximately 30 minutes from the library, paints various subjects including animals, flowers, and sailboats. Her art, displayed in such a way, creates an environment where art is very much a part of the students' daily life and ritualistic activities that take place in the library.

Malloy Performance Portico

Tying further into the theme of the library as a cultural center on campus is the Malloy Performance Portico. This area, which is circular in shape, is defined as the "cultural hub for the library" ("Highlights of," 2004). It includes a drop-down screen, built-in speakers, and the equipment necessary to support audiovisual displays. Shortly after the library opened, Baldwin envisioned this space as a future home to events such as string quartet performances, poetry readings, artwork exhibits, and screenings of student films (personal correspondence, October 30, 2004). The portico was utilized for such activities during the first year, including a publishers' reception, a new faculty reception, and the showcasing (on CD) of a student musical ensemble. A book talk and signing by one of the university's authors was an event in the planning stages in September 2005, as well as a harpist for another event reception (C. Baldwin, personal correspondence, September 20, 2005).

Art throughout the library and cultural events in the portico are the realization of the larger mission of the library — a place that stretches well beyond just a quiet place for study. According to Demas (2005):

> When the library acts as a welcoming and lively host, engaging the community in discourse and in enjoyment of the life of the mind, the community perception of the role of the library on campus begins to change. The library becomes a true cultural center and an agent in community building, and library staff and programs become engaged with the community in more and different ways [p. 34].

This idea of the library is one of collaborative spaces used for diverse campus and community activities.

Third Floor Branch Libraries

The Malloy Performance Portico provides several entranceways into the branch libraries found on this floor. The third floor houses the majority of the libraries with five total branches located here. The distinctive libraries are what truly make the building most unusual. Art, "ceiling features," colors, and, in some cases, separate entranceways are used to differentiate between the libraries.

The Leon and Olga Argyros Library of Business and Economics opens from the portico with a "ceiling feature" described as "a bronze 'bowl' embossed with a map of the northern hemisphere to symbolize international business" ("Highlights of," 2004). Colors in the space are bronze, brass, and green. In addition to individual study carrels and tables, this library provides a multimedia room for group work.

The Edgar and Libby Pankey Library of Education, located next to the business and economics branch, also includes the Peter and Mary Muth Library of Children's Literature. A large exhibit case near the entrance of the space displays part of the library's permanent toy collection. Fitting with the theme of education and children, an explanatory note near the exhibit reads: "Learning through Play, Children's Books and Toys from the Nineteenth and Twentieth Centuries." A ceiling feature is also highly visible upon entrance. Quite unlike the sophisticated bronze bowl that meets those entering the business and economics area, this area displays ceiling art that "echoes the building's paint palette in a design evoking change and lifelong learning" ("Highlights of," 2004).

The ceiling feature at the entrance to the Onnolee Elliott Ph.D. Library of Science and Technology "is a honeycomb pattern in titanium alloy to symbolize life sciences and technology" ("Highlights of," 2004). This area boasts the largest collection on the floor and includes another multimedia room and group study room. Student work was on display throughout this space in fall 2005. The work included rather large poster projects that were arranged on the tops of lower shelves and also around the perimeter. The posters, which were colorful and included references and abstracts of the students' work within layouts of text and images, were on various topics, such as DNA testing, coral reefs, global warming, deforestation of the rainforest, and conjoined twins.

The John and Donna Crean Library of Film and Television and the M. Douglas Library of Music are the final two branches on this floor. Group study rooms, a listening area, a multimedia room, and spaces for individual study are also found throughout, as well as the Dr. William E. and Katharina Bradley Film and Television Screening Room, an area permitting small groups to view and discuss films. Also located in the film and television branch is a large two-part exhibit of signed framed photographs from the original cast of the 1939 film *Gone with the Wind*.

Sala and Aron Samueli Holocaust Memorial Library

Another area that provides a different atmosphere is the Sala and Aron Samueli Holocaust Memorial Library, located on the fourth floor. This impressive space is located down the hall from an outdoor area called the Fashionables

Terrace, which includes tables and chairs with stunning views of the campus, larger city, and mountains in the distance. This outdoor area provides quite a contrast from the dramatic features of the holocaust library:

> After exiting the elevators, visitors are met by zinc-clad walls intended to evoke the harsh reality of the Holocaust and to raise awareness that one is entering into a different space within the Leatherby Libraries. The stones along the edge of the wall testify to enduring memory and the power of witness. In Judaism, stones — symbolizing remembrance and presence — are often placed upon gravestones. We hope that each person who enters the library will contribute in his or her own way to remembrance and witness ["Themes of," n.d.].

The entrance area initially resembles a museum with several large display cases. The main room provides a reference library with materials on the Holocaust and related topics. There are computers, tables, and areas for individual study.

The holocaust library, as well as the numerous other diverse spaces within the building, demonstrate the uniqueness of the Leatherby Libraries. History, culture, learning, and all the various aspects of a university education are each given space. Instead of culminating in a final, splintered creation, however, the spaces within the building wonderfully add layers to reach an ultimate, unified whole.

REFERENCES

Chapman University Leatherby Libraries 2004–2006 [yearly report]. (Available at the Leatherby Libraries.)
Chapman University. "Frequently Asked Questions." n.d. www1.chapman.edu/library/govt-docs/FAQ.html (retrieved August 23, 2005).
_____. "History." 2004a. www.chapman.edu/about/chapfacts/history (retrieved December 3, 2005).
_____. "Overview of Chapman History." 2004b. www.chapman.edu/about/chapfacts/history/history2.asp (retrieved December 3, 2005).
Demas, S. "From the Ashes of Alexandria: What's Happening in the College Library? In *Library as Place: Rethinking Roles, Rethinking Space*. Washington, DC:
Council on Library and Information Resources, February 2005. www.clir.org/pubs/reports/pub129/pub129.pdf (retrieved December 20, 2005).
Highlights of the Leatherby Libraries. Brochure, October 2004. (Available at the Leatherby Libraries.)
Themes of the Holocaust Exhibit. Brochure, n.d. (Available at the Leatherby Libraries.)

8

Daisaku and Kaneko Ikeda Library, Soka University

LIBRARY DATA

Address: One University Drive, Aliso Viejo, CA 92656
Phone: (949) 480-4105
Web site: http://ikedalibrary.soka.edu
Square Feet: 119,366
Circulation: 16,358 (2005)
Collection: 65,000 books; 200+ print journals; 8,000 electronic journals; 1,076 audiovisual materials (October 2006)
Source for above: M. Hight, personal correspondence, October 18, 2006

Soka University of America (SUA), located in the South Orange County city of Aliso Viejo, overlooks the 4,000-acre Aliso and Wood Canyons Wilderness Park. Its position allows for spectacular views of the natural landscape from almost any location on campus, including the windows of the Daisaku and Kaneko Ikeda Library. Soka, which means "to create value" (Soka, 2005d) was "founded on the Buddhist principles of peace, human rights and sanctity of life" (Soka, 2005c). Much of the promotional literature on the university's Web site (www.soka.edu) or in print around the campus includes quotes that speak to this spiritual foundation. The mottos and principles of SUA read like poetry:

> Mottos
> Be philosophers of a renaissance of life
> Be world citizens in solidarity for peace
> Be the pioneers of a global civilization
> Principles
> Foster leaders of culture in the community
> Foster leaders of humanism in society
> Foster leaders of pacifism in the world
> Foster leaders for the creative coexistence of nature and humanity
> [Soka, 2005c].

It is fitting that visitors to the university, upon driving through the entrance, will find a body of water called Peace Lake, an area surrounded by a simple and aesthetically pleasing walkway with park benches. The mottos and principles of the institution do mirror the serene and elegant campus. The university's grounding in qualities such as peace and harmony may also be found in the spaces within the Ikeda Library, a building that poises itself well between functionality and beauty.

University Origins

Before moving into an exploration of the spaces within the Ikeda Library, it is important to understand the context of the larger university to which the building belongs. Although residents of Orange County may assume SUA exists as a single, private entity, the university is actually the most recent addition to a longstanding tradition of education.

In Japan, Soka schools range from kindergartens to a large Soka University with an enrollment of 8,800 students (Soka, 2005d). The Soka educational system traces its beginnings to over 75 years ago:

> Soka education has its origins in the work of Tsunesaburo Makiguchi, a Japanese educator and Buddhist leader. During World War II, Makiguchi was arrested by Japanese military authorities for his opposition to the war and for his defense of religious freedom. He died in prison in 1944.
>
> The small education society that Makiguchi founded in 1930 has since grown to become one of the world's largest lay Buddhist organizations [Soka, 2005d].

In the United States, the first Soka university campus was established in 1987 in the Los Angeles County city of Calabasas. The Calabasas campus offers a graduate program (Soka, 2005d). SUA acquired the Aliso Viejo location in 1995 to establish a four-year liberal arts college, which ultimately led to the creation of the Ikeda Library. The library currently supports just one program: an undergraduate degree in liberal arts. Students select a concentration in Humanities, International Studies, or Social and Behavioral Sciences (Soka, 2005b).

Library History

The Ikeda Library is a significantly newer building, when compared to many of the libraries discussed in this book. The "Library Topping Off Ceremony" was held as recently as February 16, 1999, and the "Cornerstone Laying Ceremony," which was attended by 700 guests, occurred on May 3, 1999 (Soka, 2005a). The first event in the library building was held on December 31, 2000. It must be noted, however, that the library is not the only new building on the campus. Every building on the SUA campus in Aliso Viejo is similarly new. As already noted, the

The view from a window inside the Daisaku and Kaneko Ikeda Library of Soka University demonstrates the architectural symmetry found in the library and other campus buildings.

land was acquired in 1995 and the university opened on May 3, 2001 ("Facts and Figures," 2004). For a few months before the opening, staff and faculty used temporary offices located in the library.

Main Floor

A walkway from the parking lot to the Ikeda Library is lined on both sides by an abundance of lavender. Visitors on a spring or summer day may find that the warm temperature and a light breeze from the canyon creates an aroma of lavender in the air. A grand staircase leads to the entrance of the Ikeda Library. The main floor of the library is located at the top of this staircase on the second floor.

Close to the entrance on the main floor is an arrangement of overstuffed chairs around a circular table. Maryann Hight, a librarian at SUA, explained that this spot tends to be a high-use area by the students (personal correspondence, October 14, 2005). Several editions of the publication *California History* were fanned out across this table. A copy of one of the issue covers was also on the table within a small display frame. Hight explained that she uses this space to highlight a journal of the week and introduce the students to items from the print collection.

The reference desk is also located on the main floor. An arrangement of flowers sat visibly on the desk. Hight stated that she has three bouquets of silk flowers that she alternates for use in this space. Recently, however, she brought in real sunflowers. She further explained she has received several favorable comments from library users regarding the floral arrangements, demonstrating how a relatively easy form of decoration will noticeably enhance an area.

Five tables with computer workstations are set off a few feet from the reference desk. Tables also line a wall with windows that look out over the campus. The large windows provide natural lighting for these tables and much of the room.

Another wall is taken up by both a processing area and librarian offices. Library users can see through each librarian's office to a view of the canyon beyond. The librarians are fortunate to have doors that lead from their offices to a patio area with small tables and chairs. What is perhaps most unusual about the offices is the openness the spaces provide and how students and community users can see areas that are often kept hidden or much less accessible.

At the far end of the main floor is a 24-hour study room. Similar to the rest of the floor, the room is both functional, with several study tables and wireless access, and comfortable, with many overstuffed chairs. When the library is closed, Hight explained, students may access this room from an outside entrance with a key each student is provided (personal correspondence, October 14, 2005).

First Floor

Print periodical holdings, study spaces, and a mixture of furniture are found on the first floor. Windows that students may open themselves run nearly the length of one wall, allowing, once more, for views of the canyon. One larger study room is available for rent by community groups.

Also found down a corridor from the periodical holdings is a library instruction room. The instruction space has a makeshift feel. Two rows of computers and a large projector behind the instructor's station make this room not unlike similar spaces in other academic libraries.

What sets this space apart from the norm, however, is an area a few feet off from the computers. Similar to other furniture arrangements in the library, several sofas and overstuffed chairs are arranged in a circle around a low table. The space resembles a living room more than a classroom. Hight explained that she has effectively started some of her instruction sessions in this casual and comfortable space before having the students move over to the computer workstations (personal correspondence, October 14, 2005).

Third Floor

The third floor holds the circulating book collection. Interweaved with the stacks are different types of furniture. One assemblage of chairs near the staircase includes reading lights that students may adjust at desired angles and turn off and on themselves. Several of the chairs on this floor, especially those located near windows, are low to the ground and casual, providing seating similar to what one may find at a coffeehouse.

Fourth Floor

The fourth floor is the home of the beautiful Ikeda Reading Room. Hight commented that the room was recently used during the filming of the Paramount Pictures feature *Elizabethtown* (personal correspondence, October 14, 2005). This room alone would be enough to warrant inclusion of the library in this book. Its remoteness from the other areas of the library adds a sense of secrecy and intrigue. To reach the room, users must exit the main floor of the library and walk across an outdoor platform that connects one portion of the building to the other.

The reading room takes one back to an era of old-time libraries. A large window with magnificent curtains appears directly across from the entrance. The window provides a view of the campus below. A conference size table sits in front and below the large window. Sofas and other plush chairs are arranged throughout the room. The walls are lined with glass-enclosed wooden bookcases that hold various volumes, including Japanese-language art books. The room is accented by a vaulted ceiling with chandeliers. When existing the room, visitors will notice a terrace immediately across the corridor. This elevated, outdoor space supplies one of the most panoramic views of the canyon.

Outside Seating

Before concluding the discussion of different spaces found in the Ikeda Library, a few comments must be made about the significantly large sidewalk area that wraps around the side of the library building that faces toward the central campus. This area includes seating on small cafe-style chairs and tables. Students and other visitors may sit in the sun or in the shade of the library while looking out across a lawn that reaches toward other university buildings, including the cafeteria. This space provides a balance and meeting point between the serenity of the interior of the library and the often bustling student cafeteria. It mirrors the blending of dualities also found within the Ikeda library, which is home to simple beauty and user-oriented functionality.

REFERENCES

"Facts and Figures." *Soka University Update*. Soka University of America, Fall 2004.

Soka University of America. "Construction History." 2005a. www.soka.edu/page.cfm?p=217 (retrieved October 26, 2005).

———. "Mission and Values." 2005b. www.soka.edu/page.cfm?p=3 (retrieved October 13, 2005).

———. "Mottos and Principles." 2005c. www.soka.edu/page.cfm?p=411 (retrieved October 13, 2005).

———. "A Proud Heritage." 2005d. www.soka.edu/page.cfm?p=4 (retrieved October 25, 2005).

9

Silverado Library

LIBRARY DATA

Address: 28192 Silverado Canyon Road, Silverado, CA 92676
Phone: (714) 649-2216
Web site: www.ocpl.org/54brnch.asp
Square Feet: 1,119
Circulation: 1,245 (December 2005*)
Collection: 16,275 total items (as of March 2006)
*Annual circulation not available at time of inquiry
Sources for above: L. Lynch, Orange County Public Library Headquarters, personal correspondence, February 2006, and P. Bruce, Orange County Public Library Headquarters, personal correspondence, March 2006

Michael Gorman, who has had an illustrious career which includes posts as dean of libraries at California State University, Fresno and director of the American Library Association, has, no doubt, found himself within the walls of many grand and impressive libraries. It is interesting to note, based on his experience, that he finds size the "dominating factor in library user satisfaction." Small libraries, he further contends, are best-loved by their patrons:

> It is not difficult to see what makes these libraries special — the opportunity they afford for the librarians to get to know the users to create a human relationship with the librarians and the library itself. Though huge libraries can inspire awe, it is very often the small library that inspires affection [1998, p. 30].

The small, one-room Silverado Library, located in the far reaches of Orange County, is a perfect example.

SILVERADO CANYON

There are several ways to reach Silverado from the more populated areas of Orange County. One could take the 91 freeway east to the 241 toll road, a path with signs warning of deer crossings, and exit at Santiago Canyon Road. Another

rou... rd the hills, passing through
the... Canyon Road. Once travelers
rea... be roughly five miles further
int... however, what will become
qu... County turns into a wilderness
th... ets.
... mountain bikers, and those who
p... and growing Orange County
b... *Los Angeles Times*, offers the
f... brush-covered hills and
... ow from city streetlights fades as
a... rado and Modjeska canyons in
t... notorcyclist traveling on the
canyon road ... ntier of decades ago. According
to Lin, many residents still draw water from wells and use wood-burning stoves to
heat their homes.

Mountain Biking: Orange County California (1996) includes historical
information about Silverado Canyon, as well as two rides bicyclists may take
through the canyon, demonstrating the importance of the area to those who wish
to leave the city behind and pedal far on two wheels. When driving into the
canyon, one will most likely see bicyclists and also notice the bike paths that run
along both sides of sections of the main road. Multiple signs caution truck drivers
to not enter the bike path. The road leading to Silverado also passes by the
entrance to Irvine Lake. All of these elements, including the two-lane road nestled
between hills full of golden brush and trees, create a serene environment. It is here
that the Silverado Library, a branch of the Orange County Public Library, is
located at the base of the Santa Ana Mountains in a small storefront in between
Buck's Roadhouse and the Canyon Market.

Elsie McClelland, the first Silverado librarian, opens her small, historical book
on the area, *Silverado Canyon Sketches: 1853–1953* (1957), with the following
tribute:

> When the mighty forces of the universe, controlled by the Great Artist,
> were shaping this continent there was formed a little seven-mile canyon in
> the Santa Ana mountains that was destined to influence many lives.
>
> Something of the mystery of creation, the hush of unbroken silence and
> of brooding peace, was to remain for all time; an intangible influence felt
> and responded to by every dreamer who came into the canyon [1–2].

McClelland has not been the only canyon resident to feel a strong connection to
the region.

Although Silverado Canyon is a quiet community, when compared to the
lights and activity of the more populated cities below, the residents are anything
but timid if outsiders make attempts to build on their land. Wilson (2002) reports

that attempts to construct in the region have included "about 5,000 new homes, a gas station and strip mall, and an enlarged jail facility." Another more recent attempt led to a battle between canyon residents and a developer with plans to build 4,000 homes in the region (Lin, 2005). In addition to fighting urban sprawl, residents have also struggled to keep their local library open, which has been a target for closure over the years.

According to Granberry (1996), threats to the library have ranged from slashed hours to complete closure. During one threat of closure in 1995, "fiercely loyal patrons wrapped protest notes around beer and soft drink cans, sending hundreds of them through the mail to county supervisors" (Loar, 1996). Librarian Lucille Cruz, who is quoted in Loar, stated, "Everyone was upset when they thought this library was going to close." Cruz has also spoken more generally as a defender of the community: "I think people who come up here underestimate the intelligence of the community.... It's been a long-held belief that there are a bunch of hillbillies up here, backwoods people.... But you know, it's a group of fighters, very knowledgeable people" (Wilson, 2002).

Interestingly, Lin (2005) reports that in times of crisis in the canyon, "the library often becomes an impromptu gathering place," demonstrating its importance to the community. The building also "has become an Emergency Center Command Post during natural disasters" and "the communication post for the Inter-Canyon League's 'Canyon Watch'" ("A History," n.d.). In 1984, when residents were unable to reach their homes during a brush fire, they came to the library ("A History," n.d.). It is clear to see how the library's central position within the community has led the canyon residents to defend it.

LIBRARY HISTORY

Library service was first established for Silverado Canyon residents in 1929, under the direction of Elsie McClelland. The first library was housed in a log cabin along with the post office. Margaret Morrison, a friend of McClelland's, donated 60 books to begin the collection. In 1930, the library became part of the Orange County Library System. McClelland continued to provide library service from the cabin until the building was given to her in 1946 as a retirement home ("A History," n.d.).

Similar to the histories of the other libraries within these pages, the location was moved about until it eventually reached a permanent home. Following McClelland's retirement, the library was first relocated next to a dime store and then, a barber shop. In 1964, it moved to the Silverado Shopping Center, where it earned the privilege of being the only public building in the canyon, as well as the only air-conditioned structure. A creek runs quietly behind the shopping center. The Canyon Market, located next to the library, provides an array of plants and flower pots, along with a bench and two tables with chairs on the sidewalk in front.

The Silverado Library is a small, one-room library located in a shopping center.

ONE ROOM

The Silverado Library is a small, one-room building that provides a feeling of home upon entry. Much is packed into this tiny space. Immediately to the right is the reference desk. Ruth Loc, assistant librarian, explained that a collection of natural objects near the desk is comprised of fossils and coal from the area (person correspondence, March 4, 2006). The periodicals and audio books area is located to the left with two cushioned, reading chairs. A table with five chairs sits in the middle of the room. Book stacks line much of the remainder of the space with a children's area near the back.

LIBRARY CATS

The focus of much of this book is on the spaces within libraries that create a sense of place. At the Silverado Library, this holds true, especially due to the contrast between the vast natural surroundings and the charm of the interior of the small building. One element, however, has created an unusual history for the library, and it has definitely added a special quality to the small building. That element is a much-loved library cat.

Alis, named after the Automated Library Information System, was a calico who showed up as a kitten one day in 1985. Alis' story even reached the pages of the *Los Angeles Times* with a tribute article. The author, Noriyuki, found that Alis was welcomed by library patrons immediately upon her arrival:

> They visited even when they had no literary needs. When they moved away, they sent her cards, and she wrote back, a paw-shaped stamp serving as her signature. Friends brought tasty treats on special occasions, played with her, listened for her soothing purr on still days. Young people in the canyon grew up with Alis, listened to glorious tales with her during the story hours of their childhoods [2002].

This is Megan, the current library cat of Silverado Library. She carries on the library cat tradition established by Alis, a much-loved cat who lived at the library for more than 15 years.

Alis' significance to the community was perhaps best displayed in 1998 when she had to undergo surgery after suffering an attack by two pit bulls. Library patrons, current and past, and employees donated roughly $1,400 to pay for her medical bills (Noriyuki, 2002). Alis continued to live at the library after the attack, totaling the time at her library home to more than 15 years. There were two services for Alis when she passed on. Judi Davis of the Canyon Market next door to the library planted a peach tree behind the store in Alis' memory (Noriyuki, 2002).

Visitors to the library can ask to see pictures of Alis. One shows her sitting amongst a pile of books. The library cat tradition, however, continues to this day. This is evident by the "Feed the Kitty" donation container located on the reference desk. Megan, the new library cat, seems perfectly at home in her library surroundings. She relaxes on table tops and on the laps of visitors, ultimately adding to the unique sense of place that makes this small library feel like you have entered a friend's home.

REFERENCES

"A History of the Silverado Library." Document, n.d. (Available at the Silverado Library.)

Gorman, M. *Our Singular Strengths: Meditations for Librarians.* Chicago: American Library Association, 1998.

Granberry, M. "The 2,300 Residents of This Isolated Hamlet Are United by a Love of the Outdoors and a Sense of Activism. But Beware the Developer or Official Who Tries to Alter Their Way of Life: They've Proved Formidable Foes." *Los Angeles Times*, September 13, 1996.

Lin, S. "Canyon Dwellers Living on the Edge of Change: When Many in the Silverado and Modjeska Areas of Orange County Look over Their Shoulders, They See 4,000 Homes Closing In." *Los Angeles Times*, December 19, 2005.

Loar, R. "In Person: Librarian Close to Her Roots." *Los Angeles Times*, January 15, 1996.

McClelland, E. *Silverado Canyon Sketches*: 1853–1953. Historical Society of Southern California, 1957. (Reprinted from the March 1957 historical society quarterly.)

Noriyuki, D. "In the Wonderland of Libraries Are Cats Like Alis; Carrying on Feline Tradition, the Silverado Calico Found a Home in a Reading Room." *Los Angeles Times*, February 18, 2002.

Wilson, J. "Canyon People Fight on to Protect Their Quiet Land Development: In Latest Skirmish, Residents Dig in against Plans to Put Some 5,000 Homes in Their Area." *Los Angeles Times*, August 22, 2002.

10

Paulina June and George Pollak Library, California State University, Fullerton

LIBRARY DATA

Address: 800 N. State College Boulevard, Fullerton, CA 92834
Phone: (714) 278-2633
Web site: www.library.fullerton.edu
Square Feet: approximately 408,000
Circulation: 251,624 (fiscal year 2004/2005)
Collection: 1,218,727 books; 3,365 serials; 26,523 e-books; 1,147,843 microforms; 9,991 maps; 6,309 films/videos (fiscal year 2004/2005)

Sources for above: University archives and special collections at California State University, Fullerton and Pollak Library library statistics, available at www.library.fullerton.edu/content/administratio-nunit/general/LibraryStatistics.htm

Fullerton, California, is located in North Orange County near the cities of Brea, Anaheim, and Placentia. The old downtown area, which is a quick five minutes from the California State University, Fullerton (CSUF) campus features attractive tree-lined Harbor Boulevard. The area is full of unique antique markets, specialty shops, and restaurants of varying themes and sizes. Many historic buildings are located in and around the downtown section, including the 1919 Spring Field Banquet and Conference Center, formerly the Masonic Temple; the 1930 Plummer Auditorium; and the 1927–1928 Williams Company building, formerly the Fullerton Odd Fellows Temple (Morris, Richey, and Thomas, 2004). In the evening, visitors, college students, and residents may enjoy live musical performances at several bars and nightclubs near the intersection of Harbor Boulevard and Commonwealth Avenue.

Fullerton is easily accessible via the large, interlocking freeway system that connects sprawling Southern California. The busy ten-lane 57 freeway runs alongside the university campus. Some aspects of the campus library, the Paulina June and George Pollack Library, mirror the activity of the endless stream of cars passing by the university. This is especially true of the reference desk where librarians answered 1,870 reference questions during a typical week of the 2004-2005 fiscal year (Library statistics FY 2004-2005). Other places, particularly the designated quiet study area of the third floor in the north wing of the building, provide a refuge from the busy world outside.

CALIFORNIA STATE UNIVERSITY, FULLERTON

CSUF was established in 1957 as Orange County State College. A permanent site for the college was selected in 1958, but the first classes offered in 1959 were at nearby Sunny Hills High School. Classes were held on the permanent site in temporary buildings in 1960 (CSUF, 2005b). The college's name changed often within a relatively short period of time. The first change occurred in 1962 when the institution took the name Orange State College. This was followed by California State College at Fullerton in 1964; California State College, Fullerton in 1968; and eventually its current name of California State University, Fullerton in 1972 (CSUF, 2005b).

Although Orange County is typically thought of as a more conservative region than neighboring Los Angeles County, the campus witnessed student activism during its first decade. Student protests included a teach-in on February 17, 1967, by the Understanding Asia Committee to "air dissident views on the Vietnam War and other issues"; an antiwar rally on October 18, 1967, sponsored by the Jack London Society; and a series of "Wednesday Student Forums on liberalization of marijuana laws" beginning the week after the antiwar rally (Koehler, 1984, p. 32). Activism returned again to the campus on February 9, 1970, when hecklers shouted obscenities during a speech by Governor Ronald Reagan during an Associated Students' convocation. CSUF started disciplinary action against two of the hecklers, which escalated into several actions, including a sit-in on February 25; a fiery rally on March 3 that resulted in 19 arrests; and numerous incidents in April, such as the establishment of a temporary People's Park on campus, a place for dissidents to gather and the occupation of the then Music-Speech-Drama Building (Koehler, 1984).

Throughout the turbulent times and into the present day, the enrollment at CSUF has steadily increased. By the 1964-1965 school year, enrollment was at nearly 5,000. Enrollment for 1969-1970 increased to 12,835, making CSUF's student body "larger than 91 percent of the nation's colleges" (Koehler, 1984, p. 41). Total enrollment for fall 2005 was at 35,040 with 64 percent of the students attending on a full-time basis (CSUF, 2005c).

As its population has grown, CSUF has become an admirable campus within the California State University System and the nation through its strong commitment to the education of minority students. The magazine *The Hispanic Outlook in Higher Education* (Dolan, 2005) ranks CSUF fifth in the nation for awarding bachelor's degrees to Hispanics. In addition, the university was named Outstanding Hispanic Serving University by the Hispanic Association of College and Universities in 2003, an association with 359 members (Dolan, 2005). Also according to *The Hispanic Outlook in Higher Education* (Cooper, 2005), in 2004 CSUF was first in the nation in granting fine arts degrees to Hispanics. Another noteworthy item from the university's history is the appointment of Dr. Jewel Plummer Cobb, professor of biological science, to president in 1981. Cobb, who received her doctoral degree from New York University, was selected from 130 candidates. She was the first African American woman "to head a major public university on the West Coast" (Koehler, 1984, p. 74).

To meet the needs of its expanding and diverse student body, the campus has undertaken numerous construction projects. Recent projects include the January 2006 grand opening of the new 109,000 square foot Performing Arts Center (CSUF, 2005d) and the current construction of the 190,000 square foot Steven G. Mihaylo Hall to eventually house the College of Business and Economics (CSUF, 2005a). Sitting at the heart of the flurry of activity is the Paulina June and George Pollak Library, a building that offers varied services and spaces for the large population it serves. Over the years, the library has experienced many changes, renovations, and a considerable expansion.

Library History

The early history of CSUF's library is a humble one. In 1959, the original library was housed in a classroom at Sunny Hills High School where it shared space with the bookstore. Later it was housed in a temporary building until it occupied the basement of the Science Building (Langsdorf, 1962). Koehler (1984) reports that construction was delayed on a permanent library building until enrollment increased to justify a new structure to serve 10,000 full-time students. The need for this new building was evident in 1962 when William Langsdorf, president of the university at the time, stated that of all the projects to be initiated in the 1963-1964 fiscal year, the library project ranked first on his list of priorities. A press release from the campus on July 15, 1963, stated, "The new facility will form the nucleus around which the 235-acre campus is planned" (Orange State College, 1963).

At completion in 1966, the new library spanned approximately 220,000 square feet with six floors above ground and one floor below (California State College at Fullerton, 1965). The building was dedicated with a ceremony on November 30, 1966 (Koehler, 1984). Dr. Louis Booker Wright, director of the Folger Shakespeare Library in Washington, D.C. provided an address titled "Libraries, the Measure of Our Civilization." Wright was also given an honorary degree during the ceremony ("College Library," 1966). An exhibit of books, manuscripts, and drawings from the Frank V. De Bellis Collection opened on November 21, 1966, to correspond with the library dedication ("An Exhibit," n.d.).

It is important to note that not all of the interior spaces of the 1966 building, which was designed by the architectural firm Risley, Gould, & Van Heuklyn of Los Angeles, were initially designated as library space. The second and third floors, for example, were designated for academic instruction and included 28 classrooms (California State College at Fullerton, 1965). Space quickly became an area of concern.

Numerous documents provide evidence of space issues that continued over the following decades. Memoranda by librarians Zuniga (1976), Davis (1976), and Bril (1988) are just a few examples. A March 7, 1979, report by Aaron Cohen and Associates, an architectural firm, investigated the problematic nature of limited space. Although changes to the interior were made over the years to alleviate the space concerns, it became quite evident that a larger facility was needed.

In April 1990 a project planning guide for a new library addition was created by the CSUF Office of Facility Planning and Construction. The document proposed an expansion to the north of the existing building. A groundbreaking ceremony for the addition was held on February 4, 1994. Designed by the architectural firm Albert C. Martin & Associates, the library addition, completed in 1996, added about 188,000 square feet, almost doubling the size of the old south building (CSUF, 1996). The dedication for the library was held on October 21, 1996, with a ceremony titled "Frontiers of Learning." Apollo 11 astronaut Dr. Edwin E. "Buzz" Aldrin provided the keynote speech ("Frontiers of Learning," 1996). Two years later in October 1998, the library received the name Paulina June and George Pollak Library in recognition of the couple's $1 million endowment to the library (Berghouse, 1998).

Atrium and Galleries

Visitors to the library can travel between the older south wing and the newer north wing on the first and second floors of the library by crossing through an atrium that connects both buildings. Those entering the library from the east or west entrances will first enter into the atrium. It is arguably the most spectacular area of the library. The atrium is an airy space with ample natural lighting and art galleries on both the east and west sides. Librarian Veronica Chiang organized varied and intriguing exhibits for the library during her long tenure with the institution. Recent exhibits have included Geo-Garden: An Exhibition of Minerals and Fossils from the McGraw Collection of CSUF Geological Sciences Department and the Orange County Fossil Collection (Fall 2006); Designed to Sell: Nondigital Marketing Art (Spring 2006); and Works by Women Student Artists at Cal State Fullerton (Spring 2004).

Reference

Immediately off from the atrium on the first floor of the north wing is the reference area. The reference desk is located in one of the busiest areas of the

The entrance of the Paulina June and George Pollak Library of California State University, Fullerton, leads to an atrium that connects the south and north wings.

library, making assistance easily accessible. Four workstations are available at the desk. During the fall and spring semesters, the two workstations facing out toward the floor are generally staffed by librarians. Two additional workstations located further behind the reference desk have recently been set up for in-depth individual research consultations. To showcase library resources and potentially garner interest in reference materials, librarians often collaborate or work individually on reference book exhibits that are displayed along one side of the reference desk. Recent exhibits have been created around the themes of banned books, Women's History Month, National Poetry Month, African American History Month, and Latino Heritage Month.

Across from the reference desk is a highly populated zone referred to as the Electronic Resources area. This is one of the prime locations to secure a computer. Students will often wait in long lines to sit in this space, even when they are informed by librarians that computers are available in other areas of the library. In addition to the Electronic Resources area, the floor provides more computers in the Oasis North, an area adjacent to the reference desk. This new space includes two to five computers on circular and rectangular tables. To allow students to design their own work spaces on an as-needed basis, the area was recently redesigned with flexible furniture, including chairs with rolling castors. Of course, students may also bring their own laptops or check-out a laptop while in the library, since nearly every space of the entire building provides wireless access.

To make the floor more inviting, several rows of bookshelves were also recently removed during the summer of 2006 when older reference books were relocated to the circulating stacks. Although the reference book collection continues to take up a good portion of the floor, the removal of some shelving added natural lighting to the space and also dramatically improved a view of the outdoors. Cushioned seating that students can rearrange to fit their needs is now available within this newly created open space.

Other rooms within the reference area include state-of-the-art study group rooms for student use. These rooms are another recent enhancement with equipment including Webcams and microphones. A room close to the reference desk has been especially designated as a disabled students' space with assistive devices to meet the needs of students with disabilities, such as visual impairments. In addition, a large conference room that was dedicated as the Rotary Club of Fullerton Room in June 2002 (Giasone, 2002) is located immediately behind the reference desk. Due to its size and prime location, this room is often used by campus groups, which brings many faculty and staff into the library each semester. Library events are also held here. In April 2006, for example, a poetry series titled "Celebrating Diversity and the Creative Spirit" took place in the room to commemorate National Poetry Month and National Library Week. Another event focusing on writers titled "Memory and Migration: Conversations with Chinese Women Writers" was also held in the room during the spring 2006 semester.

Teaching Spaces

The Pollak Library has a strong instructional program that reaches much of the student body each year. In the 2004-2005 fiscal year, librarians taught 573 instruction sessions (Library Statistics FY 2004-2005). Although some sessions are held in classrooms throughout the campus, the majority take place in the three instruction rooms located in the north wing of the library. The first, third, and fourth floors each have one instruction room. The rooms contain an instructor computer workstation with a screen and projector and individual computer workstations for students.

Periodicals

Periodicals are located on the second floor of the north wing along with seating for individuals and groups. More student study groups room are also available on this floor. Copies and microform viewing machines were recently moved to a corner of the floor, providing ample natural light and views of the campus.

Government Documents

The third floor of the north wing houses international, federal, and state government documents. This floor is unique for its designation as a quiet study space. Numerous individual and group study spaces are found throughout the floor, as well as a few public access computers.

Audiovisual/Curriculum Materials Center

The fourth floor of the north wing is another busy area that provides access to numerous collections: audiovisual materials, including records, cassettes, DVDs, and VHS tapes; the juvenile book collection; and the curriculum materials center, which provides resources to support the university's education department. A large open space at the far corner of the floor provides striking views of the campus and generous natural lighting. Individual study carrels and larger tables for groups are both available within the large space. Rooms for viewing and listening to music, films, and other media are provided. This floor is also home to the Donoghue Children's Literature Center, which is a showcase room for award-winning children's literature. Comfortable seating and a colorful, inviting design provide for a unique space within the library.

University Archives and Special Collections

A 1995 article in the *Los Angeles Times* (Earnest) focused on special collections at two Orange County universities, including CSUF. The author described the

Special Collections room at the Pollak Library as a "sanctuary" and "best-kept" secret that is "tucked away upstairs." Special Collections has also been reported in the *Los Angeles Times* as a place where a puzzling theft occurred. A collection of rare books, letters, and prints valued at an estimated $13,000 was discovered missing from the room in 1986. Included in the missing items were handwritten love letters by George Bernard Shaw (Billiter, October 21, 1986). In a curious turn of events, the missing items, all 46 rare books and other items, were returned by mail in a package addressed to the library approximately four months after their disappearance (Billiter, November 4, 1986).

When one enters the Special Collections room of the library, which is housed on the third floor of the older south wing, it is quite evident that this is a space where mysterious and unusual discoveries can take place. Two tables are arranged in the entrance area of the room, along with a functioning card catalog. It is here that researchers may examine the rare and unique materials. Some notable collections include the Freedom Center Collection of books, pamphlets, periodicals, and ephemera related to political, social, and religious issues of the 20th century in the United States; the Science Fiction Collection, including periodicals and original manuscripts of several American authors, such as Philip K. Dick and Frank Herbert; and the Archives of Popular Culture with comic books, pulp magazines, and television and motion picture scripts, including the Fred Guiol Screen Script Collection and *Star Trek* television scripts. These collections are just a sampling of the treasures stored here.

The Patrons of the Library outdoor book sale at California State University, Fullerton's Pollak Library always draws a crowd.

Patrons of the Library

The Patrons of the Library have a presence on the first floor of the south wing of the building in a room across from the circulation desk. Visitors to the library will often see a large sign announcing the Patron's book sale. One popular event of the organization is the annual outdoor book sale, where students, faculty, and community visitors can browse book trucks in the Southern California sun.

Additional Spaces

The above descriptions provide glimpses into some, but definitely not all, of the unique spaces at the Pollak Library. Similar to other large multilevel libraries, a lengthy book could easily be written just on the interior spaces of this building. The library is part of the growing trend of academic libraries to adjust their interior spaces to meet the needs of diverse and changing populations.

References

Aaron Cohen and Associates. *A Report: California State University, Fullerton.* March 7, 1979. (Available at the Pollack Library Archives and Special Collections Department.)
Aldrin, Edwin E. "Frontiers of Learning: Dedication of Library North." Campus Focus 1, no. 7 (1996): 1.
Berghouse, L. C. "$1 Million Endowment Results in Library Naming." *Daily Titan*, 67, no. 26 (1998): 1.
Billiter, B. "George Bernard Shaw Letters Gone Rare Papers, Books Missing from Library at Cal State Fullerton." *Los Angeles Times* (Orange County edition, Metro section), October 21, 1986.
_____. "Missing Rare Books, Letters Arrive in Mail. *Los Angeles Times* (Orange County edition, Metro section), November 4, 1986.
Bril, P. L. "Priority of Capital Outlay Funds for University Library Building Addition." Memorandum, July 27, 1988. (Available at the Pollack Library Archives and Special Collections Department.)
California State College at Fullerton. Office of Public Information. *Fact Sheet: Library-Audio Visual Building.* July 1965. (Available at the Pollack Library Archives and Special Collections Department.)
California State University, Fullerton (CSUF). College of Business and Economics. *About the College of Business and Economics.* 2005a. http://business.fullerton.edu/About/mihaylo hall.htm (retrieved October 6, 2006).
_____. Institutional Research and Analytical Studies. *Student Profile At-a-Glance.* 2005b. www.fullerton.edu/analyticalstudies/student_profiles.asp (retrieved October 6, 2006).
_____. Office of Facility Planning and Construction. *Project Planning Guide, California State University, Fullerton, Library Building Addition.* 1990.
_____. Office of Public Affairs. "$30 Million Library Addition Takes Cal State Fullerton into 21st Century." Press release, October 8, 1996.
_____. *"Cal State Fullerton: Milestones."* 2005c. http://campusapps.fullerton.edu/news/press/milestones.html (retrieved October 4, 2006).
_____. *"Performing Arts Center: Fact Sheet."* 2005d.

http://campusapps.fullerton.edu/news/2005/performingarts/facts.html (retrieved October 6, 2006).

"College Library to Be Dedicated." *Los Angeles Times*, November 29, 1966.

Cooper, M. A. "California Leads State Rankings for Arts." *Hispanic Outlook in Higher Education* 15, no. 22 (2005): 12.

Davis, B. "Request for Increased Space Allocation for Freedom Center Collection." Memorandum, March 4, 1976. (Available at the Pollack Library Archives and Special Collections Department.)

Dolan, T. G. "Cal State-Fullerton Enhancing Hispanic Education." *Hispanic Outlook in Higher Education 15*, no. 16 (2005): 29.

Earnest, L. "Special-Collection Libraries Are Best-Kept Secrets on Campuses." *Los Angeles Times*, February 16, 1995.

An Exhibit of Books, Manuscripts, and Drawings from the Frank V. De Bellis Collection. Brochure, n.d. (Available at the Pollack Library Archives and Special Collections Department.)

Giasone, B. "Cal State Dedicates Room to Rotary Series: Rotary Room." *Orange County Register*, July 11, 2002.

Koehler, M. A. *Kaleidoscope 1959–1984, California State University, Fullerton: Glimpses of the First 25 Years*. Fullerton: California State University, Fullerton, 1984.

Langsdorf, W. "Proposed Library Building and A-V Center." Memorandum, February 1, 1962. (Available at the Pollack Library Archives and Special Collections Department.)

Library statistics FY 2004-2005. Paulina June and George Pollak Library. 2005. www.library.fullerton.edu/content/administrationunit/general/LibraryStatistics.htm (retrieved December 1, 2006).

Morris, K., D. Richey, and C. Thomas. *Images of America: Fullerton*. Charleston, SC: Arcadia, 2004.

Orange State College. Office of Public Relations. "A Unique College Library." Press release, July 15, 1963. (Available at the Pollack Library Archives and Special Collections Department.)

Zuniga, A. H. "Request for Additional Office Space." Memorandum, March 1, 1976. (Available at the Pollack Library Archives and Special Collections Department.)

Part III
Los Angeles County

11

Brand Library & Art Center

Library Data

Address: 1601 West Mountain Street, Glendale, CA 91201
Phone: (818) 548-2051
Web site: www.brandlibrary.org
Square Feet: 26,000
Circulation: approximately 164,000 per year (2003/2004)
Collection: 64,969 books; 120 periodicals; 25,196 compact discs; 13,448 records; 1,002 videos and DVDs; 165 slide sets; 504 art prints (August 2005)
Source for above: A. Resnick, personal correspondence, August 25, 2005

When driving down Sunset Canyon in Burbank toward Glendale, one will notice the Verdugo Mountains on the left and homes lining the streets of this community nestled in the foothills. The street signs change from green to white and Sunset Canyon becomes Mountain Street once entering Glendale. Within a short distance, a building resembling a cathedral or small castle will appear. It is a location so familiar that it must have appeared in numerous Hollywood movies and music videos. An abundance of tall palm trees march in unison for a good mile to the building's entrance. This wondrous structure is the Brand Library & Art Center, a specialized branch library of the Glendale Public Library System. According to Blair Whittington, music librarian, the library building is considered "the jewel of Glendale" (personal correspondence, August 12, 2005).

During two weekend visits to the library in 2005, I observed several wedding parties taking photographs on the lawn of the library, which only attests to the splendor of the building. Alyssa Resnick, senior library supervisor, explained that wedding parties often converge at the library, particularly during the traditional wedding season (personal correspondence, August 13, 2005). One quickly realizes, however, that it is not just the exterior of the building that the community flocks to, but also the unique treasures housed inside. In fact, the unusually shaped rooms and the various collections displayed throughout create a browser's paradise and a true sense of place. It is likely that this is why more than half of the library users come from outside Glendale and that, remarkably, some travel as far as 100 miles to use the collection (B. Whittington, personal correspondence, August 12, 2005).

BUILDING HISTORY

The Brand Library was built in 1904 (City, 2005a). The mansion, named El Miradero, was originally home to Mr. and Mrs. Leslie C. Brand. The building, according to a plaque located near the main library entrance, is a city of Glendale historical landmark. El Miradero translates into English as "a high place overlooking a wide view." Visitors to the library will surely see this expansive view when descending the 40 or so stairs leading from the entrance to the parking lot below.

Mr. Brand's history with the city of Glendale is significant. Not only did he found the First National Bank of Glendale, he also organized telephone, electric, and water companies (B. Whittington, personal correspondence, August 12, 2005). Upon his death in 1925, Mr. Brand bequeathed the mansion to the city. According to his will, the property was to be used solely for a public park and library. Until her death in 1945, however, Mrs. Brand retained the right to reside in the home. The mansion was converted into Brand Library by 1956 (City, 2005c).

The building is located in picturesque Brand Park, a 600-acre complex that includes the Doctors' House Museum and Gazebo (circa 1890). The museum was named for the chemist and three physicians who resided in the home in early Glendale. Also included is the Glendale-Higashiosaka Teahouse and Friendship Garden, a small structure located on lush grounds that entertains guests, by reservation only, a few select hours each week. Hiking trails, a baseball diamond, and a playground make up the remaining features of the park. The library, however, due to its stature and healthy activity, dominates the order of things at the park.

The original Brand mansion had "five bedrooms, a solarium, parlor, living room, dining room, and music salon.... The grounds were a virtual fairyland of running streams, miniature waterfalls, splashing fountains and tropical shrubbery" (Glendale Division of Parks and Recreation, n.d.). The original home was 5,000 square feet. Some of the rooms have historical pictures on the walls so library users can see how the room looked when it was still a residence.

Ten years after the library opened, "the city council allocated funds to construct an addition ... that would include facilities for art exhibitions, lectures and concerts, as well as art and craft shows" (City, 2005c). The addition, which provides an additional 21,000 square feet, was dedicated in 1969 (B. Whittington, personal correspondence, August 12, 2005). Visitors to the library still enter through the original mansion.

The new addition and the passage of time since the deaths of the Brands, however, have not diminished the mysterious nature of the building. During both of my visits, references were made to a ghost. One source stated that people in the library begin speaking in hushed tones when the lights are dimmed. She explained that the atmosphere changes in the dark. Another source reported accounts of a ghost are often provided by library users to the staff. Even an article from the

Glendale News Press (Garza, 1993) titled "Something Ghostly This Way Comes" is featured on the library's Web site. This article mentions a library administrator, library staff, and custodians experiencing the presence of something supernatural. Mr. Brand, who died in the building, is suspected to be the ghost still haunting his old living quarters (Garza, 1993).

ORIGINAL MANSION ROOMS

Upon entry, one may experience the feeling of being in both a home and a library. Behind the circulation desk is a fireplace that retains its original wood carving. The lobby, however, has some standard elements typical to most public and academic libraries, including a circulation desk, equipment for checking out materials, and a reference librarian's desk, which is visibly located in a room to the left.

The room to the right of the lobby includes several photocopy machines, and a large piano is directly in the middle of the small room. This piano, referred to as the "Brand Piano," was manufactured in 1918 and owned by the Brands. The piano then changed hands a few times until it was ultimately donated to the library in November 1997. Library users looking for art books, which are kept in this small room, have to maneuver around the large instrument.

An adjacent room is the former bedroom where Mr. Brand passed away. This room features a reading table, bookcases, and a cabinet housing four violins called the "George Washington Quartet." The violins, which took ten years to make, were the creation of Michael Gozzo, a former Glendale resident who died in 1967. Over his lifetime, Gozzo created some 135 violins. He claimed to know a secret about the grain of the wood that only he could recognize (Yaro, 1967). Each violin in the display case bears the inscription: "I live in silence and though I am dead, I sing." It is interesting that the inscription provides a reference to death in the room of Mr. Brand's passing. Such details only add to the lore.

Located in perhaps the smallest room of the original mansion is a collection of art videos, music videos, and DVDs. Also found here are file cabinets full of art exhibition catalogs, some international, that are publicly accessible. This room is near the former solarium, a large room in the middle of the mansion with books and periodicals, as well as a sale area where customers may purchase records, books, and other materials for prices ranging from $.10 to $3.00. Art prints line the top of the bookshelves throughout this room, as they do throughout most of the library.

Off from the solarium is a wonderful reading room with a large window, providing a view of some of the many trees on the lawn. Several tables are available in this room that was formerly the Brands' dining room. Serious researchers may want to sit with their backs to the window or they may find themselves losing time while getting lost in the majestic scenery outside.

Music Collection

A small corridor connects the original building to the 1969 addition. The first room in the new addition is L-shaped and features the library's music collection. Rows of CDs fill most of the larger portion of the room. According to Whittington, the CD collection has many strengths, including art songs, symphonic repertoire, opera, musical theater, film soundtracks, bluegrass/old-time music, and world music (personal correspondence, August 12, 2005). He further explained that Glendale is home to large Armenian and Hispanic communities. The world music collection reflects the interests of these communities. The circulation statistics speak to the importance of the collection. Most librarians would be astonished to find that approximately 98 percent of the CD collection circulates annually with over 100,000 total circulations.

Also found in this room are listening stations, music periodicals, records, sheet music, songbooks, and several shelves of miniature scores. A row of computer terminals looks out onto a courtyard. A perusal of some music periodicals revealed an eclectic assortment of titles that would likely appease a diverse audience. *American Songwriter*, *Jazz Times*, and *19th Century Music* are some of the titles noted. According to Whittington, the library serves a broad base of users that includes both music faculty and casual listeners.

The record collection provides an intriguing variety of music. Some interesting titles include *Folk Songs of Kashmir*, *The Singing Nun*, *Songs the Swahili Sing: Classics from the Kenya Coast*, and *The Bagpipe in Italy*. One could truly spend countless hours discovering all the unusual treasures. Whittington explained that university music students will often use the collection at Brand in addition to their college libraries (personal correspondence, August 20, 2005).

Art Gallery

The art gallery, housed in the new building addition, adds to the unique sense of place found at Brand. A hallway, which provides exhibit space, leads to the main gallery. Several shows are held at the gallery each year. The mission of the gallery is twofold: "to offer visitors a professional gallery experience" and "to showcase works by established and emerging artists from California, particularly from Southern California, that educate, enlighten, challenge, and enrich people's lives" (City, 2005b).

During my visit in August 2005, art librarian Cathy Billings was preparing for a new show to begin the next day. The room has a simplistic beauty. A large opening in the ceiling provides natural lighting and gives the room a soft, expansive feel. Artists' works lined the walls with select furniture pieces placed near the center of the room. The upcoming show, Tropico Redux, will present the work

The Brand Library & Art Center, a branch of the Glendale Public Library, includes a spacious art gallery with ample natural lighting.

of artists from the Tropico Artists Collective. The collective was founded by Glendale artists in early 2005. Photography, painting, and mixed media works are included in the show, along with the sculptural work of Macierz: "functional and meticulously painted 'portrait' furniture which 'pokes fun at the art of the last century'" ("Tropico Artists," 2005).

Following Tropico Redux, the gallery will showcase Opulent Splendor by the Wearable Art Connection. The newsletter published by the Associates of Brand Library & Art Center describes Opulent Splendor as "a celebration of ornamentation, pattern and fantasy through painting, fiber art, costume, fashion" ("Art, Music, and Dance," 2005, p. 1). The gallery was planning to end 2005 with Brand 34, the 34th annual exhibition of a national juried competition. Works will include watercolors, collages, prints, and photographs.

Earlier shows at the gallery further illustrate the diverse and rich use of the space. Family Matters, an exhibit featuring the work of artist Janice DeLoof in late 2004, included "theatrical like installations, assembled painted furniture and domestic objects, and small mixed media wall paintings that represent symbols and signs from the artist's memories" ("Family Matters," 2005).

It is important to note that visitors to the library may easily take a break from their reading or listening to tour the galleries. Not only is admission free, but the galleries are also open many afternoons and some evenings throughout the week. Such accessibility allows library users to experience the significantly different spaces of the original mansion rooms and the newer galleries.

Recital Hall

Located off the same hallway that leads to the art gallery is the Brand recital hall. The hall provides a service to the community by renting the space for local piano teachers and student recitals. Whittington explained that university students from the University of Southern California and California State University, Northridge have used the hall in the past for required off-campus recitals (personal correspondence, August 20, 2005). Other events include the ongoing "Los Angeles Opera Talks." These free evening talks on the world of opera, held the second Thursday of each month, are presented by the Los Angeles Opera League. Upcoming talks include "Intro to Opera" and "La Traviata." In addition, a "Community Concert with Los Angeles Opera Artists" is scheduled for the following summer. Such events demonstrate how the Brand Library & Art Center is a place that utilizes library space creatively to enrich the community it serves.

References

"Art, Music, and Dance Calendar for the Brand Library & Art Center." *Brand Arts Communique* 35, no. 1 (2005): 1.
City of Glendale. "About Brand Library." 2005a. http://library.ci.glendale.ca.us/brand/brand_about.asp (retrieved August 9, 2005).
_____. "Brand Library Art Galleries." 2005b. http://library.ci.glendale.ca.us/brand/brand_galleries.asp (retrieved August 22, 2005).
_____. "The History of Brand Library." 2005c. http://library.ci.glendale.ca.us/brand/brand_history.asp (retrieved August 9, 2005).
"'Family Matters': Janice DeLoof, Artist." *ArtScene: The Guide to Art Galleries and Museums in Southern California*, 2005.
http://artscenecal.com/Announcements/1004/BrandLibrary1004.html (retrieved August 21, 2005).
Garza, N. "Something Ghostly This Way Comes." *Glendale News Press*, October 30, 1993. http://library.ci.glendale.ca.us/brand/ghost.asp (retrieved August 9, 2005).
Glendale Division of Parks and Recreation. "The Brand Story." n.d. (Available at the Brand Library reference desk.)
"Tropico Artists Collective Inaugural Show Brand Gallery." Adam's Hill Homeowner's Association, 2005. www.adamshill.org/current/details6.html (retrieved August 21, 2005).
Yaro, B. "Time Slows Pace of Better Music Maker." *Los Angeles Times*, April 16, 1967.

12

Cerritos Library

LIBRARY DATA

Address: 18025 Bloomfield Avenue, Cerritos, CA 90703
Phone: (562) 916-1350
Web site: www.ci.cerritos.ca.us/library/library.html
Square Feet: 88,000
Circulation: 1,112,505 (2004/2005)
Collection: 211,201 books; 522 microfilm reels; 18,717 other microform; 5,613 audio; 10,313 video; 397 periodicals (2004/2005)
Source for above: California Library Statistics 2006 (California State Library, Library Development Services Bureau)

Few librarians or those interested in the world of libraries have not heard of the new Cerritos Library, a public library located in Los Angeles County. The library has been discussed in many publications, including *American Libraries* (Williams, 2002), *Library Journal* ("Reader's Digest," 2004; "Selling the Learning," 2003; Berry, 2002; "Late Bulletins," 2002), *School Library Journal* ("Introducing the 'Experience,'" 2002), and the *Los Angeles Times* (Sahagun, 2002). Called the "Experience Library," the new building, which opened in 2002, features an amazingly creative use of space. The library is the recipient of a 2003 Themed Entertainment Association Thea Award, an award given by TEA, an association that represents "the world's leading creators, developers, designers and producers of compelling places and experiences" ("2003 Themed," 2003). *Reader's Digest* also named the Cerritos Library the "Best Public Library" in its "Best of America 2004" issue ("*Reader's Digest*," 2004).

One interesting fact about the award-winning library is that the *previous* building won the National Award of Excellence from the American Library Association and the American Institute of Architects and the Southern California Institute of Architects Award of Honor in 1989 (City of Cerritos, 2005). This leads to the obvious conclusion that the Cerritos Library has always been a place of marked excellence with officials who strive to create a library with a true sense of place.

Each section of the new library is designed around a theme, including infusions of Art Deco (Young Adult Section), the traditional (Old World Reading

Room), the postmodern (21st Century Library), the environmental ("Save the Planet" themed Children's Library), and others. The themed spaces are linked by the "Main Street." Critics of such extravagance or those who have more conservative views of how libraries should be designed would be wise to first inquire if the new building is being utilized.

An expansive parking structure adjacent to the building is much needed to accommodate the numbers of users found in each hallway, study room, and crevice within the library. Although one may imagine significant availability of computers after reading that the library houses some 200 computer workstations, the majority of the workstations were occupied during a visit on a Sunday afternoon. It is not just computers that bring the crowds to the library, however, since data confirm total circulation of nearly one million during the 2002-2003 fiscal year (California State Library, 2004), an increase of over 200,000 from 2001-2002 (California State Library, 2003). This figure increased yet again during the 2003-2004 fiscal year to 1,102,323 (California State Library, 2005) and then again during the 2004-2005 fiscal year with a total circulation of 1,112,505 (California State Library, 2006). These figures put the library's activity on the same level as a major university library. People simply want to be in the library, experience its unique spaces, and use the various resources, particularly in a library with rooms suited to satisfy nearly any type of library user.

HISTORY OF BUILDING

According to the city of Cerritos (2005), a previous library building opened to the public on September 17, 1973. When the building was first conceived in 1970, the city's population was just 15,856. In 1980, only seven years after the opening, the population had increased to 53,000. In addition to the population increase, an astonishing 65 percent of Cerritos' citizenry were library cardholders. The public's overwhelming use of the library, coupled with the rise in population, led to the launch of a building expansion project in 1981. This expanded building, designed by the architectural firm of Charles Walton and Associates, added 21,000 square feet to the library, resulting in a total of 41,500 square feet. It was this expanded building that won the 1989 National Award of Excellence from the American Library Association and the American Institute of Architects and the Southern California Institute of Architects Award of Honor (City of Cerritos, 2005). All of this, of course, was before the current Experience Library.

The new library, which was dedicated to the community on March 16, 2002, and added 42,000 square feet, was also designed by Charles Walton and Associates. "Direction from elected officials, the librarians' research and suggestions from the community led to the idea of building a great library that would honor the past while embracing the future" (City of Cerritos, 2005). This new building not only includes spectacular interiors, but also provides an unusual titanium exterior. In

The titanium exterior of the Cerritos Library in Los Angeles County experiences subtle changes in color, depending on atmospheric conditions and the location of the sun.

fact, during separate visits to the library, I noted the color of the building was somewhat different each time. Research on this mysterious occurrence confirmed the following: "Titanium expresses the concept of change as it has subtle color shifts from reflecting the angle of the sun and atmospheric conditions" (City of Cerritos, 2005). What an experience it must be to the patrons of the library to arrive at a building that changes its appearance with the weather.

Fountain

Outside the library entrance is a large fountain decorated with various animal statues. This creation is titled The Amaryllis Fountain & The Ancient Art of Feng-Shui. A plague located on the rim of the fountain states: "The ancient symbols in the Amaryllis Fountain have been placed by a Feng-Shui authority using the traditional Chinese compass to identify the appropriate locations." Animals within the fountain are associated with themes and placed according to compass directions: north — turtle for business success and career development; south — swan for fame, fortune, prosperity, and beauty; east — fish for abundant prosperity, wealth, good health, and harmony; and west — frog for development, growth, creativity, children, and luck. Finding such an unusual and wonderfully crafted creation near the library entrance sets the tone for the extraordinary interior of the library.

Main Street

Visitors to the library first enter the Main Street corridor, which runs the length of the first floor. Each themed room on the floor is reached via this "street." A visibly staffed information desk is situated near the entrance. Brochures, bookmarkers, maps of the library, and other items are available at the desk. These print items are not simply photocopies, but high-quality, artistic creations. A large bouquet of fresh flowers was also at the information desk, illustrating the attention to detail displayed throughout the library.

Also found on Main Street is a large circulation desk, a public photocopy machine room, the Friends' Store, a Local History Room, and an area called City Hall after Hours. The City Hall space provides various documents, as well as an ATM machine. Several art exhibits may also be found on and off of Main Street, as will be discussed later.

Old World Reading Room

The space known as the Old World Reading Room appears just as one would expect. Upon entry into the library, it is the first room encountered off Main Street. Chandeliers hang from the ceiling in this room. Rich green carpets merge with heavy wood cases and a fireplace. Elegant chairs and reading tables provide many comfortable seats. Large windows filter natural light into much of the interior of the room. It is highly probable that the beauty and comfort of the space equally draw the users, since nearly every seat was occupied in this room during my visit in September 2005.

Internet Express

On the other side of City Hall after Hours is a relatively large room that includes Internet Express stations, which are terminals placed near the Main Street corridor for easy access. Also found in this room is an area devoted to magazines, newspapers, and paperbacks. Large windows add a wealth of natural lighting and create an atmosphere of openness. Tables and chairs are dispersed throughout the room, including several that provide rather plush seating. In fact, some of the furniture in this room looks like it belongs in a fine living room.

Young Adult Room

Across the Main Street corridor from the Internet Express stations are stairs leading to a mezzanine that serves as the shared young adult and multimedia room.

As in all of the rooms, nearly every chair in this area was occupied, by both teenagers and adults. An informational sheet on this special space states: "The Young Adult room provides a beautifully designed space for teenagers to read, study or work in small groups" ("Young Adult Services," n.d.). The description concludes: "The Cerritos Library welcomes teens to the new Young Adult room, a comfortable, friendly place to gather and study." The room has an Art Deco theme and features architecture and furniture with a style dating back to the 1920s and 1930s.

CHILDREN'S LIBRARY

Children's rooms in libraries are nearly always unique spaces. At the Cerritos Library, however, the Children's Library looks like Disneyland with books. A large aquarium takes up a large portion of one of the room's walls. The aquarium is one of the first things visitors see. The wall where the aquarium is embedded is a shared wall by both Main Street and the Children's Library. During my visits, I noticed a small shark swimming and intermingling with the various other fish.

A plaque just beyond the entrance to the children's space reads: "Take your time and explore / Watch the colorful fish / Size up a gigantic T. Rex / Relax under a rain forest tree / Stare into a starry night / Explore the wonders of our unique planet and discover ways that you can help save it." The lines on this plaque provide hints of what to expect inside.

Children will enjoy a full-size replica of a Tyrannosaurus Rex fossil, a scale-model of the NASA space shuttle, and a large, artificial tree. Some areas of this space have dim lighting, adding effectively to the mock forest atmosphere. Sounds that one would expect to hear in a rain forest also play in the background. Domes built into the ceiling change color with a spectrum of soft, warm hues, including blue and green shades.

Young visitors may also enjoy the Geologic Column drawing located on a wall near an art studio. A brochure on this display states, "The successive layers of rock formations shown here are representative of those extending from the bottom of the Grand Canyon up through the Bryce and Zion National Parks in southern Utah" (Cerritos Library, n.d.b). There is the further statement: "This is the most spectacular range of geologic formations in the world." This attractive brochure opens up to a 17 by 11 inch miniposter of the rock formations that children may take with them.

CLIO COMPUTER CENTER AND 21ST CENTURY LIBRARY ROOM

The Clio Computer Center is a three-tiered computer work area located on the second level. It is accessible via a large escalator and stairs. The center provides the largest bank of computer workstations within the library.

The Cerritos Library has numerous features in its interior spaces, such as bookshelves that light up.

Located on the same floor is the 21st Century Library Room. Those who opt to ride up the escalator from the first floor will experience a magnificent view of the 21st Century room directly in front of them, including an ultramodern looking reference desk, and the Clio Computer Center to the left. This large area houses the nonfiction, reference, fiction, older periodicals, and language materials, as well as study rooms wired for videoconferencing and personal computers. The study rooms are named after famous writers, such as George Orwell, Adlous Huxley, and Jules Verne.

SKYLINE ROOM

Located on the third floor is the Skyline Room, a space used for various community activities. This room is the largest area on the floor, measuring 3,200 square feet. It seats 250 guests and provides enough room to serve 150 people during banquet events ("Introducing the 'Experience,'" 2002). Events held in this room range from piano recitals, meetings with published authors, family science shows (Cerritos Library, 2005), to the International Film Symposium, which features monthly screenings of films from countries including the United States, China, Iran, India, Italy, France, Argentina, and Chile (Cerritos Library, n.d.c).

HI-TECH LAB

Located down the hall from the Skyline Room is the Hi-Tech Lab, a smaller, instructional space. The lab provides technology-specific programs tailored for the needs of various members of the public. Classes offered include beginning computer skills, instruction on searching the library catalog, and hour-long computer research classes for children ages 8 to 12.

Exhibit cases found on this floor showcase book art. Stanley Strauss, public service librarian, explained that the works on display are from the library's permanent collection: Art of the Book: The Book as Art Special Collection. He further commented that the library owns a large collection of book art (personal correspondence, September 11, 2005). Although the Hi-Tech Lab and Skyline Room are somewhat removed from the rest of the library, the book art displays weave this area into the artistry of the other floors and bring a symmetry to the interior of the entire library.

LEARNING CENTERS

The library has also created small and virtual spaces within the physical building. Ten Learning Center Resources (LCRs) were created on topics that users frequently conduct research on. The LCRs include Webliographies and bibliographies to advance the research of the patrons. Five of the ten LCRs have computer workstations within the library along with books and multimedia materials. Each of these five centers is devoted to one of the following topics: Printing and the Written Word, Views of the Future through Time, Dinosaurs, Parenting, World Traditions, and Aquarium and Ocean Life. It is not unusual for librarians to create bibliographies, pathfinders, or detailed research guides on topics, but it is definitely unique for a space within a library, even a tiny space consisting of a desk, computer terminal, and selected resources, to be permanently set aside and devoted to one research topic.

The five remaining LCRs do not exist in physical space, but on the library's Intranet. Topics covered in these virtual spaces include Geologic Time; Space, Travel, and Astronomy; Southern California in the 1940s and 1950s; and Rain Forest and Ecology. Highlighted topics within Southern California in the 1940s and 1950s include Beach Culture, Beat Generation, Tinseltown, and Disneyland.

EXHIBITS

If the spaces within the Cerritos Public Library do not make visitors experience the building as a hybrid between a museum and library, the exhibits will definitely do so. Beautiful and diverse artwork is displayed throughout the library. Similar to museum displays, glossy and cardstock brochures providing information on the art and artist are freely available at each display. These elegant brochures provide a reproduction of the art on the front cover, informative text on the inside, and the library's logo on the back cover, allowing visitors to take pieces of the essence of the library home with them.

While visiting the library in August and September 2005, I viewed several memorable works that are part of the permanent collection. On display was New York–born artist Al Held's vibrant acrylic on canvas titled *Quattro Centric XIV* (1990). The library brochure comments that the "primary colors and geometric shapes" of the work "reflect the contemporary forms and primary colors in the interior space of the Cerritos Library's second floor" (Cerritos Library, n.d.a).

A piece titled *Auric Field* (2001) by California-born artist Lita Albuquerque is created from plaster, pigment, and white gold leaf on a maple panel. This striking creation begins with a glowing circular shape outlined briefly by lapis lazuli and then surrounded by a thick, black background. What is most interesting about the piece is that the artist created her work with the knowledge of the library space it would be placed within: "The eight vertical gold leaf panels and discs that make up the installation are located in a space that will not be seen as a whole because book stacks and design structures obscure sight lines. Therefore, determining how to develop her imagery and make the individual parts relate to one another presented a challenge that Albuquerque, experienced in public art projects, enthusiastically accepted" (Cerritos Library, n.d.d).

In addition to the other fine pieces in the permanent collection, the library is home to the First Ladies Collection. Located off Main Street, this permanent display consists of portraits of all the First Ladies. Quotations by some of the First Ladies are also on display on bronze plaques. A special collection of books and personal donations to the Cerritos Library by certain First Ladies are other items in the collection.

The library is also a gallery for different displays off of the Main Street area. In August 2005, the lobby display case featured works from the library's permanent book art collection. Also on exhibit in the Local History Museum were colorful nature photographs by Richard Jespersen. Jespersen's subjects include flowers and clouds.

An exhibit of book art in September 2005 was spread out over the first and second floors. The exhibit, titled Ukulele Books, consisted of 22 ukuleles that had been crafted into unique representations of books by the husband and wife artist team of Peter and Donna Thomas. Each ukulele is a marvel. Strauss explained that Peter Thomas would be offering an upcoming workshop at the library on creating book art from ukuleles (personal correspondence, September 11, 2005). Thomas' lecture was scheduled to take place in the Skyline Room.

There is no easy way to summarize the art collections at the library. Similar to the spaces, the art provides an expansive range of creativity spanning from the traditional to the experimental. Such an eclectic display provides something for nearly all visitors to admire.

REFERENCES

Berry, J. N. "A Message from Cerritos." *Library Journal* 127, no. 15 (2002): 8.
California State Library. Library Development Services Bureau. California Library Statistics 2003. www.library.ca.gov/assets/acrobat/StatsAll.pdf (retrieved August 29, 2005).
_____. California Library Statistics 2004. www.library.ca.gov/assets/acrobat/StatsPub04.pdf (retrieved August 29, 2005).
_____. California Library Statistics 2005. www.library.ca.gov/assets/acrobat/StatsPub05.pdf (retrieved September 20, 2005).
_____. California Library Statistics 2006. www.library.ca.gov/assets/acrobat/StatsPub06.pdf (retrieved December 23, 2006).
Cerritos Library. Al Held. Brochure, n.d.a. (Available at the Cerritos Library.)
_____. Calendar of Events. Pamphlet, 2005. (Available at the Cerritos Library.)
_____. The Geologic Column: Cerritos Children's Library. Brochure, n.d.b. (Available at the Cerritos Library.)
_____. International Film Symposium: 2005–2006. Brochure, n.d.c. (Available at the Cerritos Library.)
_____. Lita Albuquerque. Brochure, n.d.d. (Available at the Cerritos Library.)
City of Cerritos. "Library History." 2005. www.ci.cerritos.ca.us/library/libhistory.html (retrieved August 27, 2005).
"Introducing the 'Experience Library.'" *School Library Journal* 48, no. 5 (2002): 22.
"Late Bulletins." *Library Journal* 127, no. 4 (2002): 13.
"Reader's Digest Honors Cerritos." *Library Journal* 129, no. 10 (2004): 25.
Sahagun, L. "Lavish, Futuristic Library Opens in Cerritos: It Has Titanium Exterior, a Shark-Filled Aquarium, Replica T. Rex Skeleton, 200 Computers and 300,000 Books." *Los Angeles Times*, March 17, 2002.
"Selling the Learning Experience." *Library Journal* 128, no. 5 (2003): 10.
"2003 Themed Entertainment Association Thea Awards." Themed Entertainment Association, 2003. www.themeit.com/2003_library.htm (retrieved August 29, 2005).
Williams, J. F. "Shaping the 'Experience Library.'" *American Libraries, 33* (2002): 70–73.
Young Adult Services. Flyer, n.d. (Available at the Cerritos Public Library.)

13

Central Library of the Pasadena Public Library

LIBRARY DATA

Address: 285 East Walnut Street, Pasadena, CA 91101
Phone: (626) 744-4066
Web site: www.cityofpasadena.net/library
Square Feet: 130,000
Circulation: 865,858 (2003/2004 fiscal year)
Collection: 343,591 total items (2003/2004 fiscal year)
Source for above: www.cityofpasadena.net/library

In 1889, *All about Pasadena and Its Vicinity* by Charles Frederick Holder was published. Enrobed in the elegant language of the time, Holder's portrait of Pasadena celebrates the city with a poetic and passionate tone:

> As Pasadena is the best-equipped health and pleasure resort, winter and summer, in this country, budding fair to compare in beauty with the famed watering-places of the Riviera, it has naturally attracted the attention of people in every quarter of the country; and every year hundreds of tourists and others proposing to visit Southern California, turn to the map and locate it near the thirty-fourth parallel of latitude [p.1].

He later continues his celebration with the following characterization of this city located in the San Gabriel Valley of Los Angeles County: "It is the land of the afternoon; people live out of doors, and have an inherent love of flowers" (p. 10). It is important to note that within Holder's entertaining profile of the city, he devotes several lines to the Pasadena Public Library, describing it as one of the buildings that "speak well" for the future of the city (p. 12). The library, according to Holder, had "a fine collection of books, and a reading-room containing all the papers and periodicals of the day" (p. 12). The library Holder comments on has since been replaced by a building erected in the early 20th century, yet his celebratory descriptions of both the city and the library are not unlike later accounts.

In 2002, for example, Pomeroy's *Lost and Found II: More Historic and Natural Landmarks under Southern California Skies* includes the Pasadena Public Library's Central Library. Describing the current 1927 building's "stately facade," created under the vision of architect Myron Hunt, Pomeroy states, "Generations of Pasadenans have come to this library" (p. 32–33). Commenting on an inscription by Montaigne that is found in the library's main hall, Pomeroy concludes, "and perhaps you'll agree with the philosopher Montaigne: 'Here I am in my kingdom'" (p. 33).

LIBRARY HISTORY

Pasadena has the unusual distinction of having an established library before the city itself was officially founded. The city, bordered on the north by the San Gabriel Mountains and often associated with the Rose Bowl and Tournament of Roses Parade, is located ten miles northeast of downtown Los Angeles (City, 2005j). The land that is now considered Pasadena was originally home to the Hahamogna Tribe of Indians until the arrival of the Spaniards in 1771. In the early to mid–1800s, the land changed hands from Spain to Mexico until California was ultimately admitted as a state in the Union in 1850 (City, 2005g). The Pasadena Public Library was founded on December 26, 1882. Interestingly, the founding of the library predates the official incorporation of the city of Pasadena by four years (City, 2005d).

The library has changed its appearance and location over the years as it transformed to meet the needs of a growing population. The current building is the third that the library has occupied. What is now the public library was a private subscription library, founded in 1882, called the Pasadena Library and Village Improvement Society. At its opening on February 26, 1884, the library was located on the south side of Colorado Street (City, 2005d). Although the construction of the new library was completed on September 13, 1883, the building did not open at that time, due to a lack of funds to pay the builders. The trustees held an Art Loan Exhibit to raise money. Everything from eggs to a mummified cat was donated for the exhibit. Enough money was raised to open the doors in early 1884 (Page, 1964).

Just a short time after its opening, the library was moved in 1886 to West Dayton Street (City, 2005d). According to Page (1964), in 1888 the library held 2,400 volumes that had all been donated by citizens of Pasadena. The library was a popular place with circulation over 14,000 in 1888. Due to the impressive use, a new building became essential. A second building, located at Walnut Street and Raymond Avenue, opened on September 9, 1890 (City, 2005d).

The library quickly began to grow out of this second space as the city expanded. In 1924, a competition was held to design three new buildings: a library, a city hall, and a civic auditorium (City, 2005d). The firm of Myron Hunt and

H.C. Chambers, architects of the Huntington Library, won the competition (City, 2005e). A new Mediterranean-style library building was dedicated in 1927. The current 1927 building is listed on the National Register of Historic Places (City, 2005d).

Expansions, renovations, and other architectural changes have not altered the library's firm position as a treasured institution. This is most evident through the donations the Pasadena Public Library Foundation has received specifically for architectural renovation and preservation of the Central Library. Since 1983, over $3 million has been raised for this cause (City, 2005d). Restoration of the building in the late 1980s has resulted in numerous awards: Pasadena Beautiful Foundation's Award of Merit, National Trust for Historic Preservation's National Preservation Honor Award, and the Excellence in the Design and Execution of Architecture and the Fine Arts Award from the Pasadena and Foothill Chapter of the American Institute of Architects (City, 2005e).

Not only has the building been the recipient of various awards, but its mysterious and grand interior has drawn several film crews. The following films have been made at the library: *Foul Play* (1978), *Dead Heat* (1988), *Arachnophobia* (1990), *Matilda* (1996), *Legally Blonde* (2001), and *Red Dragon* (2002) (City, 2005i). Anyone with romantic and traditional notions of what a library should look like will definitely find it here. The magnificent structure provides numerous rooms of varying sizes, as well as both indoor and outdoor spaces for reading. It has enjoyed well over 500,000 visitors in the last five fiscal years with 629,788 visitors for the 2003/2004 fiscal year (City, 2005c).

Courtyard and Patios

The perimeter around the large building provides several spaces for sitting in the sun or shade. Those entering the library from the south will first climb two sets of stairs to enter the courtyard. When the library is closed, the courtyard remains visible through ornamental iron gates. Immediately upon entry, visitors will find an open space with a fountain and four small benches surrounded by a multitude of bird-of-paradise flowers. Several inscriptions may be found carved into the front of the building. The middle inscription reads: "Be made whole by books as by great spaces and the stars."

To the east of the courtyard is the East Patio, which currently features a cafe area called Central Grounds. The cafe serves hot and cold drinks, including delicious espresso concoctions, as well as sandwiches, salads, pastries, and other snacks. Tables, providing room for several groups, are arranged throughout Central Grounds. A door off to the corner leads to the Library Store, where visitors may purchase used books and other items.

On the other side of the courtyard is the West Patio, which is essentially a wonderful outdoor reading room. This unique space provides several tables with umbrellas. Those who decide to partake of this space will enjoy a quietness interspersed with the running fountain, some sounds from the street below, and occasional voices from those gathering at Central Grounds across the courtyard. A door leading from the patio to the library allows library guests to choose between this outdoor space or an adjacent indoor reading room that has several cushioned chairs arranged in a small and cozy rectangular-shaped room.

Main Hall

Walking through the courtyard and into the library by the south entrance places one within the Main Hall. Even if the library had no other spaces worthy of mention, this magnificent hall would be enough of a reason to stop by. The hall is 33 feet wide, 45 feet high, and 204 feet long (City, 2005h). Balconies, which are reached by narrow staircases, overlook the far east and west corners of the hall, providing a striking view. Walking up the stairs to the balconies creates quite a nostalgic feeling for the hidden nooks and crannies that fill older buildings.

The floor of the hall is made of Portugal cork and laid in a decorative pattern to give the effect of dark and light shades. Not only is the floor an artistic creation, but the cork was installed to also help reduce noise, making it ideal for a library (City, 2005h). Hanging far above the attractive floor are several pendant lights, strategically placed and suspended on long cords. The lights are one of the most memorable parts of the interior. The lights that currently hang are not the originals, but "replicas of the original bronze and copper pendant lights Myron Hunt designed" (City, 2005h).

Ten oak tables with matching chairs are dispersed throughout the hall, making room for 60 people. Some of the pieces are originals, while others are reproductions. Librarian Dan McLaughlin pointed out how much effort was made during the restoration to remain true to the original appearance of the building's interior (personal correspondence, November 13, 2005). The large scale of the space provides an openness with much room for people to walk around and explore without feeling crowded. In addition, the hall is an area that opens into many other spaces within the library, which also adds to the feeling of expansiveness.

Auditorium

The auditorium is just one of the rooms that can be reached by the Main Hall. The door to the auditorium is located at the far west end of the building. Just outside the door, visitors will find what appears to be a model of a castle enclosed within a glass display case. McLaughlin commented that children often inquire about the "castle" (personal correspondence, September 13, 2005). The model is a

The main hall of the Central Library of the Pasadena Public Library is a traditional space that is equally welcoming, regal, and glamorous.

replica of the old 1890 building that was located at the corner of Raymond Avenue and Walnut Street. Interestingly, the model, created by Pasadena resident Rex Petty, was crafted out of salvaged stone from the original building (City, 2005h).

The auditorium includes fixed seating for 142. These seats were original to the Pasadena Civic Auditorium, which was built in 1932. The seats were found in storage and placed in the auditorium during a restoration project in the 1980s (City, 2005f). A wire frame located under each seat is likely a puzzling feature for visitors in the 21st century. McLaughlin explained that the wire frames are actually hat racks that were used to hold men's hats during performances (personal correspondence, September 13, 2005).

This interesting space includes a combination backstage restroom/dressing room for performers. Such a room is required, since the auditorium is a heavily used area that averages over 450 bookings per year (City, 2005f). The library's independent and foreign film program, titled 3rd Thursday Films, is one such events that takes place in the auditorium. However, lectures by scholars, recitals, concerts, and many other events are held here. The space may be used free of charge by nonprofit groups, which comprise 70 percent of the auditorium's use.

CENTENNIAL ROOM

The Centennial Room, located behind the reference desk in the Main Hall, houses the local history and Californiana collections. This room was restored in the 1980s and dedicated on June 23, 1989. It formally housed the Fine Arts and Californiana collections when the library opened in 1927, but was then the location for business and technology materials from 1970 to 1988 (City, 2005b).

Hanging pendant lamps and table lamps with similar furnishings found in the Main Hall provide a historic atmosphere. Wood bookcases with glass-framed doors line the walls of the room, as well as large flat cases for holding oversized material, such as scrapbooks and maps. Several cases are covered with grillwork doors for extra security, including the holdings in a small Genealogy Room only accessible through the Centennial Room. Although much of the space is focused on history, the room also has a Neighborhood Information Service kiosk with current information on Pasadena.

CIRCULATING SPACES

Myron Hunt's original design for the library included a four-level area for book stacks, but only two floors were completed when the library opened in 1927. A construction project became necessary in the 1980s to add more room for the books by completing the additional floors. William Henry Taylor was chosen as the architect for this project, due to "his use of the natural light from the original skylights on the fourth level and the atrium linking the upper and lower floors" (City, 2005a).

One could lose a considerable amount of time browsing the four floors that house the library's circulating books. The area is accessible from the north entrance and the main hall. An artfully crafted feature is the centrally located staircase that connects all four floors. It is impossible not to notice the appeal of the space when peering down all four floors through the open staircase on the top level.

Other Spaces

The Central Library of the Pasadena Public Library provides many more spaces than those discussed above. This chapter should be understood as just an introduction to the wonders of the 1927 building. Other areas worthy of mention include the Technology Learning Center, Humanities Wing, and Reference and Business Wing. With its mixture of historic charm and splendor, as well as both indoor and outdoor spaces, the library is a highly recommended stop for visitors to Pasadena.

References

City of Pasadena. "Book Stacks." 2005a. www.cityofpasadena.net/library/book-stacks.asp (retrieved November 26, 2005).
_____. "Centennial Room." 2005b. www.cityofpasadena.net/library/centennial-room.asp (retrieved November 26, 2005).
_____. "Central Library." 2005c. www.ci.pasadena.ca.us/library/central.asp (retrieved November 12, 2005).
_____. "Central Library Architecture: Brief History." 2005d. www.ci.pasadena.ca.us/library/brief-history.asp (retrieved November 26, 2005).
_____. "Central Library Neighborhood Profile." 2005e. www.ci.pasadena.ca.us/library/centralprfl.asp (retrieved November 12, 2005).
_____. "Donald R. Wright Auditorium." 2005f. www.cityofpasadena.net/library/auditorium.asp (retrieved November 26, 2005).
_____. "Heritage: A Short History of Pasadena." 2005g. www.ci.pasadena.ca.us/History/default.asp (retrieved November 26, 2005).
_____. "Main Hall." 2005h. www.cityofpasadena.net/library/main-hall.asp (retrieved November 26, 2005).
_____. "Movies Filmed at Pasadena Central Library." 2005i. www.ci.pasadena.ca.us/library/filming_history.asp (retrieved November 12, 2005).
_____. "Pasadena Demographics." 2005j. www.ci.pasadena.ca.us/statistics.asp (retrieved November 26, 2005).
Holder, C. F. *All about Pasadena and Its Vicinity.* Boston: Lee and Shepard, 1889.
Page, H. M. *Pasadena: Its Early Years.* Los Angeles: Morrison, 1964.
Pomeroy, E. *Lost and Found II: More Historic and Natural Landmarks under Southern California Skies.* Pasadena: Many Moons, 2002.

14

The Writers Guild Foundation Shavelson-Webb Library

LIBRARY DATA

Address: 7000 West Third Street, Los Angeles, CA 90048
Phone: (323) 782-4544
Web site: www.wgfoundation.org
Square Feet: 1,990
Circulation: Noncirculating collection
Collection: 12,000+ film, television, and radio scripts; 2,100 books on writing, writers, and the entertainment industry; approximately 3,000 tapes and discs (December 2006)
Sources for above: K. Pedersen, personal correspondence, October 20, 2005 and December 18, 2006, and The Writers Guild Foundation Web site

The Shavelson-Webb Library is located at the intersection of Fairfax Avenue and Third Street. It sits in the impressive Writers Guild of America, west (WGAw) building, diagonally across from the landmark Farmers' Market. The library is located in an area of the city that is rarely quiet, except, perhaps, between the hours of 3:00 A.M. and 6:00 A.M. It is not far from the riches of Beverly Hills, the nightlife of Sunset Boulevard, and the alternative, yet often pricey, culture of Melrose Avenue. The library is undeniably in an area where much of the mythology of Los Angeles was born. It is very fitting, due to its location, that the library, under the direction of Karen Pedersen, devotes itself solely to writers and the craft of writing for film, television, and radio. Open to the public and free of charge, the library provides informative and helpful resources for its users in beautifully designed spaces.

HISTORY OF WGAw AND WRITERS GUILD FOUNDATION

The WGAw is "a labor union composed of the thousands of writers who write the television shows, movies, news programs, documentaries, animation, CD-ROMs, and content for new-media technologies that keep audiences constantly entertained and informed" (WGAw, *Guide*, p. 1). The prehistory of the WGAw may be traced back as far as 1912. It was in the early decades of the 20th century that writers first organized into protective associations. In 1912, the Authors Guild was founded. This organization's membership included "writers of books, short stories, articles, etc." (WGAw, *Guide*, p. 12). It was also at this time that an association of drama writers (Dramatists Guild) was formed. The Authors Guild and the Dramatists Guild joined to form the Authors League (WGAw, n.d.). A third group of writers creating material for the motion picture industry formed the Screen Writers Guild in 1921, which became an additional branch of the Authors League.

According to WGAw (*Guide*, p. 13):

> Writers got organized in 1933, and they got serious. Within a few months, membership grew from just a handful to several hundred screenwriters. In 1937 the U.S. Supreme Court upheld the National Labor Relations Act, and the Screen Writers Guild called for an election. By 1939, they began collective bargaining with motion picture producers. The first contract, signed in 1941, brought protection for writers' onscreen credits.

Internal struggles during the World War II era created factions within the Screen Writers Guild that caused "screenwriters, television writers, radio writers, and others" (WGAw, *Guide*, p. 13) to unite. This unity led to the formation of the Writers Guild of America (WGA) in 1954. The organization has offices in Los Angeles (the WGA west) and New York (the WGA east). "The Mississippi River is used as the dividing line for administrative jurisdiction between the two Guilds" (WGAw, "A Brief").

The Writers Guild Foundation, founded in 1966 by prominent screen and television writers as a nonprofit, charitable corporation, works closely with the WGAw. The foundation's programs include educational seminars and panel discussions; literacy programs; oral history interviews, "including *The Writer Speaks*, a series of video interviews with the great writers of classic film and television, plus interviews with Writers Guild members about Writers Guild and labor history in Hollywood"; publishing projects; and conferences (WGAw, *Guide*, p. 9). One of the foundation's significant programs is the Shavelson-Webb Library.

OVERVIEW OF LIBRARY

Since its establishment in 1984, The Writers Guild Foundation Shavelson-Webb Library "has had a mission to collect, preserve, and celebrate the works of writers in film, television, and radio" (WGAw, *Guide*, p. 10). Pedersen, the current library director, points out that the library's mission is significantly different than other library collections that may initially seem alike. Libraries with similar materials, such as those housed at University of California, Los Angeles or the American Film Institute, typically collect within a larger context, but the

Shavelson-Webb Library is focused entirely on writers (personal correspondence, October 20, 2005).

This focus on writers carries over into acquisition policies. Pedersen explains that the library is not a museum or conservatory, but a place to preserve the writing itself. Essentially, the focus is on acquiring and preserving creative content, not original materials (personal correspondence, October 20, 2005). For this reason, copies of original screenplays are acceptable. Both current and older materials are collected. Some of the material is donated after requests the library makes to writers and agents (K. Pedersen, personal correspondence, October 20, 2005).

The library is located on the first floor of the WGAw headquarters. Its location in this building, however, is a recent occurrence. The current location of the library was formally a Washington Mutual Bank (K. Pedersen, personal correspondence, October 20, 2005). In 2005, ground was broken to create a new space for the library in the WGAw building (WGAw, "A Brief"). According to Pedersen, the library moved into its present location in June 2005. Designed by architect John Dutton, the library, though smaller than many profiled in this book, makes up for size with glamour, warmth, and attractive furnishings and arrangements.

The library receives approximately 40 reference requests per day. An estimated 30 percent of these requests are by phone, but the majority are in person. Pedersen has noticed a dramatic increase after the library moved into its new space (personal correspondence, October 20, 2005). Since the library is open to the public, an assortment of visitors come to use the collection, including WGA members and staff, students, and journalists (K. Pedersen, personal correspondence, October 20, 2005).

ENTRANCE

The writer-focused nature of the library is evident before even venturing into the main room. The entrance to the library, accessible from the Fairfax sidewalk or an elevator from the underground parking garage, includes a high-quality display area along one wall and three television screens in the opposite wall. The televisions are embedded in the wall. Scenes from *Psycho*, *Halloween*, and *The Exorcist* were playing on the televisions during my visit in late 2005. On display below each television were copies of pages from the original screenplays of each film. In October 2005, "Writers at Work," was the title of an elegant and informative display in the cases located across from the televisions. This display, located in what is called the Stephen J. Cannell Gallery, included photographs and material showcasing various writers, such as David Mamet, Garry Marshall, Dorothy Parker, Frances Marion, and Sarah Y. Mason.

Visitors to The Writers Guild Foundation Shavelson-Webb Library in Los Angeles will first be met by artfully crafted exhibits.

Main Room and Alcoves

The main space in the library, called the Billy Wilder Reading Room, is accessible through glass doors off the entrance and exhibit area. The design and interior of the room can only be described as inviting. With the collection filling the walls around the perimeter, the space has a spacious feel. A large, rectangular table near the middle of the room provides seating for 14 with overhead lighting. Deep brown-colored wooden shelves and wall-to-wall carpet accent the room.

On the wall to the left of the entrance is a collection map which provides directions on how to locate materials within the library's color-coded organizational system. Also found in this area are open shelves that contain copies of original scripts from feature films, such as *The Godfather*, *Kramer vs. Kramer*, and *Mystic River*; television shows, including *Cheers* and *Cagney & Lacey*; and radio scripts. Writers biographies finish out the area.

One side of the room contains three areas that are best described as niches or alcoves. These areas provide intimate spaces within the larger reading room. Each alcove includes a high-tech AV station with two monitors and headphones. Visitors use the library catalog to locate programs they would like to watch. Pedersen explained that viewing, for example, a television program while having the script to also review, can be a helpful use of the materials (personal correspondence, October 20, 2005). In addition to television programs, aspiring writers can view panel discussions, writer interviews, and other instructional videos from a collection of roughly 2,000 titles. Interestingly, Pedersen stated that the library was currently working on having a printout of all the titles available that visitors could look through, since some may prefer this to searching the online catalog.

The first alcove in the room, called the Barbara and Garry Marshall Room, contains film scripts in handsome glass-covered cabinets. Copies of scripts for such famous films as *Rocky*, *The Deer Hunter*, and *On the Waterfront* are found in this alcove. The second and third alcoves include copies of television scripts from such well-known shows as *Gomer Pyle, U.S.M.C.*; *ER*; *Ellen*; *The X-Files*; *The Sopranos*; and *Sex and the City*.

In addition to the alcoves, other areas within the larger room are filled with various materials, including published scripts, WGA members' published works, industry books, reference items, and books specifically devoted to the craft of writing. Periodicals are also found here with a "comprehensive periodical collection that focuses on screenwriting," (Writers Guild Foundation, n.d.) comprised of titles such as *Creative Screenwriting*, *Hollywood Scriptwriter*, and *Screenwriter*. The shelves housing these materials wrap around much of the remainder of the room, except for open entrances to a lounge and The Sidney Sheldon Room, where Pedersen's desk, a reference desk, and a work area is found.

Reading Spaces

Located slightly off from the main reading room is the Preston Sturges Lounge. This area provides windows with vertical blinds with views of Fairfax and 3rd Street. Plants are strategically placed along with red chairs and circular tables, which all coordinate together to definitely give the room the appearance of an elegant lounge. One area in this space, surrounded entirely by windows, provides seating for three around a circular table.

Final Thoughts

The library has a goal "to become the world's foremost center of writing information and inspiration to WGA members, students, and the public" (WGAw, *Guild*, p. 10). This lofty and worthy goal speaks to the heart of the library's dedication to the writer's craft. While the library strives to meet this goal, it provides beautiful spaces where fruitful investigations and frequent inspirations must surely take place.

References

Writers Guild of America, west (WGAw). "Writers Guild of America, West History." n.d. www.wga.org (retrieved October 20, 2005).
_____. *Guide to the Guild*. Brochure, n.d. (Available at The Writers Guild Foundation Shavelson-Webb Library.)
Writers Guild Foundation. "FAQ." n.d. www.wgfoundation.org (retrieved October 20, 2005).

15

Central Library of the Los Angeles Public Library

Library Data

Address: 630 W. 5th Street, Los Angeles, CA 90071
Phone: (213) 228-7000
Web site: www.lapl.org/central
Square Feet: 540,000
Circulation: 1,228,784 (fiscal year 2004)
Collection: 2.6 million items (March 2006)

Source for above: A. Connor, central library director, personal correspondence, March 13, 2006

An informational pillar located near the 5th Street entrance of the Central Library of the Los Angeles Public Library reads:

> The saga of the Los Angeles Central Library is as dramatic a tale as can be found in the books on its shelves — a unique and beloved building designed by a man who died before it could be finished, nearly torn down by city fathers, nearly undone by two arson files, only to rise from its own ashes like a phoenix.

It is fitting that a library located in a city that has historically been associated with the creation of much theatrics would provide such a spectacular rendition of its origin for visitors to read before entering the doors. Reading such a statement also leads one to believe that he or she is about to enter an extraordinary place, which is immediately proven true.

If California is a land for dreamers and travelers and those looking for a new life, then Los Angeles, one could easily argue, epitomizes this California myth. In long-time resident Waldie's *Where We are Now: Notes from Los Angeles* (2004), he states: "The power of Los Angeles is the creation of new selves from the longings of the men and women who have arrived here after crossing a boundary not marked on any *Thomas Guide* map page" (p. 13). This mythological idea of the city is one manifested in physical form within the exterior and interior spaces of the library. It is a building that provides spaces for all, including those looking to, perhaps, create a new self. The library has also been the birth place, no doubt, of many scholarly and creative endeavors. Ray Bradbury, for example, wrote his classic *Fahrenheit 451* in the basement on a rental typewriter. He was charged 15 cents an hour for use of the machine (DeCandido, 1993).

Situated amongst numerous tall skyscrapers and the bustling activities of a true metropolis, it is impossible to separate the library from its surroundings. When entering the library from the 5th Street entrance, one will notice a reflection of the spectacular Bunker Hill steps in the glass of the library doors. This reflection is more than just a trick of sunlight; it points to the interconnected relationship between the library and its magnificent neighborhood. Designed by Lawrence Halprin and located directly across the street from the library, the masterfully crafted staircase provides a graceful movement from between the tall buildings to the crosswalk that ends at the library entrance.

It is due to all of the above that writing about the Central Library of the Los Angeles Public Library is quite a challenge. Not only is the surrounding atmosphere quite remarkable, but the library resembles its own city within a city with its multiple walkways and levels, its curious twists and turns, and its escalators, elevators, and staircases. Instead of roads, its magnitude is measured in shelves; the library contains 89 miles of shelving (A. Connor, personal correspondence, March 13, 2006). While I stood taking notes near the main lobby, a fellow visitor asked me if it was my "first time." I replied it was my second. He further relayed he had visited about a dozen times, but he was still finding his way around. "They have so much," he explained. Few would disagree. It would not do justice to simply call the library big. It is grand.

LIBRARY HISTORY

In *The Light of Learning: An Illustrated History of the Los Angeles Public Library* (1993), Soter traces the idea to found a library in the city to 1844 when a society named Los Amigos del Pais "organized to provide a social gathering place where books and magazines might be read" (p. 17). A grant helped construct Amigos Hall, which included a small reading room and a larger room for dancing. This early effort to provide a library, along with another later in the 19th century, were both ultimately unsuccessful, even though they saw periods of success.

In late December 1872, an outgrowth of the Los Angeles Library Association formed. A newly created board appointed a librarian and reading rooms opened to the public in January 1873 (Soter, 1993). Numerous articles about the library's operation and collection began to appear in the *Los Angeles Times* over the next few decades. Many articles were simply lists of new books. An article dated September 8, 1882, titled "More Good Reading" confidently told readers, "Los Angeles may well take pride in her Library as it is a truly live institution, and is well managed

15. Central Library of the Los Angeles Public Library

The Central Library of the Los Angeles Public Library is located in the heart of downtown Los Angeles where it shares the neighborhood with skyscrapers.

by Miss Foy, an efficient librarian." Another article, "The Annual Report of the Secretary and Librarian," appeared on January 2, 1889, and told the story of a library that was becoming increasingly popular, although it did not have the space for its visitors: "The four rooms are over-crowded at all times and especially so in winter, making it very uncomfortable for everyone, but until our new rooms are finished in the city hall we must make the best of it."

Not unlike other libraries in this book, the early days of the library were unstable in terms of location, which often equated to cramped quarters for staff and patrons. In 1908, it was held within the Hamburger's Department Store building, where elevator operators announced the library along with carpets and furniture (Soter, 1993). In 1914, the location changed to the three top floors of the Metropolitan Building located at Fifth and Broadway. While housed at this location, the library found itself above a drugstore (Soter, 1993). Within the Metropolitan Building, the library was a crowded place that could not effectively support the growing numbers of users. It became quite clear that the city needed a more permanent solution. The library board hired architect Bertram Grosvenor Goodhue to construct a new building which opened on July 6, 1926, on Fifth Street, the library's present location (Soter, 1993).

An article appearing in the *Los Angeles Times* on July 7, 1926, reported positively on the new building, particularly regarding its size: "The library has a floor space of approximately 190,000 square feet and has a book capacity of 1,125,000 volumes. At the present time there are about 270,000 volumes in the main library, so no department is fully occupied." On June 14, 1929, after the library had occupied its new location for only a few years, a fire destroyed all magazines and some of the files in the Periodical Department (Soter, 1993). Unfortunately, the tragedy of fire was to return again in 1986 when a more destructive blaze destroyed 400,000 books and damaged 800,000. After the disaster of 1986, the library underwent a considerable renovation and a new wing was added, which increased the size of the library to 540,000 square feet ("Central Library," n.d.). When the expanded and renovated building opened on October 2, 1993, approximately 80,000 people came to explore the new spaces and investigate the restoration of the old, while several booths outside offered library cards ("The people arrive," 1993). It is from this long and often calamitous past that the Central Library of today emerges. According to the library's former director, Elizabeth Gay Teoman, who was interviewed near the time of the 1993 opening, "The Library reflects the city's culture and history, but it also reflects its future" (Siena, 1993).

Maguire Gardens and Exterior

Near the side of the library located at 5th and Flower streets, the Maguire Gardens and exterior grounds offer much to explore before entering the interior of the building. The gardens, designed by Halprin, who also designed the Bunker

Hill steps previously mentioned, include winding sidewalks, fountains, and benches that provide ample seating amongst an abundance of bushes, trees, and flowers. Found in this oasis are "some 160 trees of 13 species and fragrant plantings, from star jasmine to pittosporum" ("They unpaved paradise," 1994).

A World Peace Bell "cast from coins and medals donated by 103 countries" to represent "a common bond among the nations of the world," according to an informational plaque, is located in one corner of the gardens. The bell was dedicated on January 26, 2001, from the World Peace Bell Association of Tokyo, Japan. The association has a goal "to provide a world peace bell to all nations of the world." Also found in this attractive space is *Spine* by artist Jud Fine. Fine's creation is a 180-piece work that "employs sculptures, pools and etched quotations to trace the evolution of written language" ("They unpaved paradise," 1994). Integrated within Fine's *Spine* are letters from 19 languages.

CAFE

Depending on the entrance they use, visitors may find themselves first looking at a cafe. The Bookends Café provides not only coffee, snacks, and desserts, but entire meals. A deli counter sells hot and cold sandwiches along with salads and spectacular cakes. A small Chinese restaurant dishes out many hot items. Having such a cafe inside a library, one that goes beyond coffee and muffins, gives the impression that this is a place where people not only breeze through, but may stay for extended times. It is not a small space either, but one measuring 4,456 square feet. Perhaps it was the opening ceremony with Chinese lion dancers on February 16, 1996, that has made the cafe a successful space. In Chinese culture, the dancers "help celebrate new endeavors" ("Lionizing Los Angeles," 1996).

LOBBY AND LIBRARY STORE

The lobby opens up with over eight passageways into other areas of the library. It is a busy, central location that provides information and circulation desks. The 36 by 36 foot ceiling is enhanced with a brightly colored design of green, yellow, red, blue, and contrasting black and white hues by artist Renee Petropoulos. Petropoulos' creation combines both geometric shapes and contrasting fluid shapes with the names of Los Angeles novelists. The painting is described as providing "an active viewing experience," due to its off-center placement, which creates a "sense of movement" ("Art and Architecture," n.d.).

Items for sale at the library store, located within the main lobby, are not the usual ones visitors may expect to find. For example, jewelry in glass cases near the door, crafted by artists from Los Angeles, New York City, and Israel, is for sale along with candles, posters, T-shirts, cards, stationary, more jewelry, cookbooks, autographed books, a large array of children's gifts, and a section devoted to books about Los Angeles and California.

Popular Library

Off the main lobby is the Arnold and Blanche Winnick Popular Library. This area offers titles in mystery, travel, nonfiction, romance, science fiction, and fiction. It is well lit and spacious with wide aisles that encourage browsing. Located close to the book section is an adjacent section providing CDs, DVDs, and other audiovisual materials. This area is arranged much like the interior of a Blockbuster or Hollywood Video rental store with similarly broad aisles.

Rotunda

The Lodwrick M. Cook Rotunda, described as the "focal point of the historic Central Library building" ("Central Library," n.d.) provides visitors a gateway to several areas. It is an empty, spacious room that one could imagine dances or large parties to be held in. Located within the 1926 building, a dome above the rotunda reaches up to 64 feet, creating an even greater feeling of openness. The rotunda leads to the Getty Gallery, Children's Literature Department, and Teen'Scape. It resembles a historic version of the new main lobby.

Unlike the brightly colored ceiling full of contrasting shapes in the new main lobby, the walls of the rotunda are equally beautiful, but covered with murals of more subtle qualities. Created by Dean Cornwell, who spent five years performing research on the project, the murals were completed in 1932. They depict "four great eras of California history, including discovery, mission building, Americanization and the founding of Los Angeles: the beginnings of arts and industry: and conquering of the elements in California." The colors in the murals "were purposely restrained to harmonize with the many-colored mosaic-like dome decorations by Julian E. Garnsey" ("Art and Architecture," n.d.).

Teen'Scape

The purpose of Teen'Scape, which is accessible from the rotunda, is obvious in the name. Even if one did not know the name, however, it would be quite evident upon entering this space that the area was designed with the young adult in mind. A small nook that is part of Teen'Scape provides seating for a few behind a short wall that looks out onto the rotunda. A turn to the right from this nook leads one down a passageway into an area called Cyberspace. Blue-tinted light hovers above an area with several circular computer workstation pods.

Off the computer area is a space that resembles a television lounge. In fact, this area was quite busy and noisy with the television easily heard from any spot in the room during my visits. Two small sofas and four cushioned chairs are located in front of the television that is built into the side of the service desk. A carpeted floor invites one to sit down, much like a living room. Periodicals for teens are located within this space.

Also within Teen'Scape are three large tables that provide seating for 18. The tables are located behind three cutouts in a wall that separates this space, but only slightly, from the television area. A mirror above one of the tables has the following caption written above it: "Who are you? Who will you become?" Words attached to the mirror include "Confident," "Artistic," "Independent," "Creative," "Thinker," and numerous others.

Tom Bradley Wing

One of the most impressive features of the library is undeniably the newer Tom Bradley Wing. Visitors may take an escalator from the main lobby to the wing. Upon arrival, they will have a stunning view of the eight-story atrium that provides natural lighting to reading areas on each floor. Escalators below appear like waterfalls bringing passengers to and from the different floors.

Immediately to the right, when standing at the top floor, is the Literature & Fiction Department. A reading room that connects two sides of this floor together provides one of the most striking views within the entire building. Windows on one side of the room look out to the city street far below. Those sitting on the other side may peer down for a top-level view of the atrium.

Although the size of the wing may be quite daunting upon a first glimpse, once one travels up and down the floors a few times, it becomes quite evident that there is an overall precision and symmetry to the layout. Subjects covered on each floor of the wing are clearly marked. There is a rhythm throughout with stacks, reading chairs, tables, and study carrels that creates a welcome predictability that ultimately makes the building easy to navigate.

Programs

One need only show up at the library on nearly any random day to find programs of unusual content. During my visit on a Saturday, for example, I discovered a meeting of the Scriptwriters' Network was going on, as well as an educational event to prepare students for the Scholastic Aptitude Test. In addition, two programs related to food were occurring at the same time: "A Food Historians' Workshop: Reading Cookbooks for the Study of Social History" and "Culinary Historians Lecture — History and Lore of Olive Oil." Just these programs alone point to the numerous available spaces the library has for members of the community to gather.

As at nearly every library, flyers were located throughout the library advertising ongoing and upcoming events. Unlike other libraries, however, the booklet advertising events for September–October 2005 was 87 pages long. The booklet includes programs at all Los Angeles Public Library locations, with Central Library events spanning pages 15–25.

"ALOUD at Central Library" is an ongoing series of lectures, readings, performances, and discussions. The cultural and contextual diversity of the events clearly mirrors the community the library serves. Novelists, architects, poets, filmmakers, and academics join for talks that are typically held in the evening. ALOUD also holds musical events, including ones similar to a concert held in September 2005 that was cosponsored by the World Festival of Sacred Music. This event, titled "The Guest House A Concert" featured Obie Award–winning composer Robert Een and the Mystical All-Star Band. A description of the event stated that musicians would "draw on diverse musical and spiritual traditions to present a musical vision of a guest house, a refuge for travelers on pilgrimage" (Library Foundation of Los Angeles, 2005). A theme of refuge within a library clearly develops the essence of an inviting and warm place for all.

Another series titled the "Downtown Lecture Series" with a theme of Arts and Los Angeles, Who is Influencing Who? is sponsored by the library, the Emeriti Center College of the University of Southern California, and a community support group of the library's Business/Economics and Science, Technology, and Patents departments and the Art, Music, and Recreation departments. This series illustrates not only the library as a place for collaboration between community groups and a local university, but also the library's interconnected relationship with the city. Attendees are encouraged to bring a brown bag lunch to these series of programs that run from 11:30 A.M. to 1:30 P.M. on Tuesdays.

ART

Before closing this exploration of a grand library, mention must be made of a few of the many artistic creations that abound on every floor. One of the most clever and surprising features is uncharacteristically found in the elevators located in the Tom Bradley Wing. Artist David Bunn used cards from the old library catalog to create a collage that surrounds the elevator passengers ("Art and Architecture," n.d.). The cards are easily readable behind panels of glass, making traveling on a library elevator both informative and, depending on one's enjoyment of library lore, quite aesthetically pleasing. According to Bunn, "As the catalog dutifully classifies and finds a place for every book, so the elevators travel deep through the center of the building, encompassing and accessing all the building's holdings" ("Art and Architecture," n.d.). Perhaps it is only at a library that such a curious display would be both enjoyed and understood by many, while enhancing the experience of a small space that is commonly void of art.

After stepping out of the elevators, visitors will find three striking chandeliers designed by artist Therman Statom in the atrium of the Tom Bradley Wing. These creations are unlike typical light fixtures. Made out of aluminum and fiberglass, the chandeliers weight 2,000 pounds each ("Art and Architecture," n.d.). Meant to represent the natural, man-made, and spiritual worlds, the chandeliers include objects such as a wheel, flowers, and a large blue bird.

Statom's memorable chandeliers share space in the eight-floor atrium with large 13-and-a-half-foot-tall lanterns. Designed by artist Anne Preston, the lanterns, titled *Illumination*, are found on each escalator landing. These permanent fixtures, which are functional, were designed in the shape of an upside-down human form out of 24 radiating vanes ("Art and Architecture," n.d.).

The chandeliers, the elevator card catalog exhibit, and the tall lanterns speak to a free and creative energy that is felt throughout the atrium. The size of some of these pieces also demonstrates the openness of the space that allows room for such large pieces of art. This illustrates how far the library has come from the packed, stuffy reading rooms of its much earlier decades. For all the quirkiness of these creations, however, art located in the original, historic building could easily be described as more traditional, which would appeal to visitors who prefer more conventional works.

Found in the Children's Literature Department, which is off the historic rotunda, are California history murals by Albert Herter. The murals, which were originally hung in the Hope Street tunnel entrance in 1928, "succeed in imparting the gracious, colorful and romantic atmosphere of early California history" ("Art and Architecture," n.d.). Also within the historic building is the Globe Chandelier, a one-ton bronze creation with a diameter of nine feet. The chandelier, which hangs in the rotunda, includes signs of the zodiac along with 48 lights to represent the 48 United States at the time the building opened in 1926 ("Art and Architecture," n.d.).

In addition to art dispersed throughout the building, several galleries provide space for museum-level exhibits. From fall 2005 through spring 2006, the First Floor Galleries showcased black-and-white photographs from Nancy Crampton's Writers collection. This exhibit, which was around the corner from the Popular Library, featured 50 photographs of novelists, poets, and playwrights.

One floor up from this gallery and running at the same time as Writers, the Getty Gallery featured Far and Wide: The Golden Age of Travel Posters. The exhibition combined over 60 posters from the 1920s and 1930s. This gallery, along with the inviting and sophisticated Annenberg Gallery with features from the Special Collection, are both off the rotunda and close to Teen'Scape.

The wealth of art at the library, coupled with the impressive book and audiovisual collection and intriguingly diverse schedule of programs, truly makes the Central Library of the Los Angeles Public Library a building to visit over and over. The citizens of Los Angeles have much to be proud of in a library that wonderfully captures and extends to the public the essence of place.

REFERENCES

"Annual Report of the Secretary and Librarian." *Los Angeles Times*, January 2, 1889.
"Art and Architecture in Central Library." n.d. www.lapl.org/central/art_architecture.html (retrieved October 17, 2005).
"Central Library Self-Guided Tour." n.d. www.lapl.org/central/guidedtour.pdf (retrieved October 17, 2005).
DeCandido, G. A. "'The Thing that Keeps Us Free': Los Angeles PL Is Reopened, Restored, Revitalized." *Wilson Library Bulletin 68*, no. 3 (1993): 11.
"Library Opens New Quarters." *Los Angeles Times*, July 7, 1926.
"Lionizing Los Angeles PL." *American Libraries* 27, no. 5 (1996): 30.
"More Good Reading." *Los Angeles Times*, September 8, 1882.
"The People Arrive at LAPL." *Wilson Library Bulletin* 68, no. 4 (1993): 14.
Siena, J. S. "Rising from the Ashes: The Los Angeles Public Library: A Conversation with Elizabeth Gay Teoman." *Conservation: The GCI Newsletter 8,* no. 2 (1993). www.getty.edu/conservation/publications/newsletters/8_2/lalib.html (retrieved March 5, 2006).
Soter, B. D. *The Light of Learning: An Illustrated History of the Los Angeles Public Library*. Los Angeles: Library Foundation of Los Angeles, 1993.
"They Unpaved Paradise." Landscape Architecture 84, no. 3 (1994): 20.
Waldie, D. J. *Where We Are Now: Notes from Los Angeles*. Los Angeles: Angel City Press, 2004.

16

Philosophical Research Society Library

Library Data

Address: 3910 Los Feliz Boulevard, Los Angeles, CA 90027
Phone: (323) 663-2167
Web site: www.prs.org
Square Feet: approximately 1,500*
Circulation: Noncirculating collection
Collection: approximately 50,000 items including manuscripts, works of art, documents, and 30,000–35,000 books (October 2006)
*Exact square footage not available at time of inquiry
Source for above: M. D'Aoust, personal correspondence, October 8, 2006

An article appearing in the Los Angeles Times in 1982 (Citron) describes the Philosophical Research Society (PRS) as a "mystery" and a place that it is "not uncommon for motorists and joggers along Los Feliz Boulevard's apartment row to cast a curious eye." It is easy to see why one would look inquisitively at this structure located at the corner of Los Feliz and Griffith Park boulevards. Sitting at the corner of the property is a substantial statue of an Egyptian sage or scholar by sculptress Claire Pierpoint (Hall, 1982). The statue, which weighs nearly 2.5 tons, contains an inscription to the sun. This unusual work of art is a good indication of the unique discoveries awaiting visitors to the PRS Library found on the society's grounds.

Philosophical Research Society

The PRS was founded by Manly P. Hall as a nonprofit institution in 1934. Shortly after the society was established, the plot of land where the society stands was secured (Hall, 1982). A ground-breaking ceremony for the PRS building was attended by approximately 100 people on October 17, 1935. The first building included the library, as well as a bindery, print shop, and front office. The PRS expanded to two buildings in 1950 and finally to three buildings in 1959. In 1968, further improvements were made, including an expansion of the library to nearly twice its original size (Hall, 1982).

Hall, the society's founder, is described as "a seeker and lover of wisdom, the very definition of a philosopher" (PRS, 2001a). Hall, who was born in Canada, came to the United States at the age of two with his grandmother, settling in Los Angeles around 1919 (Citron, 1982). He traveled the world and studied art, literature, and religion in such places as Kyoto, Calcutta, Jerusalem, Cairo, and Bombay (Citron, 1982). He is the author of an astonishing number of books. The titles of just a few demonstrate his all-embracing curiosity: Mystics and Mysteries of Alexandria, Philosophy of Astrology, Dream Symbolism, Buddhism and Psychotherapy, Meditation Symbols in Eastern and Western Mysticism, and The Light of the Vedas. Hall has also published an equally amazing number of pamphlets that include topics such as magic, reincarnation, Egyptian metaphysics, and women's contribution to culture. Hall founded the PRS "for the purpose of providing thoughtful persons rare access to the depth and breadth of the world's wisdom literature" (PRS, 2001a).

One of the ways the PRS accomplishes its mission is through lectures offered to the community in its auditorium. Before his passing, Hall lectured often on diverse topics. A journalist who attended one of the lectures when Hall was 88 years old described him as "still going strong" (O'Donnell, 1989). The lectures regularly attracted 200–300 people (O'Donnell, 1989). Recently, the PRS expanded its scope to graduate-level courses leading to master's degrees in transformational psychology and consciousness studies. Courses offered in the program have distinctive titles, such as Stages of Spiritual Growth, Outer and Inner Creativity, and Consciousness and Creative Communication. In addition to these avenues of discovery, the PRS freely provides a wealth of materials to any visitor via the PRS Library.

Library History

The history of the PRS and the library go hand in hand, since the library was established at the same time as the society. It is described as "virtually unique in the United States as a wisdom literature resource" (PRS, 2001b). The library collection was built personally by Hall. He secured many unique items during his travels abroad. In his book, The Little World of PRS: A Field Tour of the Philosophical Research Society (1982), Hall entertains the reader with descriptions of how he acquired some materials, including his descent on a stepladder into the basement of a shop owned by a "kindly old gentleman" where he found "a number of treasures" that are now in the library (p. 17). Books in the library fall under several broad categories, including astronomy, astrology, philosophy, religion, alchemy, chemistry, and mysticism. Since the PRS is a nondenominational organization, materials from all traditions are found in the collection.

Over the years, the PRS Library has held many exhibits. Previous exhibits have included a display of historic autographs, mementos, and photographs, such as a signed photograph of Walt Whitman and autographs of Harry Houdini and Helen Keller ("Historical Collection," 1983); a collection of watercolor and oil paintings by artist Meredith Ann Olson ("Water Colors," 1981); and a display titled "Great Art on Japanese Postage Stamps" ("Art News," 1967). The library has also loaned its materials for exhibits at other locations in the area, including a display at Los Angeles City Hall that chronicled the evolution of the Bible with rare materials dating from 1121 ("Rare Pages," 1958); a collection of Oriental art for an exhibit at the University of Southern California; and an exhibit titled Rare and Original Writings Covering 4,000 Years that was on display at Robinson's Department Store in Los Angeles for seven weeks (Hall, 1982). The library does not need to hold a special exhibit, however, to justify a visit. The distinctive interior of the small building and the library's reading and art collection offers an enchanting experience any time.

COURTYARD AND ENTRANCE

Three buildings on the grounds of the PRS encircle an interior courtyard. A large building that faces Los Feliz Boulevard houses an auditorium. A bookstore is located in a second building. In addition to selling Hall's many books and pamphlets, the store offers used and new books on a variety of topics along with other gift items. The third building houses the library. The library entrance features a door with two wood-carved panels that were created by woodcarver Stuart Holmes. "The Oriental panel is reminiscent of Confucius, and its Western complement is suggestive of Plato" (Hall, 1982, p. 49). Additional artistic treasures are found within the library.

MAIN READING ROOM

The wood-carved door leads to the main reading room. To the right of the entrance is a hard sapote wood carving of Coatlicue, Mother of the Gods from the Aztec tradition. A carved marble head of a bodhisattva, an enlightened being from the Buddhist tradition, sits atop a card catalog immediately across from the entrance. The library does not yet have its collection accessible in an online database. Librarian Maja D'Aoust has discovered that many people find what they are looking for through serendipitous browsing (personal correspondence, October 8, 2006).

The reference desk is located to the left of the entrance along with a few other unique items. In a glass case on a wooden table across from the desk is an original copy of Hall's first journal published in the early 1920s. Also on display on the table is a beguilingly illustrated book from 1891 titled *Living Thoughts from Poet, Sage and Humorist*. Behind the reference desk several periodicals are laid out on a

The mysterious and enchanting Philosophical Research Society Library in Los Angeles has an interior balcony that overlooks the downstairs reading room and annex.

countertop. The titles reflect the nature of the library. *The Quest, Light of Consciousness, Shambhala Sun*, and *Existentia: An International Journal of Philosophy* are a few samples of the publications displayed.

The main area of the reading room includes a substantial table surrounded by approximately ten chairs. Additional chairs line the perimeter of the room, while the walls of the reading room are adorned with wooden bookcases. A wooden tray sitting on a counter includes several books for sale.

Arthur M. Young Annex

Two steps down from the main reading room is a carpeted annex. At the entrance to the annex are two busts by Hall. One bust is of Mohandas Gandhi and the other is of Hall himself. A virgin statue by Pierpoint is also located here.

The annex provides another reading table. The far wall includes a case with books that features a Buddha statue as the centerpiece. Two additional busts by Hall, one of H. P. Blavatsky and another of Albert Pike, adorn the area along with another virgin statue by Pierpoint.

INTERIOR BALCONY

An interior balcony accessible from a staircase near the reference desk is arguably the most impressive architectural aspect of the interior. Similar to the reading room, the balcony walls are lined by wooden bookcases. Matching the adornment of the main reading room is a Buddha statue located in the center of the far wall of the balcony. The balcony runs the perimeter of the room, providing views of the main reading room from varying angles. Standing at the balcony, one can take in the splendor of the library in its entirety.

REFERENCES

"Art News: Price Works to Be Shown." *Los Angeles Times*, February 5, 1967.
Citron, A. "Eclectic Philosophy Students Mull over Complexities of Life." *Los Angeles Times*, October 24, 1982.
Hall, M. P. *The Little World of PRS: A Field Tour of the Philosophical Research Society*. Los Angeles: Philosophical Research Society, 1982.
"Historical Collection on Display." *Los Angeles Times*, July 31, 1983.
O'Donnell, S. "'Last Western mystic' Thrives in Los Feliz: He Was New Age before There Was a New Age." *Los Angeles Times*, July 6, 1989.
Philosophical Research Library (PRS). "About PRS." 2001a. www.prs.org/about.htm (retrieved June 21, 2006).
_____. "The PRS Library." 2001b. www.prs.org/library.htm (retrieved June 21, 2006).
"Rare Pages from Bible on Display at City Hall." *Los Angeles Times*, March 22, 1958.
"Water Colors, Oils to Be Displayed." *Los Angeles Times*, October 25, 1981.

17

Rancho Santa Ana Botanic Garden Research Library

Library Data

Address: 1500 North College Avenue, Claremont, CA 91711
Phone: (909) 625-8767
Web site: www.rsabg.org
Square Feet: 4,732
Circulation: Noncirculating collection
Collection: 50,000 volumes, plus microfilm, journal article reprints, and other materials (December 2005)
Source for above: P. Lindberg, personal correspondence, December 6, 2005

  Indian Hill Boulevard, accessible from the 10 freeway, runs into the heart of the city of Claremont. Although Claremont seems far from the downtown Los Angeles Central Library (it is roughly 34 miles east), the city is still located within the confines of Los Angeles County. Claremont is close to the San Bernardino county line, pushed up against the border of the Inland Empire, a territory that generally includes San Bernardino and Riverside counties. Its close proximity to cities in San Bernardino County, including Montclair, Upland, and Ontario, causes Claremont to often be erroneously included as part of the Inland Empire. Visitors to Claremont will likely discover that its appearance is quite different from its neighbors. Except for the monstrous freeway nearby, the city is unlike any other in Southern California. In fact, parts of Claremont resemble a small town one may encounter on the east coast of the United States. The San Gabriel Mountains provide a striking backdrop to the picturesque city.

  Claremont is very much a college town. The prestigious Claremont Colleges, which include the institutions of Pomona College, Scripps College, Pitzer College, Harvey Mudd College, and others are found here. The campuses of the colleges, with plush, green lawns and architectural delights, can only be described as grand. The Rancho Santa Ana Botanic Garden (RSABG), an affiliated institution of the Claremont Colleges, offers a graduate program in botany leading to a master of science or doctor of philosophy degree. The research library supports the curriculum of the program.

Claremont is perhaps the perfect place for the RSABG Research Library. The Claremont Village area, located adjacent to the colleges and just a few minutes from the RSABG Research Library, sets the city apart from its neighbors. The shops and events in the village area are proof that the city is a place with a thirst for the unique and intellectually stimulating. This is evident by walking through the weekend Claremont Farmers and Artisans Market, where one can find artwork, orchids, breads, fruits, and vegetables for sale or by visiting one of the many unique shops, such as Casa Flores Florist, Folk Music Center, or Rhino Records. Imports may be purchased from Indonesia, Thailand, Nepal, Russia, Ukraine, Japan, and Tibet. Restaurants located in the Claremont Village serve California, Afghan, Italian, Mediterranean, Mexican, and Spanish cuisine. Within this creative, educational, and international milieu, the RSABG adds to the sense of place of Claremont with an amazing nature center and unusually stimulating research library located a short walk from the lively city environment.

Botanic Garden

Since the research library is located within the botanic garden, it is impossible to not see the garden and library as interconnected. This is similar to the Sherman Library & Gardens in Corona Del Mar, California, another unique place discussed within this book, yet the RSABG and its library are perhaps even more closely intertwined since the collection at the RSABG research library mirrors the garden outside.

The RSABG, according to an informational brochure available to visitors, "was founded to promote botanical knowledge, conservation, and landscape use of California's native plants" (RSABG, n.d.). The garden was started in 1927 by Susanna Bixby Bryant, who collected plants on her ranch in Orange County, California. In 1951, the garden was relocated to its current home in Claremont. Bryant, who is described as "a visionary member of one of California's pioneering families," saw the need to conserve the "incredible plant diversity" found in California, the state with "the richest flora of any state in the continental United States" (RSABG, n.d.). The mission statement of the RSABG follows the spirit and dedication of Bryant:

> Rancho Santa Ana Botanic Garden is devoted to the collection, cultivation, study and display of native California plants and to graduate training and research in plant systematics and evolution. Through all its programs, the mission of the Garden is to make significant contributions to the appreciation, enjoyment, conservation, understanding, and thoughtful utilization of our natural heritage [RSABG, January 2005].

The garden, located at an elevation of 1,350 feet on an 86-acre plot of land, has the room to execute its mission.

A pathway leading to the Rancho Santa Ana Botanic Garden Research Library allows visitors to experience the natural landscape that surrounds the library.

Visitors to the library will follow a trail through a section of the garden that leads from the parking lot to the administrative building that houses the library. The path, lined with stones and various plants, is a relatively brief and slightly elevated, winding trek. Although this portion of the garden is just a tiny patch compared to the expansive area to the north of the library, visitors will definitely notice the charm of the place and be able to discover several California plants before reaching the library entrance. Coast live oak, evergreen currant, western sycamore, Susanna coral bells, giant sequoia, California juniper, California fan palm, desert agava, desert apricot, California encelia, and island bush snapdragon are some of the plants that line the trail.

Once one reaches the level where the library is located, a shaded area with picnic benches is available. Just below the library is the small Benjamin Pond with a bench for seating. To enter the library, visitors must first go through the Garden Shop. Books, walking sticks, wind chimes, and plants may be purchased here.

Library Main Floor

The RSABG Research Library has two staff members, including Patty Lindberg, acting director of information services, and 12 volunteers. The library is a relatively small space stretched over two floors. Users enter the library on the main floor after passing through a small hallway. Photographs showcasing the garden from several decades back line the wall in the hallway.

What is quite evident upon entering the library is that this is a research facility. A large freezer containing plant specimens, for example, sits directly to the side of the main entrance. According to Lindberg, however, graduate students are not the only users; members of the community are welcome and often come to the library. It is no doubt the location and collection that draws the community.

Immediately inside the door is an exhibit case. In December 2005, an exhibit of orchid books was on display in honor of a 1959 graduate of the RSABG program. The small room contains several aisles of book stacks and a periodicals section. Lindberg pointed out a card catalog that is still functioning. The sound of a typewriter, coupled with the card catalog, can make one feel like an earlier time exists in the library. An online catalog, connecting the collection to the other Claremont College libraries, however, demonstrates that the library is a wonderfully liminal space floating between an older world and today's technological developments.

Also found on the main floor are three research tables along the windows, allowing for superb views of the garden and mountains in the distance. Care has been taken to preserve the collection, especially since much of it is fairly close to the windows. A tint on the windows minimizes the glare of the sun, providing warm, natural lighting, while reducing the fading effects on the collection. The same care has been taken with the overhead fluorescent light fixtures, which contain "sleeved fluorescent tubes" (RSABG, January 2005). Temperature is also meticulously kept between 67 and 70 degrees.

Library Downstairs Annex

Walking down the rather narrow staircase to the downstairs annex truly makes one feel like he or she is entering a researcher's cave. Once inside the small space, however, one will notice natural lighting, as upstairs, through windows with similar views of the garden and mountains. Room is available for several researchers along the window. This area, which has likely been more than one researcher's delight, holds material in several compact stacks.

Programs & Events

RSABG offers a wide-ranging program of events, making the library and garden a place to return to again and again. Community education programs

Tables in the Rancho Santa Ana Botanic Garden Research Library in Claremont look out to the expansive gardens beyond.

offered in fall 2005 range from "Bookcrafting Primer: Making Fun Books and Journals" and "Advanced Papermaking Techniques" to "Introduction to Gardening with California Native Plants," "Best Plants for Southern California Gardens," and "Introduction to Birdwatching" (RSABG, Fall 2005).

Tours for children, including "Indian Uses of Native Plants," "A Sense of California," and "Tree Detectives," instruct and delight (RSABG, 2005/2006). Adults may register for late fall and winter garden walks. Family events include the Winter Bird Fest.

Those who come to visit the garden and library may also pick up the *Field Checklist of the Birds of the Rancho Santa Ana Botanic Garden* brochure. The checklist, compiled by the Pomona Valley Audubon Society and last revised in 1997, provides a detailed chart of the 141 species of birds that have been spotted in the garden or adjacent areas. Common birds appearing throughout the year include the California quail, ring-billed gull, mourning dove, Anna's hummingbird, and several others.

It would also be wise to plan visits on a seasonal basis to experience the garden in different temperatures and see birds that only appear at select times of the year. The library has also recently established a book sale. Those who come to peruse the available titles, may find themselves leaving not only with an assortment of plants from the Garden Shop, but also a carload of books.

REFERENCES

Rancho Santa Ana Botanic Garden (RSABG). *Garden Map and Guide for Visitors.* n.d. (Available at Rancho Santa Ana Botanic Garden.)
_____. *Archival and Library Collections Policy.* January 25, 2005. (Provided by Patty Lindberg, acting director of information services, Rancho Santa Ana Botanic Garden.)
_____. *Community Education.* Fall 2005. (Available at Rancho Santa Ana Botanic Garden.)
_____. *School Tours and Programs.* 2005/2006. (Available at Rancho Santa Ana Botanic Garden.)

PART IV
Santa Barbara County

18

Joseph Campbell & Marija Gimbutas Library, Pacifica Graduate Institute

Library Data

Address: 249 Lambert Road, Carpinteria, CA 93013
Phone: (805) 969-3626
Web site: www.online.pacifica.edu/cgl/about
Square Feet: approximately 375
Circulation: Noncirculating collection
Collection: approximately 3,000 volumes (Joseph Campbell collection); approximately 1,700 volumes, 12,000 slides, and 41 boxes of research files (Marija Gimbutas collection); James Hillman manuscript collection; papers of Joseph Wheelwright and Jane Hollister Wheelwright (June 2006)
Sources for above: R. Buchen, personal correspondence, June 28, 2006, and the Joseph Campbell & Marija Gimbutas Library Web site

It is important to begin a discussion of the uniqueness of the Joseph Campbell & Marija Gimbutas Library by first reflecting on Pacifica Graduate Institute. The special qualities of the library, which are many, can best be understood within the context of the institute, since Pacifica is an entirely unique creation. The spirit of the curriculum at the institute and the natural surroundings add greatly to the sense of place at the library.

Pacific Graduate Institute

Pacifica has two campus locations in Carpinteria, a beachside community just a short drive south of Santa Barbara. The Lambert Road campus, where the Joseph Campbell & Marija Gimbutas Library is found, is a unique setting located on the former estate of late philanthropist Max Fleischmann. This historic site, which has been restored and renovated, was built in 1924 (Pacifica Graduate Institute, 2006a). In many ways, the campus resembles a retreat center. The steps one must take to reach the institute add greatly to the mystique.

Public parking is not available on the grounds, due to an effort to preserve the

The grounds of Pacifica Graduate Institute offer many surprising delights, such as this statue of the Hindu elephant god Ganesh.

land. Visitors and students must take a shuttle from a local hotel, which is provided free of charge by the institute. If this seems odd at first, once one arrives at the campus, the beauty of the surroundings will convince one of the importance of this policy. So central is the land to the institute, that its Web site not only mentions such factors as accreditation and class formats, but also devotes much space to the setting, as demonstrated by this excerpt: "The gardens and 'people paths' are arranged in such a way as to invite the birds, insects, and other animals of the area to make their homes in these places" (Pacifica Graduate Institute, 2006a). The Pacifica Organic Market Garden is located on the grounds, just a short walk from the library. According to Pacifica: "Existing orchards have been converted to organic production. By growing fresh fruits, herbs, and vegetables on campus, Pacifica moves toward its goal of environmental sustainability." Also close to the library are the California Mediterranean Gardens and a wealth of blossoming and wildly alluring plant life. Before knowing exactly what type of institute Pacifica is, a visitor will be able to detect that it is likely quite different and specialized.

Dr. Stephen Aizenstat (2006), founding president of Pacifica, states on the institute's Web site: "At its core, Pacifica is rooted in its vision: animae mundi colendae gratia *(for the sake of tending the soul of the world)*." Pacifica's mission statement reads, "Pacifica traces many of its central ideas to the heritage of ancient story tellers, dramatists, and philosophers from all lands who recorded the workings of the imagination" (Pacifica Graduate Institute, 2006d). Pacifica is grounded in the depth psychological tradition that includes the teachings of C. G. Jung, Joseph Campbell, Marion Woodman, James Hillman, and others (Pacifica Graduate Institute, n.d.). The institute offers graduate degrees in psychology (depth, clinical, and counseling) and mythological studies. Also available is a master's degree in humanities with an emphasis in mythology, education, or depth psychology. In addition to its academic programs, Pacifica offers unusual and intriguing seminars and programs that may be attended for continuing education credit. Recent programs have included "Dreamtending: A Dream-Centered Life." It is within this context that the Joseph Campbell & Marija Gimbutas Library finds its perfect home.

LIBRARY COLLECTIONS

The Joseph Campbell & Marija Gimbutas collections comprise the largest part of the library's materials. Campbell's work on mythology was brought into many homes via the 1988 PBS series *Joseph Campbell and the Power of Myth with Bill Moyers*. He is the author of classics including *Hero with a Thousand Faces*. The dynamic life of Campbell is perhaps best represented in his famously quoted phrase: "Follow your bliss." In fact, visitors to the Joseph Campbell Foundation Web site (www.jcf.org) can share their stories of how they have followed their

The small Joseph Campbell & Marija Gimbutas Library in Carpinteria houses a unique and inspiring collection that makes it a true scholar's haven.

bliss. The Campbell collection at Pacifica includes nearly 3,000 volumes from his personal library. The books fall within the fields of anthropology, literature, the arts, philosophy, religion, and mythology (Pacifica Graduate Institute, 2006c). Many of the books in the collection are inscribed with Campbell's marginalia, which will, no doubt, add to a researcher's delight. Richard Buchen, special collections librarian, specifically pointed out Campbell's copy of Jung's *Aion*, which includes a great deal of Campbell's marginal notes and underlining. The collection also consists of manuscripts, research papers, photographs, audio tapes of lectures, video tapes, and memorabilia.

Before Gimbutas died in 1994, she was an esteemed professor of archaeology at the University of California, Los Angeles. Her pioneering works include *The Language of the Goddess* and *The Living Goddesses*. Having the archives of Campbell and Gimbutas housed together is no coincidence. The work of both researchers greatly complements each other. According to Marler (1995),

> During the last few years of his life, Joseph Campbell spoke frequently of Marija Gimbutas, profoundly regretting that her research on the Neolithic cultures of Europe was not available during the 1960's when he was writing *The Masks of God*. Otherwise, he would have "revised everything."

In his foreword to Gimbutas' (1989) *The Language of the Goddess*, Campbell states, "One cannot but feel that in the appearance of this volume at just this turn of the century there is an evident relevance to the universally recognized need in our time for a general transformation of consciousness" (p. xiv). The Gimbutas collection consists of her personal library, lecture notes, figurines, manuscripts of her articles and books, research files, photographs, and approximately 12,000 slides. Perusing Gimbutas' library is truly a celebration of the life of the mind. Buchen (personal correspondence, June 28, 2006) explained Gimbutas read some 13 languages. Her book collection spans numerous disciplines, including women's studies, mythology, anthropology, philosophy, and archaeology. Some marginalia may be found within the books, but, according to Buchen, her marginal notes were not as extensive as Campbell's. Gimbutas' copy of Eisler's *The Chalice and the Blade*, however, was noted to include some underlined passages.

Other collections include the James Hillman manuscript collection. Hillman, the father of archetypal psychology and a leading scholar in Jungian and post–Jungian studies, selected Pacifica as the repository for his papers. Hillman's original manuscripts for nearly all of his lectures, articles, and books are housed here (Pacifica Graduate Institute, 2006b). The library also cares for the papers of Jungian analysts Joseph Wheelwright and Jane Hollister Wheelwright. The Wheelwrights trained with Jung and were founding members of the C. J. Jung Institute in San Francisco (Joseph Campbell, n.d.).

Colorful and freely available handouts in the library are not only informative, but interesting. In addition to brochures for the library that include biographical information on Campbell, Gimbutas, Hillman, Hollister, and Wheelwright, more detailed handouts include a bibliography of Campbell, *The Life & Work of Marija Gimbutas*, *James Hillman: His Life and Work*, a chronology of Campbell's life, and the especially fascinating *Joseph Campbell Canon* that provides a list of books Campbell typically assigned to his students while teaching at Sarah Lawrence College.

Garden & Exterior

Surprises await visitors approaching the library or those who elect to take a break from their research and go out for a stroll. Just a short trek from the building, for example, one will come across a statue of Ganesh, the Hindu elephant god. Numerous offerings were found around the statue during a summer visit.

As mentioned previously, the library is surrounded by an abundance of plant life. The gardens and lawn around the library are immaculate with winding paths and many quiet places to stop for reflection. The abundant vegetation is also quite aromatic. Adjacent to the side of the library and enveloped by the plant life, is a circular area with two stone benches. Another outdoor space is a patio behind the library with tables and chairs that look out to the garden.

Foyer

A wood door, which is the main entrance to the library, opens to a small foyer, composed of hardwood flooring, that ultimately leads to the main room of the archives. This tiny space resembles the interior of a cottage. Just inside the door is an exhibit case displaying three shelves of materials from the Marija Gimbutas collection. Included on the shelves are numerous replicas of goddess figurines, including birthing figures. A final fourth shelf is devoted to Campbell with such interesting objects as an open copy of Allen Watts' *Myth and Ritual in Christianity* with Campbell's own underlining, as well as a yellow legal pad containing Campbell's notes. The objects in the exhibit are displayed attractively by Buchen, who artistically designed all the exhibits in the library. For those conducting research on Gimbutas or Campbell, being able to view items actually owned by them would be extraordinary. Having such an exhibit placed near the entrance causes one to pause for at least a brief examination. It also provides a nice introduction to the archives.

Main Room

The main room of the library is quite small, resembling a private study. Size is of no consequence here, however, since what is found inside is simply amazing. Wood bookcases that line all of the walls add decoration and warmth. The bookcases extend up toward a white ceiling that contains a fan. Two small work stations are placed in opposite corners. One station provides researchers equipment for the use of audiovisual material; the other is a computer station. A round table is also available for researchers near the entrance. It is on this round table that a second exhibit case is located.

Within the exhibit case are Campbell's original notes on Carleton Coon's anthropological study *The Story of Man* and a page of notes from one of James Hillman's speeches. A lower bookshelf set up behind the table runs nearly the length of the middle of the room, yet there is still space for a few researchers to walk about. Several books and other items of note are located on the top of this shelf. A bust of Campbell by Angela Gregory (circa 1928) sits on one corner; a bust of Gimbutas by Sapkus sits on the other. At the far end of the bookshelf sits a third exhibit case.

Due to its placement away from the wall, this tall, rectangular case may be viewed from all four sides. Four shelves of Campbell's artifacts are on display. Included are various figurines and objects, an eagle feather that was given to Campbell by a Native American elder, and Campbell's New York City Library ruler.

Although the collections at the library, particularly the Gimbutas and Campbell personal libraries already described, cannot be considered exhibits, they do add significantly to the sense of place. One is simply surrounded by books in this small space. The archives cannot provide room for large groups, but that is clearly not the purpose. What it does provide is a sanctuary for a few or the solitary researcher. It is, without doubt, a scholar's haven.

References

Aizenstat, S. "President's Greeting." Pacifica Graduate Institute, 2006. www.pacifica.edu/president.html (retrieved July 17, 2006).
Gimbutas, M. *The Language of the Goddess*. San Francisco: Harper & Row, 1989.
Joseph Campbell & Marija Gimbutas Library. Brochure, n.d. (Available at the Joseph Campbell & Marija Gimbutas Library.)
Marler, J. "Marija Gimbutas: Life and Work." Pacifica Graduate Institute, 1995. www.online.pacifica.edu/cgl/Gimbutasbio (retrieved July 27, 2006).
Pacifica Graduate Institute. *2006–2007 Course Catalog*. n.d.
_____. "Educational Environment." 2006a. www.pacifica.edu/about_edu_environ.html (retrieved July 17, 2006).
_____. "The James Hillman Collection." 2006b. www.online.pacifica.edu/hillmancollection (retrieved July 21, 2006).
_____. "The Joseph Campbell Collection." 2006c. www.online.pacifica.edu/cgl/Campbell (retrieved July 21, 2006).
_____. "Mission Statement." 2006d. www.pacifica.edu/mission.html (retrieved July 17, 2006).

19

Central Library of the Santa Barbara Public Library

LIBRARY DATA

Address: 40 E. Anapamu Street, Santa Barbara, CA 93101
Phone: (805) 962-7653
Web site: www.sbplibrary.org
Square Feet: 52,000–54,000
Circulation: 630,286 (fiscal year 2006)
Collection: 207,421 (July 2006)
Source for above: J. Turner, personal correspondence, July 14, 2006

A small volume titled *Santa Barbara and Around There* written in 1887 by Edwards Roberts described in enthusiastic prose the many merits of the region. Roberts began, "Santa Barbara does not need to have untruths published regarding its climate, surroundings, and natural attractions. They are so nearly perfect, so varied and beautiful, that it is superfluous to exaggerate them" (p. 5). Writing about the city with poetic character, Roberts continued, "Santa Barbara may be described as having her feet bathed by the warm blue waters of the Pacific, and her head pillowed on the mountains of the Santa Ynez" (p. 11). Characterizing the city as a resort with growing popularity, he even compared Santa Barbara to "what Nice and Mentone are to Europe" (p. 5). Near the end of his book-length tribute, Roberts pointed out, "The public library is one of the best in the State" (p. 188).

Well into the next century, the Southern California Writers' Project's *Santa Barbara: A Guide to the Channel City and its Environs* (1941) aptly stated, "Santa Barbara's chief business is simply being Santa Barbara. Her cool, healthful climate, the sea and the mountains attract people of wealth, social position, and leisure" (p. 58). The wealth of Santa Barbara continues to this day and is not a secret by any means. In fact, one can purchase a postcard at a local tourist shop that shows a picture of a shack with the caption, "Affordable housing in Santa Barbara."

Although the city is one of the most expensive to live in the state, if not the country, there is nothing stuffy about Santa Barbara and all can feel welcome walking its streets. Many of the areas where tourists flock, such as the popular State Street, have the allure of a semibohemian beach town. The city has also been the home to many poets. In an early 1970s anthology of Santa Barbara poetry, Rexroth (1973) stated, "What is good for literature is an environment which fosters recollection in tranquility." This is an environment that may be found in previous decades in Santa Barbara and one still available, but, perhaps, more elusive in the 21st century. Santa Barbara is home to many locations that are steeped in beauty and wonder, permitting "recollection in tranquility." Among these one may include the Santa Barbara Botanic Gardens, the Santa Barbara Mission, and, of course, the historic public library.

LIBRARY HISTORY

Listed as a point of interest for visitors in the aforementioned 1941 guide, the Santa Barbara Public Library can trace its origins to 1870 when Sarah A. Plummer set up shop with a small lending library. In 1880, the Odd Fellows purchased Plummer's library and moved the collection to their lodge (Nesselrod, 1990). On February 16, 1882, the city council established a free library and reading room (Southern California Writers' Project, 1941). A few years later in 1888, the library moved from the Odd Fellows Lodge to a floor of the Upper Clock Building at State and Carrillo streets (Nesselrod, 1990).

In June 1892, the library moved once more to a new building on East Carrillo designed by architect P. C. Barber. As is often the case, space quickly became an issue. The trustees of the Carnegie Corporation were successful at procuring a Carnegie grant of $50,000 (Nesselrod, 1990). In November 1917, a new building opened to the public. The new library, originally designed by architect Francis W. Wilson and Carleton M. Winslow, has experienced many challenges, including a 1925 earthquake and a need in the 1970s to demolish portions that were found to be seismically unsound, yet it has remained undeniably resilient. A Web site devoted to Carnegie libraries states, "The Santa Barbara Public Library has long been considered a community treasure, noted for its collection, architecture, interior comfort, visual amenities, and cultural events" (Carnegie Libraries, 1999). Once one walks inside the equally majestic and welcoming building, it is quite easy to see why.

ENTRANCES AND FOYER

Visitors may enter the foyer of the library from two different directions. One entrance is positioned conveniently near a large parking garage that leads not only to the library, but also to shops and restaurants; the other entrance is reached after walking through a small garden area that faces into the street. Before entering the building from the latter, one can sit and relax within the exterior garden space.

Once inside, visitors will note murals by artists Howard Warshaw and

A wood carving above the original entrance to the Central Library of the Santa Barbara Public Library includes the city's coat of arms, the figures of Plato and Aristotle, and the shields of four famous libraries: University of Bologna, Bibliotheque Nationale in Paris, University of Salamanca, and the Bodleian Library at Oxford University.

Channing Peake accenting the foyer. The murals were originally painted on a wall in the garden patio, and they were removed, preserved, and restored in the foyer during remodeling and expansion of the building in the late 1970s (Nesselrod, 1990). The foyer of the library is quite large with benches for seating in the middle and entranceways leading to interior spaces on both sides. One entrance from the foyer leads to the building that houses the reading rooms, collection, and reference and circulation services, or the primary business of the library; the other leads to exhibit galleries. The foyer is the space that connects these different realms.

GALLERIES

Immediately off the foyer is the large Faulkner Gallery, which leads to the smaller Faulkner Gallery East and West rooms. These rooms, which were not part of the original building, but completed in 1930, were made possible through a donation of a parcel of land by a trustee, Clarence A. Black, and a gift of $55,000 by Mary Faulkner Gould (Nesselrod, 1990). The gallery was designed by architect Myron Hunt, who also designed the famous Huntington Library in San Marino, California.

Gallery exhibits in June 2006 included a student display of life drawing in the large gallery and two smaller exhibits of work by the Santa Barbara Art Association's Past Presidents and Board of Directors. Included in the smaller galleries were oils, collages, acrylics, and pastels. Long tables with chairs in the center of both the east and west galleries provide interesting spaces for gathering within a quiet and creative environment, as well as spaces devoted to showcasing local artists. During an afternoon visit in June 2006, both gallery tables were occupied by tutors and their students.

Main Floor

The entrance across from the gallery leads to the main floor of the library. A striking double staircase is visible near the center of the library upon entering the main floor off the foyer. According to Nesselrod (1990), the staircase divides the new building and the old. It is clear that the main floor is a gateway to various other spaces, depending upon one's needs. New fiction and nonfiction books are available for browsing immediately after passing the circulation desk near the entrance. To the right is the children's room that includes a fish aquarium and small study carrels along the window. Stairs and an elevator to the right can take one to the upper floor where reference services and administrative offices are housed, as well as a large display titled "Freedom Shrine," which was "created by the exchange clubs to strengthen citizen appreciation of our American heritage." The shrine consists of reproductions of numerous historic documents, including the Emancipation Proclamation, Gettysburg Address, Bill of Rights, and the Constitution.

Reading Rooms

Two spectacular two-story reading rooms are accessible from the main floor. The first reading room to the left of the circulation desk includes a fireplace and windows facing out to the garden courtyard. Many tables and chairs are arranged throughout the space for individual or group seating. The second two-story reading room includes large windows that run the length of the room and provide ample natural lighting. The windows allow for a view of the city street where one may take a break from reading to watch the passersby.

LOWER LEVEL

Stairs to the right of the main entrance lead to a lower level where newspapers, audio visual material, and periodicals are kept. Due to its location, arriving downstairs feels as if one has located a secret, but welcoming, place. Tables and chairs, as well as cushioned seating is available here. This space also provides an outlet for community publications. A significant area is set aside not far from the staircase for free community papers and announcements, as well as publications from Santa Barbara City College, Parks and Recreation, and numerous other organizations. Although the lower floor is not as glamorous as the reading rooms or galleries, it illustrates, perhaps best, the core qualities of the library: hospitality and community spirit.

REFERENCES

Carnegie Libraries of California. "Santa Barbara, Santa Barbara County." 1999. www.carnegie-libraries.org/california/regions/centralcoast/santabarbara.html (retrieved December 4, 2005).

Nesselrod, P. K. *Biography of a Library*. Santa Barbara, CA: Friends of the Santa Barbara Public Library, 1990.

Rexroth, K. Foreword to *20 Times in the Same Place: An Anthology of Santa Barbara Poetry*, by ed. L. Mallory. Carpinteria, CA: Painted Cave Books, 1973.

Roberts, E. *Santa Barbara and Around There*. Boston: Roberts Brothers, 1887.

Southern California Writers' Project. *Santa Barbara: A Guide to the Channel City and Its Environs*. New York: Hastings House, 1941.

Part V

Central Valley and Mariposa County

20

Beale Memorial Library

LIBRARY DATA

Address: 701 Truxtun Avenue, Bakersfield, CA 93301
Phone: (661) 868-0701
Web site: www.kerncountylibrary.org/beale.html
Square Feet: 127,041
Circulation: 463,055 (fiscal year 2004/2005)
Collection: 294,466 (fiscal year 2004/2005)
Source for above: Kern County Library Web site

The cities of Los Angeles and San Francisco are often what come to mind when one thinks of California, yet there is a significant area of California that contains 25,000 square miles: the Central Valley. This region, which is sometimes called the Great Valley or the Great Central Valley, is agricultural territory that produces numerous crops including fruits, vegetables, grains, nuts, rice, and cotton (Hart, 1978). It spans 450 miles from roughly Bakersfield in the south to Redding in the north. It is unfortunate that the area is often neglected or considered a sort of secondary California, one minus the glamour and culture, because such views do not do justice to a region with considerable history, to the land that sustains so many with its bountiful harvests, and to a landscape that has inspired countless writers.

John Steinbeck, whom some consider the quintessential California writer, is perhaps the most obvious example of where the Central Valley has played a role in the formation of literary excellence. Although Steinbeck spent much of his time in areas along the Central Coast, his *The Long Valley*, a collection of stories, is one example of the appearance of Central Valley areas within his fiction, such as the city of Salinas.

Some recent literary anthologies also celebrate the region, including *How Much Earth*, an anthology of the Fresno Poets who primarily come from the city of Fresno or smaller surrounding communities and *Highway 99: A Literary Journey through California's Great Central Valley*, which includes such notables as Maxine Hong Kingston, Joan Didion, and Philip Levine. James D. Houston (1996), California novelist and nonfiction writer, commenting on this often forgotten part of the state in the latter mentioned anthology, writes: "To see this other part of California, the resource-full part, it helps to get away from the coast from time to time, and head inland, which is why I found myself on the road to Bakersfield again, over there in Kern County" (p. 262).

The Central Valley also appears with its own section in *Unfolding Beauty: Celebrating California's Landscapes*. It is described as a "huge valley, which can be as much as seventy-five miles wide, includes grassland, riparian forests, tule marshes, chaparral, and acres and acres of farmland" (Beers, p. 331). Anthologized within these pages is an excerpt from John Muir's "The Mountains of California," that clearly demonstrates his awe of the land:

> The Great Central Plain of California, during the months of March, April, and May, was one smooth, continuous bed of honey-bloom, so marvelously rich that, in walking from one end of it to the other, a distance of more than four hundred miles, your foot would press about a hundred flowers at every step. Mints, gilias, nemophilas, castilleias, and innumerable compositae were so crowded together that, had ninety-nine percent of them been taken away, the plain would still have seemed to any but Californians extravagantly flowery [p. 338–339].

It is near the southern tip of this Great Valley that the Beale Memorial Library sits at the intersection of Q and Truxtun Avenue in Bakersfield, a city that can be reached in roughly just two hours from Los Angeles. Jim Wasserman, writing on the current library building shortly after its grand opening in the late 1980s for the *Fresno Bee*, states, "Any city or county that can build something as beautiful and forward-thinking as that structure and fill it full of books, music and computers is a place carving out a whole new image and vision of itself." The library, a member of the San Joaquin Valley Library System, is a place of elegant and carefully planned spaces.

History of the Library

The story of the Beale Memorial Library can be traced to May 1883 when an article appeared in the *Kern County Californian* in support of establishing a library. The author claimed "nothing would contribute more to the morals, thrift and advancement of our community. With an 'unbounded faith in the ... elevating influence of books,' towns having 'free circulating libraries' take great pride in them" (quoted in Boyd and Rump, 1987). The Kern Library Association was formed, but not until six years after the appearance of the *Kern County Californian* proclamation. The first attempt to open a two-room library with books and magazines tragically ended when a July 1889 fire in downtown Bakersfield destroyed several structures, including the building the library was to be housed in (Boyd and Rump, 1987).

In March 1892, the Salvation Army opened a public reading room in its barracks. This was followed in May 1894 with a well-stocked reading room in the Kern County Land Company that provided the community with books and periodicals. In 1898, two circulating libraries were established in the Woman's Christian Temperance Union and the Woman's Club (Boyd and Rump, 1987). These early steps to create a true library ultimately culminated in 1900 with the dedication of the Beale Memorial Library at 17th Street.

The library was originally a gift to the city by Mary Beale and her son Truxtun Beale in memory of their husband and father, General Edward Fitzgerald Beale ("Beale Memorial Library," 1972). Similar to the history of other libraries, overcrowded conditions shortly appeared. In November 1914, the library moved the adult books to the City Hall, due to overcrowding. The library then had a serious setback when an earthquake on July 21, 1952, caused irreparable damage, forcing the permanent closure of the building later that summer ("Beale Memorial Library," 1972). The library remained in temporary quarters for several years until a new building opened in 1957 ("Fact Sheet," 1988).

The next chapter in the library's story began in the mid–1980s when the need for more space for court activities resulted in the idea to relocate the library. County officials found a solution to the burgeoning judicial system problem with the decision to move the law library, jury services, and public defender offices into the library building (Hardisty, 1984). These initial resolutions ultimately resulted in the fine library building the citizens of Bakersfield have today.

After the decision was made to relocate the library, a task force formed to work out recommendations (Hardisty, 1984). At one point in the planning process, a fundraising foundation was assembled to raise money to furnish the building. Foundation president Don Murfin was quoted as saying the library furnishings should be "special" and "go beyond a basic library." He further stated, "We want it to be a fine cultural statement for Kern County" (quoted in Hardisty, 1986). Designed by San Francisco architect Scott Danielson, the new Beale Memorial Library, which opened in 1988, is a roughly 127,000 square foot building, offering considerably more space than the previous 56,872 square foot library ("Fact Sheet," 1988). Writing for the *Fresno Bee*, Wasserman states, "It is unusually elegant and airy for a county government building, full of windows and light, an interior landscape that says browse and stay awhile, linger in the presence of books" (Wasserman, 1989). The feeling Wasserman comments on begins as soon as one steps inside.

Periodicals, Paperbacks, and Reading Spaces

Directly to the right of the main entrance and on the first floor of the library are several open spaces that invite visitors to browse or spend time reading. Large windows that run the length of the building provide ample natural lighting. One of the spaces carved out in this expansive area provides newspapers on wood bookshelves. Several seats are arranged in between the shelves with a plant directly in the middle. For those wanting more privacy, desks are located along the windows. Following the newspaper area is another inviting space with a similar design of seating, but here one will find shelves with magazines and books for sale. Immediately after the areas designated for newspapers and magazines is a large reading space.

Mezzanine

Off the first floor and near the back of the library are stairs leading to a mezzanine full of book stacks. This is one of the most interesting areas on the first

The Beale Memorial Library in the Central Valley city of Bakersfield has an interior mezzanine that overlooks the lower level.

floor. While perusing the stacks, visitors may look down to the first floor below. The mezzanine provides a good view of the library's different spaces, including the audio visual section near the far back.

Children's Room

Off to the left of the main entrance and circulation desk is the Children's Room. Immediately before entry to the room is a bronze sculpture by Gary Price titled *Storytime*. Price's work is meant

> to portray a strong and simple silhouette showing children's love of storybooks and the fantasy they find within the pages of their reading.
> The wonderful thing about this sculpture is the way children relate to it and huddle around its base, feeling the heads and bodies of the figures, and trying to emulate the position of the brother and sister ["A Little History," n.d., p. 7].

During a visit to the library in April 2006, I noticed a father with two children sitting on the floor with Price's piece, as if they were, in fact, interacting with the art. It is clear that the placement of the sculpture in front of the Children's Room was a wise choice.

The Children's Room has the anticipated small bookshelves, tables, and chairs, but what is also found here in the back corner is a storytelling pit. Discovering the area is like coming across a secret and mysterious alcove. Sitting perfectly within its corner, the pit features a television, VCR, stereo, and a screen for an overhead projector, as well as a stage for puppet shows ("Fact Sheet," 1988).

The storytelling pit is complemented by two etchings titled *Dazzie* (1985) and *Marvin* (1979) and a lithograph titled *Walt Badger* (1989) by Beth Van Hoesen, a San Francisco–based artist who received training at Stanford University and California School of Fine Art. These drawings of animals add a gentle elegance to this carefully designed space.

Atrium

Adding to the feeling of openness is an outdoor atrium located within the center of the building. Since this area is only accessible once one is inside the library, visitors may take library materials outdoors to read. The atrium boasts an abundance of trees, plants, and places to sit. Unlike many similar structures that eventually have some form of a roof, this area opens completely to the sky. Of course, this limits the use of the space during rainy days, but it also adds to its overall attraction. The atrium brings plentiful amounts of natural lighting to the interior spaces. It also has "excellent acoustics which makes it desirable for readings and for small concerts" ("Fact Sheet," 1988).

Special Collection Rooms

Located on the second floor are several rooms full of rich and unique collections to delight researchers. To reach the rooms, one can walk up carpeted stairs or take the glass elevator. One room on the second floor, the Geology, Mining, and Petroleum Room, is devoted to materials concerning geology, mines and mining, and the oil industry, including topographic and geologic maps, journals, books, and government documents. Adjacent to this room is the volunteer-staffed Genealogy Room. Finally, the second floor is home to the Jack Maguire Local History Room. Found here are materials that tell the story of Kern County and neighboring counties. Other treasures include books written by Kern County authors, historical photographs, Bakersfield city directories that date from 1899 to the present, and material on John Steinbeck, especially items related to his masterpiece *The Grapes of Wrath* (Kern, 2004b).

Each of the special collection rooms are stylish in their design, making the second floor visually appealing. Each room also includes maps from the Curtis Darling Map Collection, which is a collection donated to the library by Darling. These maps, many dating back to the 19th century, provide an interesting history of the county. The collection includes such treasures as the *Official Map of Kern County* (1888, 1892, and 1898) and *Expeditions to Central California* (1875, 1878) (Kern, 2004a).

Art

In addition to the various spacious within the building, a clear, dominating feature that adds to the overall attractiveness of the library is the art collection. A brochure titled *The Beale Memorial Library Fine Arts Collection* invites visitors to take a self-guided tour with a map of the two floors and brief commentaries on each work of art. The library's art was not collected in a haphazard fashion; a thoughtful selection process which spanned from 1987 to 1995 was conducted by members of the Art Acquisition Committee. "The focus of the collection is work by California artists who created during the 19th and 20th centuries" ("A Little History," n.d., p. 1).

One collection worthy of mention is the Carleton Watkins Photography Collection. Watkins, who was born in upstate New York in 1829, moved to California at a young age. By 1861, he was working as a landscape photographer, which included seven trips to photograph the natural wonders of Yosemite ("Carleton Watkins," 2004). He also traveled the Southern Pacific Railroad line in

1876 and 1880 to photograph the scenery. Many of the photographs from his railroad trips were taken in Kern County. In 1888, Watkins returned once more to Kern County for the purpose of photographing the region ("Carleton Watkins," 2004). The Beale Memorial Library was fortunate to receive a donation of Watkins album of photographs titled "Photographic Views of Kern County California." Many of Watkins' photographs are on display throughout the library.

Another artistic treasure is the Society of Six collection. The society was a group of California post–Impressionist painters from the 1920s. The society also served as a sort of artistic support network. The painters created together, critiqued each other's works, partied, and even lived together at times. They practiced "plein-air" (out-of-doors) painting and reveled in "speed and spontaneity," including the desire "to finish a painting in one sitting" ("A Little History," n.d., p. 24).

The Society of Six and Carleton Watkins collections are just a fraction of the art owned and displayed by the library. Bronze sculptures, pastel watercolors, oil paintings, black-and-white photographs, and etchings fill the building. The generous interior allows for the works to be dispersed gracefully throughout the various spaces, making the visit to the library a visually gratifying experience.

REFERENCES

Beale Memorial Library. "A Capsule History." January 26, 1972. (Provided by the Beale Memorial Library.)
_____. *Fact Sheet*. April 22–30, 1988. (Provided by the Beale Memorial Library.)
Beers, T., ed. "The Central Valley." In *Unfolding Beauty: Celebrating California's Landscapes*, by ed. T. Beers, 331–33. Berkeley: Heyday Books, 2000.
Boyd, W. H., and M. Rump. "New Library Building for Bakersfield." *Historic Kern: Quarterly Bulletin Kern County Historical Society* 36, no. 4 (1987): 1–5.
Buckley, C., D. Oliveira, and M. L. Williams, eds. *How Much Earth: The Fresno Poets*. Berkeley: Heyday Books, 2001.
Hardisty, D. "City Gives $50,000 for Library Furnishings." *Bakersfield Californian*, July 8, 1986.
_____. "Group Sets Meeting on Library Relocation." *Bakersfield Californian*, February 6, 1984.
Hart, J. D. *A Companion to California*. New York: Oxford University Press, 1978.
Houston, J. D. "In Search of Oildorado." In *Highway 99: A Literary Journey through California's Great Central Valley*, by ed. S. Yogi, 262–77. Berkeley: Heyday Books, 1996.
Kern County Library. "Carleton Watkins Photography Collection. (2004) www.kerncountylibrary.org/HTML/ about/bea/spcol/Watkins.html (retrieved March 20, 2006).
_____."Curtis Darling Map Collection." (2004) www.kerncountylibrary.org/beale_spcol_map.html (retrieved March 20, 2006).
_____. "Jack Maguire Local History Room." 2004b. www.kerncountylibrary.org/beale.html (retrieved March 20, 2006).
"A Little History about the Art and the Selection Process." n.d. (Provided by the Beale Memorial Library.)
Muir, J. "The Mountains of California." In *Unfolding Beauty: Celebrating California's Landscapes*, by ed. T. Beers, 338–45. Berkeley: Heyday Books, 2000.
Wasserman, J. "Bakersfield's Library Leaves Fresno in Dust." *Fresno Bee*, March 30, 1989.

21

Visalia City Library

LIBRARY DATA

Address: 200 West Oak Avenue, Visalia, CA 93291
Phone: (559) 733-6954
Web site: www.tularecountylibrary.org/branch/visalia.htm
Square Feet: 31,600
Circulation: 271,779 (fiscal year 2004/2005)
Collection: 146,591 (fiscal year 2004/2005)
Sources for above: Tulare County Library Web site and M. Drake, personal correspondence, March 28, 2006

Writing about the large territory that the city of Visalia is located within, the late local historian Annie R. Mitchell (1976) reports: "In some dim geologic time, according to Indian legend, an inland sea broke through the surrounding hills and flowed into the ocean of the West. The space that it left is our San Joaquin Valley" (p. 1). Visalia, a San Joaquin Valley city positioned approximately 75 miles from Bakersfield in Tulare County, is located within a region that Mitchell defines as a "geological laboratory." The city, founded in 1852, is the county seat and oldest town between the cities of Stockton in the north and Los Angeles in the south.

Visalia is often thought of in relation to the wondrous national parks located just a short drive from the city limit. Writing over a half century ago in *The Story of Tulare County and Visalia*, Robinson (1952) states:

> Sequoia and Kings Canyon National Parks are Tulare County's "back country," which is not a region of big hotels or lush restaurants, but one that draws people who like to get away from "civilization," who enjoy hiking, scenery, wild life, fishing, and winter sports. The mountains provide a thrilling backdrop, too, for the towns of the foothills and Valley [p. 25].

The connection between the parks and Visalia, however, is not just due to proximity. The history of the city and efforts to conserve the wilderness are intertwined. Mitchell (1963), citing the names of many pioneers who were involved in the protection efforts, states, "The battle to save the giant redwoods as part of the conservation of natural resources began in Visalia" (p. 41). Mitchell comments on letters and editorial efforts made by George Stewart, a local newspaper editor, as well as the work of John Muir.

Visitors traveling to see the marvels of the parks, such as Mount Whitney, the highest peak in the continental United States, or the giant sequoias, including the largest tree in the world, the General Sherman Tree, will often pass through Visalia, especially those traveling from southern parts of California. Travelers, however, should consider staying, or, at least, pausing. Mitchell (1976) writes that the city's "history permeates the entire history of the lower valley as well as that of Tulare County" (p. 146). She further contends, "Visalia has always been the trading center of a large surrounding area.... Its geographical location on the delta of the Kaweah River has provided an incredibly fertile soil where almost any crop may be grown" (p. 146). Its history, according to Mitchell, is also one of considerable business with saloons, saddle shops, blacksmiths, lumberyards, wagon shops, and various other establishments. Downtown Visalia is alive with this history.

Visitors may begin their discovery of the city by first picking up the brochure titled *Historic Visalia Walking Trail* from the Visalia Library. Sites along the walking tour include the Visalia House, a brick hotel dating from 1859; an 1853 log residence, the first house in Visalia, built by former district attorney Samuel C. Brown; a Methodist Episcopal Church dating from the 1850s; and Visalia's first store built circa 1854. The Visalia City Library is located within this historic milieu.

History of the Library

The rumblings of a need to establish a library in Visalia came as early as 1861, according to Vicenti (2000). The minutes of a board of supervisors meeting in February 9, 1861, reveal an interest in the founding of a reading room. Vicenti, however, reports that it was not for many years that the desire came to a short-lived fruition. At the corner of Court and Center streets in 1879, a reading room was opened by the ladies of Visalia in the Good Templars Hall. This initial reading room was open in the afternoons and provided books donated by local families. Although the ladies volunteered their time for the project, the operation was ultimately not successful and saw a quick closure. A few years later in June 1893, the Women's Christian Temperance Union established a second reading room. The room remained open for several years, although the location changed twice since its initial opening (Vicenti, 2000).

In 1902 information was provided to the Carnegie Foundation in order to receive funding to erect a library building. After funding was successfully obtained, construction plans were put in place. The Visalia Carnegie Free Library opened its collection to the public on May 31, 1904 (Vicenti, 2000).

By 1916, plans were in motion to build a new building, but the funding did not materialize. To deal with space issues, tables and chairs were placed on the sidewalk, when the weather permitted, to allow library users more places to read (Vicenti, 2000). Efforts to construct a new building were not realized until the 1930s with Roosevelt's Works Progress Administration. Vicenti describes the building that was soon constructed under the creative direction of architect Judson Steele as a structure in the Spanish Colonial Revival style with a two-story, eight-sided central tower with four wings radiating from the center. The library was decorated with plaster bas-relief ornamentations above the doors, stucco walls, a tiled gable roof, and other adornments.

This new building was dedicated on August 27, 1936. The next major phase of the library's saga was the construction of the 1976 building, which is still in use today. The 1976 building sits next to the historic 1936 building, which has been used for many years as a storage facility for the library.

ONE LARGE SPACE

The current 1976 building is primarily one large room with an unusually tall ceiling. It would be incorrect to describe the interior of the building as elegant or stylish, but it is a highly welcoming space. The "home-away-from-home" appeal is immediately noticeable, which probably explains why the library was bustling with activity and had few vacant seats during my visit on a rainy Monday afternoon in April 2006.

To the right of the main entrance is a community bulletin board. Found in this area are also framed flyers promoting events, including a visit by poet Gary Soto. Also near the front of the library is a display of new books in print and audio formats, as well as an "Exchange Paperbacks" area with a sign reading: "Please exchange 1 for 1." Dispersed throughout the remainder of the large room are book stacks, a periodicals section, a children's area, and numerous tables and seating for groups or individuals. Everything about the entrance and the rest of the library lacks pretension and seems to say "all are welcome here."

ANNIE R. MITCHELL HISTORY ROOM

Located on the second floor is the small Annie R. Mitchell History Room. Mitchell, described as both a "member of a pioneer family" and "pioneer historian" was born in 1906 and died in 2000 (Tulare County Library, 2005). She was educated at both Fresno State College and the University of California, Berkeley, before serving as a teacher and in other educational occupations in Visalia from 1931 to 1964. She published several works on Tulare County. The history room is appropriately named after her.

The room is furnished with two tables for individuals or groups to assemble. There are also four reading chairs. Wood bookcases run the length of one wall, providing access to a wealth of materials. Included in the collection are sound recordings of oral histories relating to World War II–era Tulare County and aerial maps of the region from 1937, 1952, 1956, 1967, and 1977 (*Annie R. Mitchell*, n.d.). The research collection also includes books on the history of the county, the Sierra Nevada, and neighboring Kern, Kings, and Fresno counties; annual reports of county agencies and Sequoia National Park's early days; photographs, high school and college yearbooks dating back to as early as 1891; and telephone and business directories (Tulare County Library, 2006). Quiet and set off from the busy interior downstairs, the history room feels like a secret place.

Renovation of Historic Building

If this book were being written just two years into the future, this chapter on the Visalia City Library would likely be quite different. The library is currently in the midst of a considerable change. On December 19, 2002, the Tulare County Library received grant funds through the Library Bond Act Board to remodel and expand the library, which includes a renovation of the 1936 building that has deteriorated considerably over the years (Tulare County Library, 2005–2006).

As mentioned previously, the 1976 building and the 1936 building sit next to each other. The renovation project includes the construction of a lobby that will connect the two buildings. The historic building will also be the new home to the children's wing (Tulare County Library, 2005–2006). These changes will surely change and enhance the overall experience of visiting the library well into the future.

References

Annie R. Mitchell History Room. Pamphlet, n.d. (Available at the Visalia City Library.)
Mitchell, A. R. *Visalia: Her First Fifty Years*. Exeter, CA: 1963.
_____. *The Way It Was: The Colorful History of Tulare County*. Fresno, CA: Valley Publishers, 1976.
Robinson, W. W. *The Story of Tulare County and Visalia*. Los Angeles: Title Insurance and Trust, 1952.
Tulare County Library "Annie R. Mitchell." 2005. www.tularecountylibrary.org/hisres/annie.htm (retrieved February 20, 2006).
_____. "Visalia Library Building Project." 2005–2006. www.tularecountylibrary.org/visaproj.htm (retrieved May 21, 2006).
_____. "Partial list of the historical research collection." 2006. www.tularecountylibrary.org/hisres/historylist.htm (retrieved May 27, 2006).
Vicenti, J. L. *The Tulare County Library: From the Days of the Pioneer to the Millennium: A Historical Examination of the Institution and Those Who Made It Great*. 2000. (Available at the Annie R. Mitchell History Room, Visalia City Library.)

22

Mariposa County Library

LIBRARY DATA

Address: 4978 10th Street, Mariposa, CA 95338
Phone: (209) 966-2140
Web site: www.mariposalibrary.org/hours-mainbranch.php
Square Feet: 8,120
Circulation: 86,538 (July 2005–April 2006)*
Collection: not available at time of inquiry
*Circulation statistics are for a ten-month period.
California Library Statistics 2006 (California State Library, Library Development Services Bureau) confirms Mariposa countywide holdings of 49,931 books; 37 microfilm reels; 5,250 other microforms; 4,204 audio; 6,014 video; 90 periodicals.
Source for above: J. M. Dodd Meriam, personal correspondence, June 12, 2006

The *Mariposa Gazette* (1954) reports that "Mariposa ('Butterfly') was named when early Spanish explorers returned to tell of the great clusters of beautiful butterflies found in the Sierra foothills" ("Mariposa: The Mother"). Mariposa was one of the original 27 counties of California in 1850. Often referred to as the "Mother of Counties," Mariposa County in 1850 covered one-fifth of the state (Radanovich, 2005). Hart (1978) reports that the county "stretched over to the Coast Range and back to the Nevada state line and down to Los Angeles ..." until "its lands were whittled away to help form ten other counties" (p. 259–260). In 1850, Mariposa "included the entire present-day counties of Mariposa, Merced, Madera, Fresno, Kings, Tulare, and Kern, as well as portions of San Benito, San Bernardino, Mono, Inyo, and Los Angeles Counties" (Wood, 1954, p. 11).

Other facts about Mariposa County, which are quite impressive, illustrate the special qualities of the region. The county is home to the three tallest waterfalls in North America, including Yosemite Falls (2,425 feet); it contains the largest rock monolith in the country (El Capitan at 3,593 feet); and it is home to the Jordan Oak, the country's largest canyon oak tree (Mariposa County Visitors Bureau, n.d.). Fifty-five percent of the county's acres are actually owned by the federal government, due to Yosemite National Park, the Bureau of Land Management and the Sierra/Stanislaus National forests falling within county lines (Mariposa County Chamber of Commerce, 2006). Beyond these natural wonders, Mariposa is also credited with having the oldest weekly newspaper in continuous publication (the *Mariposa Gazette*, which dates to January 1854) and the oldest courthouse in continuous use west of the Rockies (Mariposa County Visitors Bureau, n.d.). The Mariposa County Courthouse, established in 1854, is located in the historic gold mining town of Mariposa, the county seat.

It is a relatively short drive from Yosemite Valley in Yosemite National Park, approximately 45 miles or one hour on Highway 140, to the community of Mariposa. Mariposa resembles a small, historic village with an "old West" style main street. Although Mariposa is a land steeped in history, it is also an area where new and innovative ideas are welcome. A recent feature article in the free newspaper *Central Sierra Good Life*, demonstrates this openness to experimentation with information on alternative and sustainable homes in the region (Dusek, K., 2006). The article and another of a similar theme in the same issue (Dusek, B., 2006) both illustrate the free spirit that is alive in the community with information on area homes that have been built with clay and straw bales. In fact, the second annual Tour of Innovative Homes, an event to "showcase five of Mariposa's most innovative, creative and well-planned dwellings" ("Tour of Innovative," p. 10) was to take place in June 2006 along with other events such as the 18th Annual Cannonball Cowboy Poetry Gathering and the Mariposa County Pioneer Wagon Train event where "period costume is encouraged but not required," according to an advertisement in the *Central Sierra Good Life*. It is within the eclectic culture of this 19th-century mining town that the new Mariposa County Library building is found.

The Mariposa County Library is a member of the San Joaquin Valley Library System. Mariposa County is the northernmost of the six counties in the system. Libraries are not new to Mariposa. Per Library Director Jacqueline M. Dodd Meriam, library service started in Mariposa in 1894 (personal correspondence, June 12, 2006). According to Meriam, the previous library building was located in the Museum and History Center. The new building, which opened on December 19, 2000, was funded through Mariposa County, the Library Services and Construction Act Grant, and the Friends of the Library Building Fund (Mariposa County Library, n.d.). It has a prime location next to the historic courthouse.

ENTRANCE

The bell on the courthouse chimes on the hour and can be heard from the library. Ample parking is available on the street or in a lot between the library and the grounds of the courthouse. One element noticed almost immediately is an inviting sign on the front of the library that reads "Home of Books Galore Books for Sale." The charm of the library building within the context of a historic town with a "books for sale" sign likely makes it nearly impossible for most bibliophiles to pass up a visit.

The Mariposa County Library, located next to a historic courthouse, features Books Galore bookstore, various interior spaces, and an outdoor patio.

Benches are available for sitting immediately to both sides of the main entrance. After passing through the door, the Books Galore bookstore is in the first room to the left. Once one has passed through the lobby area into the main interior, the library opens up to primarily one large room with various spaces. The first area greeting visitors is a new books display to the right. The display includes fiction and nonfiction books.

DISPLAYS

Different exhibits are noticeable upon entering the library or after walking around a bit. An exhibit in June 2006 featured artwork from Yosemite Renaissance XXI, "an annual competition/exhibition intended to encourage diverse artistic interpretations of Yosemite" (Yosemite Renaissance, 2006). Included in the exhibit was an impressive and beautifully crafted textile by Bonnie Peterson titled *Muir Trail Lakes, Peaks and Passes,* which won the top Best in Show Award. Another textile by Peterson titled *Lyell Canyon & Emerald Lake* was also on display along with an unusually stimulating work by Kathyanne White titled *Eclectic*

Configuration Yosemite Falls. White's piece utilized digitally manipulated photographs, earning an honorable mention. Not only did the exhibit add vibrant colors and creativity to the library's main space, but it also reflected Mariposa's long and close relationship with Yosemite Park.

Other displays that illustrated community involvement included a small exhibit in the young adult section by the Book and Art Club titled Books Made into Movies. In addition to the display that is a result of the young adults' efforts, the "young adult section regularly undergoes improvements suggested by local teens" (Mariposa County Library, 2001). The 4-H Club also had a display on Jane Austen that was informative and artistically arranged. The Austen display included a chronology of the writer's life along with books and a collage.

CHILDREN'S ROOM

The Children's Room includes a Parent Corner that "features a collection of books, magazines, and videos on subjects of interest to parents raising young

A space in the Mariposa County Library that features mysteries demonstrates the charm of the small library.

families in today's world" (Mariposa County Library, 2001). The library's goals for the children's space include regularly updated displays. In addition to books and magazines for children, library computers have "interactive learning games, word processing, and reference programs" for a young audience of toddlers to preteens (Mariposa County Library, 2001). Equipment also includes an audio station with headphones for children to use.

REFERENCE AND ADULT BOOKS SPACE

To the right of the entrance is one of the largest areas that includes reference, paperbacks, mysteries, fiction, nonfiction, and a collection of maps in one corner. Wood paneling throughout greatly accents the space. The library provides several sizes of tables for visitors to choose from: large rectangular, small rectangular, or small round. Individual study carrels equipped with computers are another option. Although the library is a new building, the adult area resembles the interior spaces of libraries from earlier periods, making it a charming space with the ambiance of history.

OUTDOOR PATIO

A final space to mention is an outdoor patio. Near rose bushes and a small garden courtyard with additional bench seating, the library's outdoor area provides three tables with matching chairs. This space, as well as many others throughout the library, provides diverse options, depending on users' needs and preferences, and invites visitors to sit and stay for awhile.

REFERENCES

California State Library. Library Development Services Bureau. *California Library Statistics 2006*. www.library.ca.gov/assets/acrobat/StatsPub06.pdf (retrieved December 23, 2006).
Dusek, B. "A Couple Finds Paradise in Their Straw Bale Home." *Central Sierra Good Life*, June 2006.
Dusek, K. "Area Residents Feel at Home with Alternative Styles of Building." *Central Sierra Good Life*, June 2006.
Hart, J. D. *A Companion to California*. New York: Oxford University Press, 1978.
Mariposa County Chamber of Commerce. *Business Directory and Community Information*. 2006.
Mariposa County Library. Project information, n.d. (Unpublished document provided by the Mariposa County Library.)
_____. "Library Areas." 2001. www.mariposalibrary.org/using-areas.php (retrieved June 10, 2006).
"Mariposa: The Mother of Counties." *Mariposa Gazette Centennial Edition*, April 1954.
Mariposa County Visitors Bureau. *Mariposa County: Home of Yosemite: Gold Country and Yosemite Vacation Planner*. n.d.

Radanovich, L. *Mariposa County.* Chicago: Arcadia, 2005.
"Tour of Innovative Homes Set for June 24." *Central Sierra Good Life,* June 2006.
Wood, R. F. *California's Aqua Fria: The Early History of Mariposa County.* Fresno, CA: Academy Library Guild, 1954.
Yosemite Renaissance. "The Competition and Show." 2006. www.yrhome.org/theshow.html (retrieved June 17, 2006).

23

Bassett Memorial Library

LIBRARY DATA

Address: 7971 Chilnualna Falls Road, Wawona, CA 95389
Phone: (209) 375-6510
Web site: www.mariposalibrary.org/wawona.php
Square Feet: 1,800
Circulation: 4,432 (July 2005–April 2006)*
Collection: not available at time of inquiry
*Circulation statistics are for a ten-month period.
California Library Statistics 2006 (California State Library, Library Development Services Bureau) confirms Mariposa countywide holdings of 49,931 books; 37 microfilm reels; 5,250 other microforms; 4,204 audio; 6,014 video; 90 periodicals.
Source for above: J. M. Dodd Meriam, personal correspondence, June 12, 2006

Writing in *The Yosemite*, John Muir (1912/2003) states that "no temple made with hands can compare with Yosemite. Every rock in its walls seems to glow with life" (p. 8). It is a favorite vacation spot for many Californians who typically reach the park by driving through a section of the Central Valley. The most reliable route that remains open through the winter more regularly than others is the Arch Rock entrance. Approaching the park from Merced on Highway 140, one will pass the town of El Portal just before the park entrance, which leads directly into the Yosemite Valley. Other entrances include the Hetch Hetchy and Big Oak Flat to the north and the Tioga Pass entrance to the far northeast. The south entrance welcomes travelers to the park through the historic town of Wawona.

Attempting to describe nearly any part of Yosemite in words is a difficult task that is likely best left to poets, nature writers, and John Muir. First called Pallahchun by Native Americans, meaning "a good place to stop," and later changed to Wawona, meaning "Big Tree" (Yosemite National Park, 2003), the town provides a magical and breathtaking landscape. After traveling through Oakhurst and the small village of Fish Camp on Highway 41, one will reach the south park entrance and the town of Wawona. It is home to the Mariposa Grove of Big Trees. Muir comments that "everybody who visits Yosemite wants to see the famous Big Trees." He then adds that most visitors will select the Mariposa Grove in Wawona: "a beautiful place on the South Fork of the Merced River" (p. 225–226). While in

Wawona, Muir wrote letters to friends from an ink he made from the sap of the Mariposa Grove Big Trees ("Wawona," 1954). Wawona is also known for some of its man-made structures, including the still-operational Wawona Hotel, a National Historic Landmark and Historic Hotel of America thought to have opened in 1879 (Yosemite National Park, 2003), as well as a series of bridges.

Phillips (1999) provides information on many of the town's bridges, including those that have been long destroyed by floods, in his small pamphlet *Bridges of Wawona*. This includes Indian Bridge, first built in 1921 and rebuilt twice until it was washed out by a flood in the late 1930s. Other bridges are the Swinging Bridge, built in the early 1960s and still standing, and the Chilnualna Bridge, first built around 1948 and replaced in the 1960s and 1990s. It is in this "beautiful place," to use Muir's description once more, a land of giant trees and historic structures, that the Bassett Memorial Library, a branch of the Mariposa County Library, sits at 7971 Chilnualna Falls Road.

History of the Library

Rankin (n.d.) reports that Wawona first had a library in late 1926. Stability of library service, however, did not occur until much later. According to Rankin, "Libraries came and went, in 1937, 1941, 1946, and finally stayed in 1983 — although in recent years the library was in a tiny old hamburger stand." Newton (1997) further confirms that prior to the library's current location, it was, indeed, housed within 300 square feet of available space at the Hungry Bear Sandwich Shop.

The fate of Wawona's library changed for the better in May 1996 when ground was broken for a new library on Chilnualna Falls Road. The location of the library is approximately two miles off of Highway 41, the main road leading from Wawona to Yosemite Valley. Driving down Chilnualna Falls Road, one will pass a few residences, stables, a school, and several other small structures with the wondrous wilderness as a backdrop.

A fund for the creation of the Basset Memorial Library was established in 1994 by Russell and Teresa Bassett. The fund was created in memory of their son, Edward Bassett (1945–1994), who had a love for Wawona and Yosemite National Park that grew from time spent at the Bassett Family's cabin (Bassett Memorial Library, n.d.). The Bassetts were intricately involved in the planning of the library. Russ Bassett, Sischo (n.d.) reports, "likened the library building to a 'Field of Dreams.' 'Our benefits are yet to come from the library,' he said at the 1997 library dedication ceremony, 'when children who use the library dream dreams that will shape their lives.'" Sischo also reports that Bassett encouraged friends and organizations to donate books. By the time the library opened, the family had a garage full of books. Bassett was even successful at receiving book donations from the president of the Michigan university he attended. He received one book, "a nice one," from a librarian in the Czech Republic (Rankin, n.d.).

The Bassett Memorial Library in Yosemite National Park is one large room divided into several spaces. The library also has an outdoor deck.

In addition to donating and acquiring materials for the collection, Russell and Teresa Bassett visited libraries during their travels, bringing ideas back to share in the formation of the Wawona library (Sischo, n.d.). Russell Bassett, who passed away April 22, 1999, just a little over two years after the library's dedication on April 12, 1997, stated at the ceremony, "'I felt if we built a library, we could count on people coming'" (Rankin, n.d.). Maurie Hoekstra, Mariposa County librarian at the time of the ceremony, dedicated the library "to the community's children as a challenge to your minds, comfort to your souls." Nearly 300 people attended the dedication. Although the number in attendance may not sound significant, it represented "more than half" of Wawona's permanent population (Rankin, n.d.).

ONE ROOM WITH DISTINCT SPACES

The exterior of the library resembles a home more than a public building. In fact, signage and a small parking lot are the only indicators that one has, in fact, reached a library. A wooden bench is available for sitting in the shade immediately before the entrance. Once stepping inside the library, the feel of home does not dissipate. The interior is one, airy large room with several distinct spaces.

An intriguing piece of art is displayed in a case directly to the right of the entrance. This is the first hint of the art collection found throughout the interior. Included in the case is a small piece described as "Replica of Bronze Chariot and Horses in Tomb of Qia, 1st Emperor of Qin Dynasty in China." Shortly after viewing the chariot and horses, a watercolor from the Miriam Loberg collection appears to the left. Titled *Afternoon in the Library*, the watercolor shows a child clearly submerged in the realm of reading.

In addition to these two pieces, during a visit in June 2006, the library was displaying, and offering for purchase, the work of photographer Carol Bliss Thomas. Branch Head Virginia Blackburn pointed out how the library rotates artists three to four times per year (personal correspondence, June 3, 2006). Indeed, two binders chronicling the history of the library through photographs and documents reflect the various exhibits the library has provided for the community, including those of Yosemite artist Letty DeLoach, creator of paintings, drawings, and mixed-media compositions and Wawona watercolor artist Mary Jane Ehrman (Bassett Memorial Library, n.d.). It is clear from the representation and support of local artists' works that the library is a place providing much more than library resources.

The reference desk is located to the right of the entrance. Two tables with chairs are arranged in the middle of the room. To the left of the entrance is a small area with four computer stations with Internet access and a photocopy machine. Above the workstations are more nature photographs by Thomas.

Near the center of the room is a large display of resources on Yosemite. Books offering different information on the park are featured along with many more items. Materials found here include hiking guides, photographic books, works on John Muir, and numerous other items.

A young adult space near one of the corners includes cushioned window seating. A large window provides a view of the natural surroundings. A table and four chairs provide additional seating.

An oak silver inlay desk sits regally near the young adult area and a door leading to an outdoor deck. Displayed on the desk are library tote bags available for purchase, as well as other items. This unique piece of furniture has a history that includes not only Yosemite National Park, but several regions of California (Bassett Memorial Library, n.d.).

Although the name, date of manufacture, and the original location of the desk are not known, the history of the desk can be traced as far back as 1928 when it was located in the offices of a savings and loan company in Los Angeles. Ownership of the desk changed during the Depression when it fell into the possession of the Title Insurance and Trust Company. In 1950, the desk was shipped to the company's Independence, California, office, where it remained from 1950 to 1961. In 1961, the desk was traded to the Bassett Business Interiors Company in Whittier, California. Recognizing the unusual nature of the desk, the company stored the desk in their warehouse until a suitable location could be determined (Bassett Memorial Library, n.d.).

The surrounding wilderness of Yosemite National Park adds to the uniqueness of Bassett Memorial Library's sense of place.

On December 7, 1980, the desk found its new place as a concierge's desk at the luxurious Ahwahnee Hotel in Yosemite National Park. It remained at the Ahwahnee for many years. In 1996, the hotel donated the desk to the Bassett Memorial Library (Bassett Memorial Library, n.d.). Visitors to the library may notice the beauty and customized nature of the desk, but may be unaware of its mysterious origin and the interesting history it represents.

Outdoor Deck

A final area that speaks to the uniqueness of the library is an outdoor deck that may be reached through an interior door. Not unlike a deck that may be attached to cabins and mountain-style homes, this space provides a location for outdoor reading and other activities. The view from the deck, which looks out into the dense wilderness beyond, is also undeniably stunning. This addition shows how the Bassett Memorial Library has a sense of place that ties it directly and harmoniously to the natural wonders of Yosemite. Indeed, it is impossible to separate the library from its majestic location.

References

Bassett Memorial Library. n.d. Unpublished documents regarding Edward V. Bassett, the Bassett family, the silver inlay desk, and the formation of the library (available at the Bassett Memorial Library).

California State Library. Library Development Services Bureau. *California Library Statistics 2006.* www.library.ca.gov/assets/acrobat/StatsPub06.pdf (retrieved December 23, 2006).

Muir, J. *The Yosemite.* New York: Modern Library, 1912/2003.

Newton, J. "Wawona Opens a New Page on Town Library." *Sierra Star,* April 3, 1997.

Phillips, T. B. *Bridges of Wawona.* Pamphlet, 1999 (Available at the Bassett Memorial Library.)

Rankin, J. "Wawona Celebrates Its First Permanent 'Library of Dreams.'" n.d. (Article available at the Bassett Memorial Library.)

Sischo, P. "Russell L. Bassett: In Memoriam." n.d. (Article available at the Bassett Memorial Library.)

"Wawona and the Mariposa Grove of Big Trees." *Mariposa Gazette Centennial Edition,* April 1954.

Yosemite National Park. "Wawona History." 2003. www.yosemitepark.com/content2col.cfm?SectionID=25&PageID=339 (retrieved June 11, 2006).

24

UC Merced Library

LIBRARY DATA

Address: 500 North Lake Road, Merced, CA 95344
Phone: (209) 724-4444
Web site: http://library.ucmerced.edu
Square Feet: 180,000
Circulation: not available at time of inquiry
Collection: 216,200 items as of June 2006 (40,450 books; 15,000 electronic journals; 160,750 electronic monographs; 900 DVDs; 250 databases)
Source for above: S. Davidson, personal correspondence, June 2, 2006

In a recent editorial piece, former Harvard librarian Alex Wright (2006) wrote on the continuing need for physical library space. Comparing contemporary reading rooms to monastic libraries of medieval Europe, Wright stated,

> Even in the silent reading rooms of our modern libraries, a kind of quiet collaboration takes place among readers, librarians, and authors. There is a tacit sense of community, and a reassuring solidity in the shared physical space that seems to provide an antidote to the specter of loneliness [p. 9].

It is quite apparent after visiting the UC Merced Library at the University of California, Merced (UC Merced) that those involved with the planning of a 21st-century high-tech research library are acutely aware of the need for such traditional community spaces. The UC Merced Library, with a motto of "Not what other research libraries are ... what they will be," includes numerous reading rooms and other spaces, as well as an array of nonlibrary services that are typically housed in other administrative buildings on most university campuses. Assistant university librarian Barclay (n.d.) states that "despite UC Merced Library's reputation as an online/electronic/virtual/paperless Library, we have done our best to give the Library building a real sense of place, a place that is comfortable, inviting, and adapted to many different uses." It is within the context of this vision that the library has truly been designed as the heart of the campus.

UC MERCED

UC Merced is the tenth campus of the University of California statewide system. The campus opened on September 5, 2005. It has the distinction of being the first American research university to be built in the new century. The location of the campus is near the center of the state.

Merced, the county seat, is a Central Valley city located approximately 60 miles north of Fresno and 120 miles south of Sacramento. It is also uniquely positioned in close proximity to Yosemite National Park. The drive to Yosemite Valley can be made in roughly two hours, resulting in Merced often being referred to as the "Gateway to Yosemite." It has historically been a center for agriculture, although its economy in recent years has become more diversified. Still, Bianchi and Sons Packing, a fresh tomato shipping company, is ranked second in terms of top Merced manufacturing employers. Interestingly, UC Merced is already ranked sixth in terms of nonmanufacturing employers (City of Merced, 2005).

Although UC Merced is a new campus located within a traditionally

The view from a window of the UC Merced Library at the University of California, Merced illustrates the expanse of land that surrounds the newest campus of the University of California system.

agricultural community, the fact that it is part of the prestigious University of California system may cause one to imagine it as other more known campuses, such as Berkeley or UCLA. A visit to Merced, however, quickly demonstrates its uniqueness. In June 2006, the campus was literally a few buildings situated on a large field. It is quite astonishing to first approach the campus from a distance. Once one is walking around the campus or within the library, it is impossible not to be aware of the expanse of surrounding land.

The importance of land to the region has not been forgotten in the planning of the university; environmental concerns have been central. Chancellor Tomlinson-Keasey made this clear when she stated in January 2002 that UC Merced should "set the standards for sustainable use of energy and other scarce resources and to be a model of development in the great San Joaquin Valley" ("Environmental Stewardship Program," 2004). Goals were outlined in numerous areas, including recycling, energy efficiency, water conservation, and transportation, with a specific focus on bicycling and "the opportunity to develop a bicycle-friendly community adjacent to the campus." Even food was considered in the long-range plan: "Products that are fresh, locally grown and produced, and environmentally friendly will be included in the campus' food offerings" ("Environmental Stewardship Program," 2004).

The university's noble efforts were highlighted in "The Greening of Academe," an article by Jeff Yoders that appeared in *Building Design and Construction* (2005). According to Yoders, UC Merced is the first campus in the United States "to aspire to LEED Silver certification from the U.S. Green Building Council" (p. 40), although several universities are requiring that new buildings be LEED certified. LEED, which stands for "Leadership in Energy and Environmental Design," is defined by the U.S. Green Building Council (2006) as "a voluntary, consensus-based national standard for developing high-performance, sustainable buildings." LEED provides a framework with an emphasis on "state of the art strategies for sustainable site development, water savings, energy efficiency, materials selection and indoor environmental quality." Yoders reports that working within the confines of LEED has been no easy feat for Merced thus far, due to a climate that he characterizes as the most severe of any of the UC campuses with temperatures often exceeding 100 in the summer and reaching below freezing in the winter.

The sustainability factor is complemented by other aspects discussed in the university's *Long Range Development Plan 2002*. The section "Planning Principles" highlights such goals as creating a "social heart" on campus and "identifiable neighborhoods," including "residential neighborhoods" and "academic neighborhoods." For example, "The social sciences, humanities and arts, with their high levels of student activity, will be focused in the most central locations on campus near the library" (p. 4–14). These principles tie into the theme of a "sense of place" on campus, as outlined on pages 4–17 of the plan: "The campus must capture the greatness of the University of California in its physical plan by creating a sense of place from the beginning, and by assuring a sense of beauty which contributes to attracting faculty and students." This sense of place will be accomplished through "a sequence of memorable views and spaces" (p. 4–17). A tour of the UC Merced Library clearly illustrates these campus-wide goals.

NEW LIBRARY

Construction of the library began with a groundbreaking ceremony in October 2003. A UC spokeswoman, Sheryl Lichtig Wyan (quoted in Turner, 2003), stated that the ceremony for the library was particularly significant, since the groundbreaking was "for the building that really is the heart of any campus, the library." Even with the Internet and other options that technology affords today's students, such as remote-access databases, it is significant that the physical library building was still recognized as central to a new university.

Wyan's sentiments echo those of students who are deciding which university to attend. In a recent study titled *The Impact of Facilities on Recruitment and Retention of Students*, Cain and Reynolds (2006) surveyed 13,782 students from 27 different states on the importance of various campus facilities. The library ranked second, only behind facilities for one's academic major, as a facility that was "extremely" or "very important" to consider during the university selection process. After facilities for one's major and the residential facilities, the library came in third when students were asked which facilities were important to see during a campus visit. The authors conclude that the library, along with academic major facilities, classrooms, and technology "will be important areas to continue to address to ensure keeping higher satisfaction levels" (p. 60). Creating a structure like the UC Merced Library meets this demand with open, diverse spaces that are well-balanced and aesthetically pleasing.

CAFE AND SERVICES

The first floor of the library includes a large, open space and coffee shop along with various types of furniture, including cafe-style seating. Student service offices and the campus bookstore are both housed here, demonstrating an interesting merge of traditional library space with the more business-orientated aspects of the university. There is a definite blending across certain conventional boundaries, since food and drink are permitted throughout the library.

READING ROOMS AND STUDY SPACES

The UC Merced Library is definitely not lacking in reading rooms and other study spaces. One of the most impressive spaces is the McFadden Willis Reading

Room located on the fourth floor. The elegant room, designed with darker and richer tones than many of the other spaces, is simply enrobed in natural light. The window fixtures are designed in such a way that it makes one feel as if all of the windows are open. Tables and chairs, as well as movable cushioned furniture, are spread out throughout the room. Some of the furniture appears to be leather, but librarian Sara Davidson (personal correspondence, June 2, 2006) pointed out that all the textures are synthetic and special efforts were made to only purchase environmentally friendly products, including those not made with animal products. The library newsletter does a superb job at describing the room as "a great place to tackle a big project in a quiet, spacious, pleasant environment." Furthermore:

> As the highest room in the Library, you can look out across miles of rolling fields. The rich colors evoke a sense of the Library in a Victorian house, but the modern amenities let you know that you are in one of the newest research libraries in the country ["The McFadden Willis," n.d.].

Another impressive space is the reading room and study area on the third floor. Providing more amazing views of the landscape, the space is accented in tones of green, tan, and cream, with a mixture of movable furniture. At least two dozen plush chairs and eight or so sofas are found here, along with the more standard tables and chairs. According to Davidson, a project is underway to include uncatalogued "fun" magazines that would be available in the third floor space for students to peruse (personal correspondence, June 2, 2006).

In addition to the furniture found within the reading rooms and other spaces, the library also has many individual study carrels. These, however, are different than the norm. While pointing out carrels on the fourth floor, Davidson (personal correspondence, June 2, 2006) commented that the carrels were customized to be four feet wide to allow for roominess that traditionally smaller carrels do not permit.

Not only are aesthetically pleasing spaces provided, but predictable and functional spaces, as found at many university libraries, are also on the second, third, and fourth floors. These small areas provide photocopy machines and printers.

Free Technology

Unlike many university libraries that have extensive areas filled with desktop computers, UC Merced is attempting to be less stationary and more free with its technology. Although there are some desktop terminals, the library primarily provides computers to its students through laptop checkouts. As with the movable furniture, students are able to create their own spaces within a wireless environment. The free laptops are available for four hours at a time, with the

The interior of the UC Merced Library provides several study spaces and reading rooms, such as this area that features different styles of furniture.

option to renew. Not only does this provide freedom within the library, but also across campus. Students do not need to remain in the library, but can take the laptops around campus. Laptop checkout is described as being "as easy as checking out a book" ("Library Loaner Laptops," n.d.).

Place for Art and Events

Although the library has been open just a short time, it has had a lively and impressive schedule of diverse events to celebrate literature and the arts, efforts that may culminate in the creation of a strong campus community. Events have included a reading by artist, author, and founding member of the Rebel Chicano Art Front, Jos Montoya ("Around the Region," 2005); a Mexican folk-art exhibition and family art show titled Miracles on the Border: Folk Paintings of Mexican Migrants to the U.S. that included art by students, faculty, and relatives of campus employees ("UC Merced Art," 2006); a Java Art Walk to celebrate "art, music, food and coffee" ("Around the Region," 2006); and Asian Fest, an event to promote Asian-American cultural awareness ("It's Happening," 2006).

Many staff work areas have framed artwork, demonstrating an importance of creating a sense of place even beyond the public spaces. Davidson stated that the library's overall plan is to have 20 art displays throughout the building (personal correspondence, June 2, 2006). On May 8, 2006, an exhibit titled David Johnson Photography: Past and Present Images opened. Johnson, who was the first African American student of Ansel Adams, "became an important chronicler of black life in San Francisco in the middle part of the 20th century" ("Photographer David Johnson," 2006). The exhibit filled several walls, intermingling with open spaces and book stacks, while providing a visual portrait of history.

The university's vision for creating a campus with a sense of place, as outlined in the *Long Range Development Plan 2002*, states that "within the campus there will be comfortable and memorable gathering places and opportunities for sculpture, water features, and other landmarks as the campus grows" (University of California, p. 4–17). Some of these aspects, of course, will be found outdoors, but others will be experienced within university buildings. Those involved with the planning of the UC Merced Library have already demonstrated that the library is one location on campus that will prominently contribute to the cultivation of place.

References

"Around the Region: Merced." *Modesto Bee*, November 24, 2005.

"Around the Region: Merced." *Modesto Bee*, March 4, 2006.

Barclay, D. "A Different Library, a Different Tradition." *The Kolligian: UC Merced Library Newsletter*. n.d. (Available at the UC Merced Library.)

Cain, D., and G. L. Reynolds. "The Impact of Facilities on Recruitment and Retention of Students." *Facilities Manager*, March–April 2006. www.appa.org/files/FMArticles/fm030406_f7_impact.pdf (retrieved June 26, 2006).

City of Merced. "Working In." 2005. www.cityofmerced.org/services/business.asp (retrieved June 20, 2006).

"Environmental Stewardship Program." University of California, Merced, 2004. www.ucmerced.edu/about_ucmerced/environmentalstewardship.asp (retrieved June 19, 2006).

"It's Happening This Weekend." *Modesto Bee*, April 12, 2006.

"Library Loaner Laptops." *The Kolligian: UC Merced Library Newsletter*, n.d. (Available at the UC Merced Library.)

"The McFadden Willis Reading Room." *The Kolligian: UC Merced Library Newsletter*, n.d. (Available at the UC Merced Library.)

"Photographer David Johnson to Exhibit Historic, Current Works at UC Merced." University of California, Merced, May 4, 2006. www.ucmerced.edu/news_articles/05042006_photographer_david_johnson_to.asp (retrieved June 19, 2006).

Turner, M. "Groundbreaking Paves Way for 'Heart' of Merced Campus." *Modesto Bee*, October 8, 2003.

"UC Merced Art Events." *Modesto Bee*, March 3, 2006.

University of California, Merced. *Long Range Development Plan 2002*. www.ucmercedplanning.net/information/finaluclrdp.html (retrieved June 19, 2006).

U.S. Green Building Council. "LEED: Leadership in Energy and Environmental Design." www.usgbc.org/DisplayPage.aspx?CategoryID=19 (retrieved June 26, 2006).

Wright, A. "Libraries as Places to Linger and Mingle." *Christian Science Monitor* 98, no. 34 (2006): 9.

Yoders, J. "The Greening of Academe." *Building Design and Construction* 46, no. 9 (2005): 40–49.

Part VI
Monterey County

25

Henry Miller Memorial Library

Library Data

Address: Highway 1, Big Sur, California 93920
Phone: (831) 667-2574
Web site: www.henrymiller.org
Square Feet: 700
Circulation: Noncirculating collection
Collection: archival collections of letters, original manuscripts, manuscript copies, postcards, ephemera, books, and pamphlets totaling several thousand items
Source for above: M. Torén, personal correspondence, December 18, 2006

The sense of place of the Henry Miller Memorial Library (HMML) in Big Sur, California, extends well beyond the boundaries of the library building. As travelers approach the library from Highway 1 along the California Coast, they are met by tall redwood trees and sharp cliffs that drop far down to meet the Pacific Ocean. So challenging are the steep, hairpin turns leading to Big Sur, that T-shirts are available at a local gift shop that read: "I survived Highway 1." The curves of the narrow, two-lane highway do not allow for speeding. Drivers must also share the road with bicycle enthusiasts. One cannot easily get to the library; the journey requires a commitment. Perhaps this is why the library feels like a place unlike any other.

In *The Natural History of Big Sur*, Henson and Usner (1993) affirm: "In Big Sur, where the mountains of the Santa Lucia Range rise abruptly from the Pacific Ocean, the two utterly opposed elements of rock and sea contrast more dramatically than anywhere else in the United States" (p. 7). They continue their assessment of Big Sur as a place of "diverse rocks" with "some of the most complicated geology in California" (p. 7). One cannot visit the library without noticing the landscape, and surely memories of a visit will mix the interior of the library building with the ocean and surrounding forest. As it is often impossible to separate a library from its community, the HMML demonstrates how a library building cannot be separated from its natural surroundings.

BIG SUR

Big Sur is located in Monterey County, along the Pacific coastline between the cities of Carmel and Lucia. Traveling through Big Sur, one quickly realizes how much of the territory remains wild. There are few homes and no resemblance to the bustling city life often associated with California. The 2000 population of Big Sur was estimated at just 996 residents (U.S. Census, 2000).

Those looking for artistic inspiration may find it in Big Sur. It is clearly a land that speaks to the free spirit. The stock at a local grocery store down the street from the library indicates the character of the clientele with its array of organic and vegetarian foods. An art gallery showcasing the work of local artists and a large shop full of candles, incense, artwork, and brightly colored clothing from India are both located a few paces from the grocery store. Those seeking long-term inspiration from the region would be wise, however, to heed Miller's warning that few of the artistic variety remain for long (1957, p. 13). Similar to the journey to the library requiring a commitment on the part of the traveler, an artist hoping to relocate must have the dedication required for silence and the absence of city-life stimulation.

In *Big Sur and the Oranges of Hieronymus Bosch*, Miller wrote that comparisons between the region and others are "vain." He continues: "Big Sur has a climate of its own and a character all its own. It is a region where extremes meet, a region where one is always conscious of weather, of space, of grandeur, and of eloquent silence" (p. 4). Further demonstrating the polarities of the land, Miller views it as "an inviting land, but hard to conquer. It seeks to remain unspoiled, uninhabited by man" (p. 6). He finds himself thinking, "This is the California that men dreamed of years ago ... this is the face of the earth as the Creator intended it to look" (p. 6).

Other writers and artists have shared in Miller's enthusiasm. Two of the more famous include Beat Generation author Jack Kerouac and poet Robinson Jeffers. In *Big Sur*, Kerouac writes about the mystery of the land: "I gulp to wonder why it has the reputation of being beautiful above and beyond its *fearfulness* ... those vistas when you drive the coast highway on a sunny day opening up the eye for miles" (p. 403). A recent collection of the poetry of Jeffers (2001) includes poems inspired by Big Sur, along with photographs of the land by Morley Baer. From the collection, Jeffers writes of the region's music, which includes the music of the sea and the silent music of the mountains in the poem "Meditation on Saviors" (p. 133). The fact that such creativity and poetic inspiration is tied so closely to the region illustrates the sense of place one will experience before arriving at the door of the library.

HENRY MILLER AND THE HISTORY OF THE LIBRARY

Henry Miller is the author of such modern classics as *Nexus*, *Tropic of Cancer*, and *Tropic of Capricorn*. He lived in Big Sur for 18 years, which was a time of great inspiration. While living in the region, "he turned out some of his finest work,

25. Henry Miller Memorial Library

The Henry Miller Memorial Library in Big Sur was once the home of Miller's good friend, Emil White.

including *The Rosy Crucifixion*, a three-volume epic about his life with his second wife, June" (HMML, 2005). Miller's name is often tied to author Anais Nin, with whom he had a longstanding affair. Miller pushed the limits of artistic expression, resulting in some of his writings being labeled obscene, or, at the least, controversial. Charged with obscenity, in 1963, a Los Angeles bookseller was sentenced to a year's probation and 30 days in jail for selling Miller's *Tropic of Cancer* ("Hearing Is Granted"). In 1961, authorities in seven New Jersey counties moved to ban *Tropic of Cancer* ("Tropic of Cancer"). These are just a few of the incidents surrounding Miller's literary legacy.

The property that is now the HMML was once the home of Miller's good friend, Emil White (HMML, 2005). So fond of White was Miller that he dedicated *Big Sur and the Oranges of Hieronymus Bosch* to him, describing White in the inscription as "one of the few friends who has never failed me." After moving to Big Sur, Miller requested White move to the land also. White became Miller's personal secretary and caretaker. He was also an artist who painted oils and watercolors of Big Sur. His ability to create and sell tour guides of the region eventually helped him secure the funding to purchase what is now the HMML in the 1960s (HMML, 2005).

White's loyalty to Miller is realized today through the existence of the library. According to the HMML (2005),

> After Miller died in 1980, Emil decided to maintain his property as a memorial to his friend and as a gallery where local artists could show their work. In 1981, with the assistance of the Big Sur Land Trust (BSLT), he converted his home into the library. Emil spent the rest of his life as director of the new institution, which evolved into a local center for the arts.

White died in 1989, and he bequeathed the library to the BSLT. The library's mission remains twofold: "first, to champion the literary, artistic and cultural contributions of Henry Miller; and, second, to be a cultural center for local and county residents and visitors from all over the state, the country and the world" (HMML, n.d.b).

Not unlike the Big Sur region with its contrasting elements, the HMML is difficult to define. It has the elements of an archive, museum, community and art center, library, bookstore, and, simply put, a general hangout. Entrance to the library is free and the atmosphere and friendly staff, including library director Magnus Torén, make it quite clear that all are welcome to visit and stay for awhile.

LIBRARY VISITORS

Now that a description of the unique location and background of the HMML has been outlined, one has to ask who the library's main visitors are. The library does serve the surrounding community and 40 percent of the visitors are local residents from Big Sur and the surrounding cities of Monterey County. The other 60 percent of the users are divided evenly between California residents and foreign tourists, especially from Germany, Japan, and France (HMML, 2005).

It is also interesting to note that many visitors to the library are there to attend events, making use of the library as a space for promotion and cultivation of art. Poetry workshops and readings, painting workshops, art exhibits, concerts, film screenings, and lecture series are held at the library. Unique, planned events at the time of this writing include the 3rd Annual Listening Room International Songwriters' Retreat in February 2007 and the 4th Annual Big Sur Writing Workshop for Fiction, Young Adult Fiction, and Narrative Nonfiction in March 2007. Participants of the songwriters' retreat will share in a "group meal" and a Listening Room Concert Series presentation at the library (HMML, 2006). In addition to the retreats, the local Buddhist center utilizes space at the library and the Big Sur Volunteer Fire Brigade holds first aid classes on the property. Weddings and memorials are also held at the library (HMML, 2005). All of these events significantly enhance the library's sense of place.

FENCE

Visitors to the HMML will first be met by a large wooden fence that surrounds the grounds of the library. The fence does not clash with the natural environment, but manages to diminish the barrier effect while still creating the feeling of crossing a threshold. A hole carved into the fence allows visitors to peer into the grounds even when the library is closed. During a visit to the library in June 2006, signs hanging on the fence announced short film screenings on Thursday evenings and open mic on Wednesday evenings.

When entering the large door built into the fence, one experiences the liminality of crossing into a space that is connected, yet, different on either side. The fact that the fence is tall, measuring approximately six feet, also creates the feeling of being in a special place that is easily accessed, yet closed off from the outside. It is most fitting that the entrance to the library creates these dualities, since the landscape of Big Sur revels in such opposites.

WALKWAY AND LAWN

Once inside the fence, visitors will notice a meadow that is surrounded by large redwood trees. A walkway leads from the fence to the porch entrance to the library. The walkway curves closely to the left side of the property. To the right of the trail is a green lawn that includes an outdoor stage for events. Torén explained that the library recently held a successful outdoor film festival in the lawn area that drew approximately 70 people (personal correspondence, June 30, 2006).

The entrance to the Henry Miller Memorial Library along Highway 1 features a rustic fence with announcements of upcoming events.

Curious items line the walkway, which add to the experience of being in a place devoted to artistic personality. An old white sofa is likely the first item a visitor will see. The sofa is not typical outdoor furniture, which provides a humorous effect. It is not clear if the sofa is on display, as a museum object may be, or if it is intended as a place for visitors to rest. The wear-and-tear of the natural elements on the fabric of the sofa, however, put into question if anyone would actually take a seat.

In addition to the sofa, to the right of the walkway stands a large cross, measuring approximately ten feet, that is structured out of old computer monitors. This cross greatly clashes with the natural landscape. A curious visitor who knows nothing about Miller or the library will immediately be able to tell that he has entered a place that is quite unique and difficult to pin down. The cross and sofa serve a similar function that display cases and art galleries located close to library entrances provide. Utilizing space in this way illustrates the expansive possibilities of library space.

Porch

The porch that leads into the building appears more like an entrance to a home than a library. During a recent visit on a Saturday morning, a man sat on the porch with his acoustic guitar and entertained the visitors with an assortment of songs. Conversation amongst visitors on the porch was interspersed with the music and could be heard from the interior of the library.

A table set up on the porch had free coffee for guests. An unusual assortment of cups was available that appeared to come from various private kitchens. Two vases of live flowers were also arranged on the table. This display added to the homelike feel of the library by extending an unspoken invitation to sit and relax.

Interior Space

Once entering the interior of the library, it becomes quite clear how small the structure is. The library that the public sees is just one room with a small wood-burning stove. Tables and shelves with books, sometimes arranged in piles, line the walls of the library. The books are both new and used. The collection is equally purposeful and eclectic. In addition to the large number of Miller titles, I noted quite a few titles on various musicians, including Neil Young, Jim Morrison, Bob Marley, and Tom Waits. I also found many titles of an esoteric religious nature, such as the writings of the famous Trappist monk, Thomas Merton.

The walls of the library are lined with an unusual assortment of materials. Some of the artwork on display is specific to the Big Sur region, but Miller's work may also be found. One example is his 1970 watercolor titled *The Lovers*. A sign near this painting mentions that prints of Miller's art are available for purchase.

A small wood display case off to one side of the room includes some of Miller's books with inscriptions. Although these items remain behind glass, other materials hang on the walls with no protection from the elements. Envelopes and postcards mailed to Miller's Big Sur residence are attached to some walls just above the book arrangements, making them easily accessible to the visitors.

Along another wall where a clerk sits is a computer terminal that is available for free for visitors to browse the Internet or check e-mail. Literature on the library states that before the "development of this community resource, residents without computers and access to Internet had to travel to the Monterey-Carmel area for service" (HMML, 2005). Computer users can take in the view of the surrounding forest through a window directly in front of the monitor.

Deck

In addition to the porch, the library offers a deck along the backside of the building. Found here is a sofa and several cushioned chairs. One can sit and hear the creek running behind the library, while reading or relaxing in the outdoors. According to Torén, there is a goal to add an Internet station to the deck.

Archives

A small structure located next to the main library houses the archival collections in a climate-controlled environment. The collection includes materials related to Henry Miller and Emil White, as well as materials on the history, both cultural and natural, of Big Sur. In 1999, a significant acquisition was finalized when the library bought the Miller/Schnellock Archive. This collection contains letters spanning 40 years between Miller and his boyhood friend Emil Schnellock, as well as original manuscripts, postcards, and other items. The library is also in possession of the William Ashley Collection, which is considered the most complete collection of Miller's published works (M. Torén, personal correspondence, December 18, 2006).

A project is underway to catalog, preserve, and digitize the collections. After finalization of the project, the library will have a complete catalog of its holdings. In addition, future "interesting exhibits" are promised with use of the archival material (HMML, n.d.a). This will only add to the unique utilization of space within the small library and likely increase the number of Miller researchers and scholars to this oasis in the wilderness.

References

"Hearing Is Granted to 'Tropic' Seller." *New York Times*, April 30, 1963.
Henry Miller Memorial Library (HMML). "About the Henry Miller Library." 2005. www.henrymiller.org/library.html (retrieved June 17, 2005).
_____. "Songwriters' Retreat." 2006. www.henrymiller.org/SWW1.html (retrieved December 22, 2006).
_____. Letter, n.d.a. (Available at the Henry Miller Memorial Library.)
_____. Pamphlet, n.d.b. (Available at the Henry Miller Memorial Library.)
Henson, P., and D. J. Usner. *The Natural History of Big Sur*. Berkeley: University of California, 1993.
Jeffers, R. "Meditation on Saviors." In *Stones of the Sur*, by ed. J. Karman. Stanford: Stanford University Press, 2001.
Kerouac, J. "From Big Sur." In *The Portable Jack Kerouac*, by ed. A. Charters, New York: Viking, 1995.
Miller, H. *Big Sur and the Oranges of Hieronymus Bosch*. New York: New Directions, 1957.
"'Tropic of Cancer' Upheld in Jersey." *New York Times*, October 18, 1961.
U.S. Census Bureau. "Fact Sheet: Zip Code Tabulation Area 93920 Census 2000 Demographic Profile Highlights." 2000. http://factfinder.census.gov (retrieved June 30, 2005).

26

Harrison Memorial Library and Park Branch Library

LIBRARY DATA

Addresses: Harrison Memorial: Ocean Avenue and Lincoln Street, Carmel, CA 93921
Park Branch: Mission Street and Sixth Avenue, Carmel, CA 93921
Phone: (831) 624-7323 (Harrison Memorial)
(831) 624-4664 (Park Branch)
Web site: www.hm-lib.org
Square Feet: 7,266 (Harrison Memorial)
6, 214 (Park Branch)
Circulation: 104,077 (2004/2005)
Collection: 81,638 books; 2,712 audio; 1,892 video; 131 periodicals

Sources for above: D. Sallee, personal correspondence, July 5, 2006, and *California Library Statistics 2006* (California State Library, Library Development Services Bureau)

Harrison Memorial Library and the library's Park Branch are both located a short walk from the Pacific Ocean in a setting with streets and walkways that often resembles a fairy-tale world. A highly illustrated volume titled *Cottages by the Sea: The Handmade Homes of Carmel, America's First Artist Community* (Paul, 2000) is a work that captures the essence of the town through images of the many unique and strikingly beautiful homes that line its quiet streets. Paul cleverly states, "Carmel is one answer to the ancient quarrel between the poets and the philosophers about human life and how to live it" (p. 10). Reflecting on the present-day citizens, Paul reports, "Carmel is home to poets, painters, thinkers, musicians, dancers, and writers. It is home to those who share a creative and simple spirit" (p. 195). This "spirit" is one that is grounded in tradition.

Poet Robinson Jeffers (1887–1962) is often the first literary figure who comes to mind when one thinks of Carmel. In *Themes in My Poems* (1956), Jeffers credits the Monterey Coast with being the "simplest and commonest theme" in his poetry. He continues, "I should say that this rocky coast is not only the scene of my narrative verse, but also the chief actor in it" (p. 35).

Jeffers moved to Carmel with his wife and built his famous residence Tor House, a landmark that remains open today for hourly Friday and Saturday tours.

Although he may be the most celebrated of the writers and artists who found both home and inspiration in the town, he is just one of a rather substantial, eclectic bunch. Walker's (1973) *The Seacoast of Bohemia* traces the early years of the group. In his chapter titled "Arrival in Eden," Walker discusses the "three pioneers" of the artist community, including the poet George Sterling, the photographer Arnold Genthe, and, who he considers the "true bellwether of the flock" and "central character," the novelist Mary Austin (p. 13). According to Walker, the town was a "great discovery" for the bohemians. Within such a creative and artistic beachside community, Carmel's library was founded. Gilliam and Gilliam (1992) state, "The town's literary origins are symbolized in the handsome Harrison Memorial Library" (p. 188).

Library History

Library service in Carmel was established in 1906 with the Carmel Free Library Association. The library lent books from a small redwood building (Harrison Memorial Library, n.d.). It is interesting to note that Ida Johnson, who was president of the library board in 1906, reflected the artist community of the time. Johnson supported herself by hand painting China, but she was also a water colorist who created over 100 paintings of California native plants (Harrison Memorial Library, n.d.).

The original library association had 70 members in 1907. Although the number may sound small, it was nearly the entire population of Carmel at the time. The library was open daily for just two hours in the afternoon and had a volunteer staff the first two years (Hess, n.d.).

In 1918, Carmel resident Mrs. Ralph Chandler Harrison presented the possibility of donating land for a new library to the Trustees of the City of Carmel. A few years later in 1921, an anonymous gift provided the funds to secure a lot for the library. A lot at the corner of Lincoln and Sixth was purchased and the library moved to this new location (Hess, n.d.). The following year, Harrison, who had previously appeared before the trustees with a land donation opportunity, passed away. According to Hess, her will left money and land to be used for construction of a new library. In addition, the library was to be named after Ralph Chandler Harrison, her late husband. On March 31, 1928, the Harrison Memorial Library was dedicated. Carmel's population at the time was approximately 2,000. The library had 1,400 card holders (Hess, n.d.).

The library was designed by noted architect Bernard Maybeck, who created many wondrous buildings, including the Palace of Fine Arts in San Francisco. M. J. Murphy built the library under Maybeck's direction. Harrison Memorial Library (n.d.) reports that Maybeck's design is a reflection of California Mission style with an exterior in the style of Spanish Colonial Revival. The building features stuccoed exterior walls, low-pitched red tile roofs, and Carmel stone columns. A plaque titled "The Maybeck Plaque" designed in the "ornate style often employed" by the architect hangs in the library's lobby (Carmel Public Library Foundation, 2002). The plaque, created by Gretchen Flesher and stencil artist Stephanie Crabb, includes a quote by Maybeck: "Here you can reach all that is within you." Names of donors who contribute $10,000 to the Carmel Public Library Foundation Endowment Fund are on the plaque. It includes names of individuals, families, and businesses.

The Park Branch Library opened in February 1989 in a building that previously housed a bank. The Henry Meade Williams Local History Department, located within the Park Branch, was dedicated on 1991. The Harrison Memorial and Park Branch libraries are just a five minute walk from each other. During a visit to both buildings, it was quite apparent that these structures create one library for the community, even if they are separated physically. This is perhaps best demonstrated by the fact that Harrison Memorial does not include a children's library, but Park Branch does. Therefore, it is quite probable that families with children use both locations.

Located in a city with a history tied so directly with art and literature, it is no surprise that the library has received considerable support and use from its community. The nonprofit Carmel Public Library Foundation, comprised of a group of citizens, provides all the funding for the library's books and audiovisual materials. This is quite different from the government funding typically received by many public libraries. In addition, the group funds special programs, maintenance of the online catalog, and Internet workstations (Harrison Memorial Library, n.d.).

The spaces of both buildings are clearly appreciated by those who maintain them. This is evident by the handsome brochures, created by the Carmel Public Library Foundation, that are on display and freely available at the library. The content of each brochure is devoted to one of the library's rooms. These documents tell the history of the individuals the spaces are named after, while also providing sketches of the interiors.

Garden (Harrison Memorial)

Visitors to the library will first encounter the library garden, a space of sidewalks, alternating shade and sun, and places for sitting. A pamphlet in the library by the Carmel-by-the-Sea Garden Club indicates a current fund drive soliciting donations to "re-create" the garden with new walkways, benches, and plants. This effort further demonstrates the ongoing community involvement between the city's residents and the library.

BARNET J. SEGAL READING ROOM (HARRISON MEMORIAL)

It is purported that Maybeck designed the library to be more like a club than a library (Harrison Memorial Library, n.d.a). This is best demonstrated with a visit to the Barnet J. Segal Reading Room, named after the former Carmel resident who organized the Bank of Carmel and founded the Carmel Art Association, for which he coordinated the purchase of a studio to be the association's permanent home (Carmel Public Library Foundation (n.d.a).

Steps to the right of the entrance lead down to the reading room. The room is glamorous, yet welcoming. Bookcases in the space are built into the wall. A large window provides a view out into the garden. Seating for 18 is available around three tables. There are also cushioned chairs and a table situated in front of a fireplace.

JAMES L. AND PRIMROSE BILLWILLER REFERENCE ROOM (HARRISON MEMORIAL)

James L. and Primrose Billwiller were staunch supporters of the Harrison Memorial Library. They believed the library "was both symbol and substance of the free marketplace of ideas and images" as well as "a repository of Carmel's communal identity" (Carmel Public Library Foundation, n.d.c). Both were devoted to literature. With English degrees from San Jose State University and the University of California, Berkeley, James Billwiller was dean of instruction at the City College of San Francisco where he also taught English. Prior to their marriage, Primrose Billwiller ran a bookstore in Seattle and worked as an editor. The couple retired in Carmel where their common passions and beliefs culminated into support for the library. They joined the Friends of the Library and James Billwiller later helped establish the Carmel Public Library Foundation and the Park Branch (Carmel Public Library Foundation, n.d.c).

It is no surprise, based on the couple's devotion to the library, that the reference room, where visitors go for assistance, is named in their honor. This space is located to the left of the lobby. It provides computers and two tables with chairs for reading or studying.

ROBERT CAMPBELL BALCONY (HARRISON MEMORIAL)

The balcony, one of the most unique spaces within the library, was dedicated on February 12, 2003. Robert Campbell, former Carmel resident and writer, described the Harrison Memorial Library to his friend as "the heart and soul of

Carmel" (Carmel Public Library Foundation, n.d.d). Campbell moved to Carmel in 1978 after living previously in both New Jersey and Malibu. His Carmel residence became a location for creativity and literary expression. His writing achievements were many, including a 1957 Academy Award nomination, a 1976 National Book Award nomination, a 1987 Edgar Allan Poe Award, and a 1988 PEN Award nomination ("Robert," 2002).

Beyond his literary life, Campbell was actively involved with the library, serving on the Board of Trustees for the Harrison Memorial Library. One of his lobbying efforts, keeping the library open seven days a week, was successful. According to the Carmel Public Library Foundation (n.d.d), the balcony was dedicated "in appreciation of his generous bequest to the Foundation and to honor the memory of this talented and colorful friend of Carmel and of the Harrison Memorial Library." The balcony houses many rows of book stacks. If standing at the railing of the balcony, one has a grand view that overlooks the main reading room and stretches even beyond the library into the library's garden.

The view from the Robert Campbell Balcony in Carmel's Harrison Memorial Library overlooks the Barnet J. Segal Reading Room.

Art (Harrison Memorial)

The library does not have an actual gallery, yet its walls are adorned with art created by artists who lived in Carmel, with many works by those who were members of the Carmel Art Association. The library provides a free booklet titled *The Art and Artists in the Art Collection at the Harrison Memorial Library* (2006) that visitors may refer to while walking throughout the building. The booklet also includes a bibliography of books that provide information on Carmel's artists.

The library lobby includes such works as Paul Dougherty's *Coast of California*. Dougherty moved to Carmel in 1928 and was president of the Carmel Art Association in 1940 (*The Art and Artists*, 2006). Also found here is *Point Lobos* by M. DeNeale Morgan, who moved to Carmel in 1907 and was "instrumental in founding the Carmel Art Association in 1927" (*The Art and Artists*, 2006). The reading room includes many unusual works, including the *Statue of Father Serra* by Howell Armor. Portraits of Ralph Chandler Harrison and Ella Reid Harrison by an unknown photographer and a clock owned by Ms. Harrison, along with other art works, are found in the reference room.

Children's Library (Park Branch)

The lobby of the Park Branch is an entranceway to two distinctly different spaces. To the left is the local history room; the children's room is to the right. The children's room is one of the larger, if not the largest, spaces found in either library building. It includes a substantial story-time area, numerous rows of bookshelves spread throughout the room, and different types of seating, ranging from a sofa to standard tables and chairs.

Henry Meade Williams Local History Room (Park Branch)

It is fitting to conclude this chapter with a discussion of the local history room where one can find a treasure of manuscripts, personal papers, photographs, and books documenting Carmel's distinctive history. The room is named after Henry Meade Williams, who was born in New York City in 1899 and was a resident of Carmel from 1936 until his death in 1984. His life was a celebration of the written word and the life of the mind. His wife, Mona Williams, was a novelist and poet. Williams was a member of the Friends of the Harrison Memorial Library and the group's president for a time. In 1958, his love of books led to his purchase of Carmel's Wells' Bookshop, which was located on Ocean Avenue (Carmel Public Library Foundation, n.d.b).

In addition to naming the room after Williams, the library also features the Henry Meade Williams Lecture Series. The lobby of the Park Branch includes a display case with exhibits corresponding to the lectures. In 2006, lecture topics included "The Essential Mary Austin," a talk featuring the Carmel resident and author; "Big Sur Bohemians," which included a discussion of Henry Miller, Jack London, Langston Hughes, and others; and "Etchings from the Ella Reid Harrison Collection" (Harrison Memorial Library, 2005).

The local history room is elegant and welcoming with a comfortable workspace for many researchers. The main space includes cushioned window seating along with the customary table seating. A bookcase lines the length of one wall.

As mentioned previously, the Park Branch Library is located within a former bank building. The manuscript collection is kept in what was originally the bank vault. Although this space is somewhat hidden, researchers who are permitted to enter will be surprised to find displays. One display with a theme of the history of Carmel provides information on creative and interesting residents in a collage of photographs and small biographies. The collage includes Pal, Carmel's dog, who was a much-loved former "citizen" of the town and part of Carmel's history. Pal is buried up the road from the Park Branch at the Forest Theatre. Beyond this room is the inner vault, which also houses manuscripts and an art collection. According to local history librarian Denise Sallee, the vault contains works by many local artists who have donated art to the library (personal correspondence, June 29, 2006). Once again, significant community involvement is demonstrated, which is the over-arching theme to the sense of place found at both the Harrison Memorial Library and the Park Branch Library.

REFERENCES

The Art and Artists in the Art Collection at the Harrison Memorial Library. Booklet, June 2006. (Available at the Harrison Memorial Library.)

California State Library. Library Development Services Bureau. *California Library Statistics 2006.* www.library.ca.gov/assets/acrobat/StatsPub06.pdf (retrieved December 23, 2006).

Carmel Public Library Foundation. *Barnet J. Segal Reading Room.* Pamphlet, n.d.a. (Available at the Harrison Memorial Library.)

_____. *Henry Meade Williams Local History Room.* Pamphlet, n.d.b. (Available at the Harrison Memorial Library.)

_____. *James L. and Primrose Billwiller Reference Room.* Pamphlet, n.d.c. (Available at the Harrison Memorial Library.)

_____. *Robert Campbell: The Balcony.* Pamphlet, n.d.d. (Available at the Harrison Memorial Library.)

_____. *The Maybeck Plaque.* Pamphlet, 2002. (Available at the Harrison Memorial Library.)

Gilliam, H., and A. Gilliam. *Creating Carmel: The Enduring Vision.* Salt Lake City: Peregrine Smith, 1992.

Harrison Memorial Library. "HML Lecture Series Calendar." 2005. www.hm-lib.org/pages/lh/events.html (retrieved August 13, 2006).

_____. Document on the history of the library. n.d. (Provided by the Henry Meade Williams Local History Department.)

Hess, A. "Harrison Memorial Library: An Outline of Its History." n.d. (Provided by the Henry Meade Williams Local History Department.)

Jeffers. R. Themes in My Poems. San Francisco: Book Club of California, 1956.

Paul, L. L. *Cottages by the Sea: The Handmade Homes of Carmel, America's First Artist Community.* New York: Universe, 2000.

"Robert Wright Campbell." *Contemporary Authors Online* (retrieved July 14, 2006; this online database requires subscription for access). Farmington Hills, MI: Thomson Gale, 2002.

Walker, F. *The Seacoast of Bohemia.* Santa Barbara: Peregrine Smith, 1973.

27

Pacific Grove Public Library

LIBRARY DATA

Address: 550 Central Avenue, Pacific Grove, CA 93950
Phone: (831) 648-5760
Web site: www.pacificgrove.lib.ca.us
Square Feet: 12,593
Circulation: 228,763 (2004/2005)
Collection: 96,535 total items (2004/2005)

Sources for above: Pacific Grove Public Library comparative statistics (provided by Acting Library Director Ellen Gill Pastore), and *California Library Statistics 2006* (California State Library, Library Development Services Bureau)

Pacific Grove is located on the northern tip of the Monterey Peninsula. It was a Methodist tent city in 1875 and the location, in 1879, of the first chautauqua in the western United States (Hart, 1978). Each October for over 100 years, thousands of monarch butterflies have traveled to Pacific Grove "from the Northern Pacific States, British Columbia and Southern Alaska to winter in the groves of trees, only to become restless and fly away to the north in March" (Knox and Rodriguez, 1978, p. 34). This phenomenon, that sounds like an event created by a novelist of magical realism, is, no doubt, the reason so many tourists travel to the region. Visitors who happen to wander into the Pacific Grove Public Library can pick up a "Butterfly Books" reading list and soon find themselves immersed in a book with a title as wondrous as *The Moon of the Monarch Butterflies* (George, 1968) or *The Butterfly Trees* (Shepardson, 1952).

Pacific Grove is a short drive from Cannery Row, an area made famous by John Steinbeck. It is interesting to note that Steinbeck lived in a Pacific Grove cottage that was built by his father around 1900. Knox and Rodriguez (1978) report that much of Steinbeck's research for *Cannery Row*, *Tortilla Flat*, and *Sweet Thursday* was completed while he resided in the cottage.

In addition to the draw of butterflies and Steinbeck, Pacific Grove's attractions are numerous, including Point Pinos Lighthouse, Lovers' Point Park and Beach, and Asilomar State Beach, where Steinbeck's *Cannery Row* character Doc Ricketts "gathered specimens from the 'Great Tidepool'" (Knox and Rodriguez, 1978, p. 41). Davenport (1964) characterizes Pacific Grove as a town with a "persistent cultural civic mindedness" (p. 50). He follows his compliment with a list of "excellent" features. The public library is first on his list.

Library History

A Pacific Grove Public Library (n.d.a) colorful, glossy brochure titled *How to Support Your Pacific Grove Library* intermingles a drawing and photographs of the library with text calling for investments to this "community resource." Funds are requested to expand the building by 8,000 square feet, allowing for a community room, additional seating "for study and leisure reading," more shelving, and various refurbishments. This expansion would add to a growing list of earlier enlargements in 1926, 1938, 1950, and 1978 (Pacific Grove Public Library, n.d.b). Such enhancements point to the importance of the library to the community. As is often the case, the library has an almost constant need to expand its physical space to meet the demands of the community and burgeoning collections. It is this reality that appears again and again when examining the library's history.

"Pacific Grove Library: The Chautauqua Years" (2005), an unpublished document provided by librarian Jean Chapin, is perhaps the most thorough, recorded history of the library. According to Chapin, library service in Pacific Grove began in 1886 with a reading corner in the Old Parlor, a building that served as the community hall from the early 1880s until 1910. This small space consisted of chairs and less than 100 titles arranged on corner shelves. Those who paid $1.00 per year could use the library during its hours of just 2 P.M. to 4 P.M. on Saturdays.

According to Chapin, the library remained at the Old Parlor for only two years. In 1888, the collection moved to a shared space with the museum in an octagon-shaped building. Hours were expanded. Shortly, however, in 1901, it was determined that the room provided for the collection was too small and a larger facility was sought. An initial appeal for funding was presented to Andrew Carnegie at this time by the Ladies Library Association. Chapin reports there were no results from the appeal. The issue of space, of course, remained. A new location was found at a building on Grand Avenue. The collection of less than 100 books had grown to roughly 500 by this time.

A significant change came to the organization of the library in late 1905 when the Pacific Grove Free Public Library and Board of Trustees was established. The library opened at its Grand Avenue location in 1906, which was the same year that a second appeal for funds was requested of Carnegie. This time, a promise of $10,000 for a new building was received. The Carnegie building was designed in the mission style with characteristic arches by the McDougall Brothers. Chapin states that at least 2,000 people attended the laying of the cornerstone. Nearly all town businesses were closed to allow everyone to attend. The building opened the evening of May 12, 1908. It consisted of three large rooms.

Slightly a decade after opening, the collection was at 10,000 volumes. The first expansion to the building, a new children's wing, was completed in 1926–1927. In 1938, a west wing housing a new reading room was added. Another expansion occurred in 1950 when two new wings were added. The largest expansion occurred when the building nearly doubled its size in 1978. This latest expansion also brought the library its steep gable roof (Carnegie Libraries, 1999).

ENTRANCE AND INTERIOR SPACES

The entrance to the library, located just a few blocks from the ocean, has a large garden area in front. A covered, arched walkway leads to the front door. The various expansions have been executed well, making the library still feel as if it is one, grand room, yet the areas in the front are actually the newer additions. If one continues to walk straight to the back of the building, interior arches will mark that one is entering the older Carnegie building.

Immediately to the right of the entrance is the circulation desk. The audio visual area is to the left in a space that provides seating at four tables. Down the center aisle, directly in the path of the entrance, are displays of paperbacks. Stacks are also to the right and left as one begins to walk further into the interior of the large room. Young adult and large type books are clearly marked to the right. Art books are located behind glass on shelves along one wall near the entrance to the older building.

Two areas are devoted to community postings and literature. Near the circulation desk is a special events bulletin with several posts. Some of the information gathered on the bulletin board is related specifically to the library, such as an upcoming benefit that includes chocolate and wine tasting. Along the wall just prior to entering the children's room is a large shelf offering an abundant, eclectic mixture of community publications and additional postings. Here one can pick up a free Pacific Grove Directory or find notices to attend meetings of the Pacific Grove monthly book club (P.G. Reads!), the Monterey Peninsula Quilters Guild, or the Robert Louis Stevenson Club of Monterey.

As mentioned before, a straight path from the front door to the other end of the building leads to the interior of the original building. A sign reading "This is a quiet study area" is posted near the entrance. Three archways lead to a periodicals section. Following the periodical shelving area are several chairs positioned along windows that overlook the street below. Plants are intermingled with the chairs.

Also found in the original building is the reference desk and reference materials. A summer reading display was positioned in between the stacks of the reference area and another space full of book stacks during my visit in late June 2006. A most interesting addition to the space near the reference desk, that is both functional and decorative, is a coat rack. The coat rack is an example of an addition that is quite simple, but one that dramatically changes the atmosphere to

The Pacific Grove Public Library includes archways that lead to the periodicals and a reading space with windows that overlook the street.

that of a welcoming space. The message is clear that visitors may feel comfortable and not rushed.

CHILDREN'S ROOM

The children's room is to the right of the entrance after passing the circulation desk. The room is set off from the rest of the library, providing a separate, special space. It is decorated by a colorful mural by artist Harold Landaker, which spans 40 feet long by six feet wide (Chapin, 2005). Landaker originally donated the mural in 1950 for the expansion of the new children's room. During an additional expansion of the children's wing in 1978, the mural was removed from its old location, restored, and mounted in the expanded room (Chapin, 2005). Also found in the room are an aquarium and large display of dolls from several countries, including Japan, Guatemala, and Mexico.

A calendar of events for June 2006 illustrates the many activities that take place in this room, including stuffed animal pet shows, the expected story times and puppet shows, as well as themed events, such as "Oink! Stories about Pigs." This room reflects the overall experience of being in the Pacific Grove Public Library, a library with a noble history of devotion to the community it serves. Perhaps it is a common history, shared by many libraries, but each library's story, as the one found here, is unique.

REFERENCES

California State Library. Library Development Services Bureau. *California Library Statistics 2006.* www.library.ca.gov/assets/acrobat/StatsPub06.pdf (retrieved December 23, 2006).

Carnegie Libraries of California. "Pacific Grove, Monterey County." 1999. www.carnegie-libraries.org/california/regions/centralcoast/pacificgrove.html (retrieved December 4, 2005).

Chapin, J. "Pacific Grove Library: The Chautauqua Years. History of the Pacific Grove Public Library Presented at the Pacific Grove Museum of Natural History." September 27, 2005. (Unpublished document provided by Pacific Grove Public Library.)

Davenport, W. *The Monterey Peninsula.* Menlo Park, CA: Lane Books, 1964.

Hart, J. D. *A Companion to California.* New York: Oxford University Press, 1978.

Knox, M., and M. Rodriguez. *Making the Most of the Monterey Peninsula and Big Sur.* San Rafael, CA: Presidio Press, 1978.

Pacific Grove Public Library. *How to Support Your Pacific Grove Library.* Brochure, n.d.a. (Available at the Pacific Grove Public Library.)

_____. *Serving the Community for 100 Years.* Brochure, n.d.b. (Available at the Pacific Grove Public Library.)

Part VII
San Francisco Bay Area

28

Charles Franklin Doe Memorial Library and Gardner Stacks, University of California, Berkeley

Library Data

Address: University of California, Berkeley, CA 94720
Phone: (510) 642-3773
Web site: www.lib.berkeley.edu/doemoff
Square Feet: 90,779 (Doe Library); 132,583 (Gardner Stacks)
Circulation: 751,934 (Gardner Stacks, June 2005–June 2006)
Collection: 2.1 million onsite; 2.8 million off-site at the UC Northern Regional Library Facility (June 2006)
Source for above: I. Abalos, personal correspondence, July 25, 2006

In her novel *Tripmaster Monkey*, noted author Maxine Hong Kingston (1997) describes Berkeley as a city with air "so filled with poems" (p. 217). Ishmael Reed (1997) characterizes Berkeley mysteriously as "the city of unfinished attics and stairs leading to strange towers" (p. 174). Each neighborhood, every street, and nearly all corners have stories to tell. The challenge to writing about Berkeley as a city or Berkeley as a university is not in finding items to include, but in eliminating the abundance of available information. Ultimately, Berkeley is not a place to read about, but a place to experience, which makes writing about it most difficult. Considering the magnitude of Berkeley's personality, it is appropriate that it would have one of the world's major research libraries. Before touring the library, however, it is important to understand the flavor of the surrounding community and campus.

Berkeley

Telegraph Avenue is the main street leading from the entrance of the University of California campus to neighboring Oakland. The avenue and surrounding streets are lined with cafes, restaurants of nearly any ethnic cuisine imaginable, and numerous bookstores. From the four floors of used and new books at Moe's to the blissful bianca mocha served at Caffe Strada, Berkeley is an international city that nourishes the senses and the intellect.

Many who arrive at Berkeley come to study. Traveling to the city is often recorded as a pilgrimage, as if one has a calling that must be satisfied. For some, it is a place to begin anew. Margot Adler (2002), writing on her journey, states, "Living in New York City, I looked upon Berkeley as so many Americans have looked throughout history upon the West — as an escape from everything that defined my past" (p. 111). She continues, "I was determined to enter this mythological realm and to claim it as my own."

Jo Freeman's (2004) memoir *At Berkeley in the Sixties: The Education of an Activist: 1961–1965* also begins with a journey. She titles her first chapter "The Train to Berkeley." Freeman's journey from the San Fernando Valley in Los Angeles is much shorter in distance than Adler's coast-to-coast trip, yet, she states, "almost everything was an adventure because I had never done it before" (p. 3). Freeman describes the area where student political groups would arrange their tables to pass out literature as "1,000 square feet of political space which nourished the student marketplace of ideas" (p. 11). Freeman and Adler's stories are part of a significant collection of countless descriptions and memories of the campus and surrounding city that have culminated into the drama that is Berkeley.

Berkeley: A Literary Tribute (La France, 1997) is an anthology that captures many writers' experiences. Not all of the writers speak highly of Berkeley, which is also part of its larger story. Although many become lovers of the city, others experience disillusionment and some may even feel disenfranchised by the political environment. Debate, however, is always welcome.

In "Berkeley in the Thirties," Galbraith (1997) writes, "At Berkeley I suddenly encountered professors who knew their subject and, paradoxically, invited debate on what they knew" (p. 46). Hinting at the politicization of the area that was to only grow into a furor in later decades, Galbraith reports, "The graduate students with whom I associated in the thirties were uniformly radical and the most distinguished were Communists" (p. 49). Simone de Beauvoir (1997), however, experiences something quite different in the "austere dining room" of the Berkeley Faculty Club where "serious old gentlemen" gather. For de Beauvoir, "The universities," which clearly includes Berkeley, "only confirm these young people in their apathy and conformity" (p. 72–73). Beat Generation writer Jack Kerouac (1958) provides yet another portrait by writing of his Berkeley cottage in *The Dharma Bums*:

> The yard was full of tomato plants about to ripen, and mint, mint, everything smelling of mint, and one fine old tree that I loved to sit under and meditate on those cool perfect starry California nights unmatched anywhere in the world [p. 16].

Berkeley has also been the site where many poets have honed their craft, including Jack Spicer and Allen Ginsberg. Several famous poems in Ginsberg's (1991) collection *Howl and Other Poems* were penned in Berkeley between 1955 and 1956, including *Footnote to Howl, A Supermarket in California,* and *America.*

Perhaps the best way to understand Berkeley is to realize that one cannot really define it. The answer hides in the paradoxes. The final lines of Janice Gould's (1997) poem captures this beautifully chaotic truth: "Every day / the structure of our Berkeley life / promises to give way" (p. 230).

UNIVERSITY OF CALIFORNIA AND DOE LIBRARY

Sibley (1928) writes:

> There has always been about California and her history something that has stirred the imagination of men. But in all of her story no chapter has been more filled with romance than that which deals with the founding of ... the University of California [p. 11].

The Berkeley campus of the University of California, the flagship campus, was established in 1868. Walking around the campus grounds, one will notice some symmetry, particularly with several of the older, core buildings, yet, taken as a whole, it is an eclectic mixture of time periods and architectural designs. Freeman (2004) experiences the campus as not giving "the appearance of having been planned but of expanding in response to need, like a medieval town" (p. 7). The hilly nature of the grounds is not lost on Freeman: "There are many ravines and few plains. One is always walking up or down, entering the large buildings at different levels" (p. 6–7). This somewhat haphazard characterization of the campus is accurate to a certain degree, and mirrors the overall nature of the city's poetic, yet chaotic, climate. A feeling of evenness, however, may be experienced when standing near the center, or heart, of the campus at the main library. One admirer of the library has enthusiastically proclaimed this "center of University thought and life" will "doubtless out last the pyramids" (Sibley, 1928, p. 60).

Architect John Galen Howard's vision is behind many of the campus buildings, including Doe Library. Before his involvement with UC Berkeley, where he was the supervising architect from December 1901 to 1924 and professor of architecture and head of the newly founded architecture department in 1903, Howard was educated at the Massachusetts Institute of Technology and the Ecole des Beaux–Arts in Paris (Partridge, 1978). Partridge reports, "One of the greatest strengths of the Ecole des Beaux–Arts had always been large-scale ensemble planning, since its main *raison d'etre* was the training of architects to carry out monumental projects for the French state" (p. 3). Howard brought his lasting influence to the campus with the creation of individual campus buildings in various modes: Greco-Roman, Italian Renaissance, and French Baroque. "Like all Beaux-Arts architects, Howard believed that 'architectural detail and composition of each individual building must indicate its special character'" (Partridge, p. 26). The Boston Public Library was Howard's principal model for the Doe Library, but ideas were also drawn from other American and French Beaux-Arts libraries (Partridge, 1978).

Doe Library is considered "the Greco-Roman centerpiece of Howard's classical ensemble. Sited on an elevated bluff and projecting slightly into the great central axis, the 225-foot wing assumes a position of prominence, the Parthenon on the Acropolis of the Athens of the West" (Helfand, 2002, p. 55–56). Placing the library near the center of campus was desired from the beginning. In 1903, Howard wrote the library should be "almost equally accessible from each and every department" (quoted in Woodbridge, 2002, p. 98).

The library is named for Charles Franklin Doe, "who left a quarter of his estate to the University for a library in 1904 (*A Visitor's Guide*, n.d.). Construction of the library began with a first phase from 1907 to 1911. The completion of the first phase was dedicated in March 1912. The final construction phase ran from 1914 to 1917 (Woodbridge, 2002). Restorations, interior alterations, and seismic improvements have taken place over the years. In 1992–1994 the new, underground Gardner Stacks were constructed (Helfand, 2002). Doe Library is a City of Berkeley Landmark and a California Historical Landmark, listed in the California Register of Historical Resources. It is also listed on the National Register of Historic Places (Helfand, 2002). The exterior presents a wondrous and majestic building composed of "Sierra granite and roofed with red Mission-style terra cotta tiles" (*A Visitor's Guide*, n.d.). The words "The University Library" are inscribed in a stone plaque above the entrance. According to Woodbridge (2002), the plaque, which weighs about 14 tons, was reportedly "the largest stone mounted on a Western building" at the time (p. 100). The awe-inspiring nature of the exterior is profound and enough to leave its mark on one's memory, but the interior spaces is where the sense of place truly lives. Several, but not all, of the unique spaces are discussed below.

NORTH READING ROOM

The North Reading Room, designed for 400 readers (Helfand, 2002), is the most dynamic space in the library. Many graduates of the campus consider the room "one of their favorite campus locations" (*A Visitor's Guide*, n.d.). It carries within its walls all the tradition and magnificence that one may expect from a large reading room in a major research library. Conversations rarely rise above the level of whispers. Even when the room is full of visitors and students, it remains a quiet space. Partridge (1978) writes, "Majestic scale, unity, dynamic tension between transverse and longitudinal axes, integration with the exterior articulation, and functional logic made the reading room the greatest architectural space on the Berkeley campus and one of the greatest of the Beaux-Arts period" (p. 27).

Bronze doors provide the central entrance to the room. Above this entrance is a clock and a biblical inscription from Proverbs. The translation of the inscription reads: "Wisdom has built herself a house; come and eat my bread, drink the wine I have prepared" (*A Visitor's Guide*, n.d.). Upon entry, one may immediately look up and gaze at the crowning splendor of the 210-foot-long room: "the soaring, bronze gilt and white coffered ceiling" which "evokes both grandeur and welcome" (*A Visitor's Guide*, n.d.). The ceiling, with three skylights, rises 45 feet above rows of evenly planted oak tables with matching chairs. Large windows along one wall and at both ends of the room provide soft, natural lighting. Trees may be seen through the large, arched window at one end.

The North Reading Room was reportedly the second largest reading room in an American library at the time of its construction. Only the New York Public Library reading room was larger (*A Visitor's Guide*, n.d.). All who walk down its middle aisle, hearing their shoes click on the tiles, or curl their legs up in one of the generous oak chairs may feel like a scholar here.

Roger W. Heyns Reading Room

A few steps from the North Reading Room is the striking Roger W. Heyns Reading Room, which was modeled "after an Italian Renaissance palace" (*A Visitor's Guide*, n.d.). The two-story room features "a carved polychromatic plaster ceiling, twelve chandeliers, and a surrounding frieze decorated with marks of historic publishers and the names of fifteen notable writers and thinkers" (Helfand, 2002, p. 60). A large 1854 painting by Emanuel Gottlieb Leutze titled *Washington Rallying the Troops at Monmouth* hangs on an end wall. The room provides tables and chairs for studying. In addition, during my visit in July 2006, several cushioned chairs were situated on a rug in front of a browsing periodicals section that offered such popular titles as *Ms.* magazine, *Time*, and the *Progressive*. With all its grandeur, the room remains a space where one can comfortably relax and browse.

Gardner Stacks

Quite unusual at Berkeley are the Gardner Stacks, which were designed by Esherick Homsey Dodge and Davis and completed in 1994. The Gardner Stacks consist of a significant, underground space of three levels of stacks with an astonishing 52 miles of shelving. The construction of this underground "city" was a result of a seismic safety study (Helfand, 2002). The Gardner Stacks replace the mysterious and rickety stacks that earlier generations of students used. The stacks connect Doe Library to the Moffitt Undergraduate Library. This underground space extends beneath part of Memorial Glade, a large, green clearing in front of the main entrance to Doe Library that students often use for sleeping, studying, and playing Frisbee.

The magnificent North Reading Room of the Doe Library at the University of California, Berkeley is a grand space that many graduates remember as one of their favorites.

The underground floors, each spanning a length longer than a football field, provide many study spaces for students. Traditional study carrels, tables, cushioned seating, and group study rooms are all on hand. Wireless access is available throughout and the library provides 450 Ethernet hubs for laptop use ("Resources: Libraries," 2006).

Although the main business of this subterranean area is to store the large book collection, it is also a place where art may be found. In 2005, artist J. Ignacio Diaz de Rabago installed *Babel Library IX* in the staircase atrium (Maclay, 2005). This ethereal creation is composed of hundreds of books that are interspersed on cables and give the illusion of floating books. The books included in the installation were unsalvageable volumes that had been withdrawn from the library (Maclay, 2005). The installation adds a dreamlike quality to the otherwise utilitarian space.

BERNICE LAYNE BROWN GALLERY & HISTORY GALLERY

Galleries in Doe Library provide other areas for informative and stimulating exhibits. The Bernice Layne Brown Gallery is an elegant corridor composed of white marble floor and wall panels that is located just off from the main entrance. According to Helfand (2002), the space "was influenced by a similar passage in the Palazzo Farnese in Rome" (p. 58). The gallery provides a display area for diverse exhibits of materials from the university's many libraries. "Past exhibits have featured such topics as the environmental movement, children's books, Chinese stone rubbings, and departments such as anthropology, Asian studies, music, physics, and others" (*A Visitor's Guide*, n.d.).

A small walk from the Brown Gallery is the History Gallery where visitors may discover the history of Berkeley's libraries through a permanent exhibit. Doe Library and other subject specialty libraries are represented. Library staff and changes to the library catalog are just two of the topics included in the exhibit. An architectural model in the center of the room shows Doe Library and other campus buildings. Quotes are painted directly on the gallery walls. One of former Berkeley president Benjamin Ide Wheeler's statements on the library appears on a gallery panel: "Give me a library, and I'll build a university about it." Having a permanent exhibit devoted to the library itself is a clever and creative method for introducing students and visitors to this "heart" of the campus.

REFERENCES

Adler, M. "My Life in the FSM: Memories of a Freshman." In *The Free Speech Movement: Reflections on Berkeley in the 1960s*, ed. R. Cohen and R. E. Zelnik, 111–28. Berkeley: University of California Press, 2002.
De Beauvoir, S. "Berkeley." In *Berkeley: A Literary Tribute*, ed. D. La France, 72–73. Berkeley: Heyday Books, 1997.
La France, D. ed. *Berkeley: A Literary Tribute*. Berkeley: Heyday Books, 1997.
Freeman, J. *At Berkeley in the Sixties: The Education of an Activist, 1961–1965*. Bloomington, ID: Indiana University Press, 2004.
Galbraith, J. K. "Berkeley in the Thirties." In *Berkeley: A Literary Tribute*, ed. D. La France, 44–55. Berkeley: Heyday Books, 1997.
Ginsberg, A. *Howl and Other Poems*. San Francisco: City Lights Books, 1991.
Gould, J. "A Berkeley Life." In *Berkeley: A Literary Tribute*, ed. D. La France, 225–30. Berkeley: Heyday Books, 1997.
Helfand, H. *The Campus Guide: University of California, Berkeley: An Architectural Tour and Photographs*. New York: Princeton Architectural Press, 2002.
Kerouac, J. *The Dharma Bums*. New York: Signet, 1958.
Kingston, M. H. "Tripmaster Monkey." In *Berkeley: A Literary Tribute*, ed. D. La France, 214–18. Berkeley: Heyday Books, 1997.
Maclay, K. "Campus Art Installations Feature 'Flying Books,' Foam Balls." Press release, UC Berkeley, April 11, 2005. www.berkeley.edu/news/media/releases/2005/04/11_artinstallations.shtml (retrieved September 4, 2006).
Partridge, L. *John Galen Howard and the Berkeley Campus: Beaux-Arts Architecture in the "Athens of the West."* Berkeley: Berkeley Architectural Heritage Association, 1978.
Reed, I. "The Last Days of Louisiana Red." In *Berkeley: A Literary Tribute*, ed. D. La France, 174–77. Berkeley: Heyday Books, 1997.
"Resource: A Reference Guide for New Berkeley Students; Libraries." October 2006. http://resource.berkeley.edu/r_html/r04_06.html (retrieved September 4, 2006).

Sibley, R. ed. *The Romance of the University of California.* San Francisco: H. S. Crocker, 1928.
A Visitor's Guide to the Architecture and History of the Doe Library. Brochure, n.d. (Available at the Doe Library.)
Woodbridge, S. B. *John Galen Howard and the University of California: The Design of a Great Public University Campus.* Berkeley: University of California Press, 2002.

29

Flora Lamson Hewlett Library, Graduate Theological Union

Library Data

Address: 2400 Ridge Road, Berkeley, CA 94709
Phone: (510) 549-2500
Web site: http://library.gtu.edu
Square Feet: 39,012
Circulation: 118,531 (2004/2005)
Collection: 744,637 (2004/2005)
Source for above: L. Glenn, personal correspondence, September 26, 2006

Quite different from the activity and crowded sidewalks of Telegraph Avenue located in Berkeley's south side is the calmer and hillier Euclid Avenue of the north side. Although one will encounter fewer cars and businesses, a limited number of cafes, small restaurants, and other shops are located on the north side. Euclid Avenue may be reached on foot by cutting across the UC Berkeley campus. It is a short walk from the steps of the grand Doe Library to the tranquil sidewalks of the north. When walking around the various winding and narrow streets, one can enjoy views that stretch from the city of Berkeley to San Francisco Bay. It is an enchanted landscape that is home to an area known as "Holy Hill," due to the number of religious institutions located in the neighborhood. The Graduate Theological Union (GTU) is located here with its Flora Lamson Hewlett Library placed at the intersection of Ridge Road and the appropriately named Scenic Avenue.

Graduate Theological Union

GTU is an ecumenical institution described as "the largest partnership of seminaries and graduate schools in the country" (GTU, 2006a). Member schools include American Baptist Seminary of the West, Church Divinity School of the Pacific, Dominican School of Philosophy & Theology, Franciscan School of Theology, Jesuit School of Theology at Berkeley, Pacific Lutheran Theological Seminary, Pacific School of Religion, San Francisco Theological Seminary, and

Starr King School for the Ministry (GTU, 2006a). Certain member schools date back considerably. The American Baptist Seminary of the West, for example, was founded in 1871 and the Pacific School of Religion traces its roots to 1866. Several of the seminaries are located within a few blocks of each other in the Berkeley north side community. Helfand (2002) explains: "This grouping of small campuses includes a number of distinctive buildings—embracing a range of architectural styles from eclectic turn-of-the-century revivalism to modernism—that characterize the neighborhood" (p. 128). The origins of this impressive union can be traced back to 1958.

In 1958, an ad hoc committee comprised of four of the theological institutions listed above was assembled to investigate a cooperative graduate program (GTU, 1982). These early negotiations ultimately culminated in the incorporation of the GTU in 1962. At the time of its founding, the union included four Protestant seminaries. Within two years, Roman Catholic participation was added. When the union celebrated its 20th anniversary in 1982, two Protestant and three Roman Catholic seminaries had joined the four original schools (GTU, 1982). The union continues to thrive today, offering master's and doctoral degrees. GTU has several academic centers and affiliates that broaden its ecumenical and interdisciplinary reach, including the Center for the Study of Religion and Culture; the Richard S. Dinner Center for Jewish Studies; the Center for the Arts, Religion, and Education; the Center for Theology and the Natural Sciences; the Institute of Buddhist Studies; and others. The unique research of the students at GTU is supported by the Flora Lamson Hewlett Library, an institution with a history as interesting as the union.

LIBRARY HISTORY

Glenn (2002) explains that even before the GTU existed, seminaries in the state and Bay Area were participating in "cooperative library programs." After the establishment of the union in 1962, a committee was appointed to determine library needs for the seminaries. The GTU Bibliographical Center was created in 1964 after one of the alternate plans provided by the committee. Glenn (2002) states the center was not a library, but a facility that performed various functions, such as creating a union catalog and assembling a reference collection.

In 1969, the Common Library was established with seven of the member schools initially signing the agreement (Glenn, 2002). "In the following school year, the library of the Church Divinity School of the Pacific became the Common Library's temporary quarters, which served as the center for reference services, book selection, and integration of the library collections of the member schools" (GTU, 1982). Glenn (2002) states these "temporary quarters" were actually in the basement. Although the Common Library was now in existence, plans for the library were not final.

A site for a new library building at Ridge Road and Scenic Avenue was secured not much later. During the initial planning stages, the library was conceived as becoming "both the central learning and teaching facility of the GTU" (McTaggart, 1974). "The new building was envisioned not simply as a place to house books. It would also be, in the words of Dean Welch, 'a teaching instrument that will be the major physical symbol of the common effort that the GTU represents'" (GTU, 1982, p. 13–14). Philadelphia architect Louis I. Kahn was appointed in 1972 to design the structure. Some of his earlier buildings included the Phillips Exeter Library in Andover, Massachusetts, the Yale University Art Gallery, and the Kimball Museum of Art in Fort Worth, Texas (McTaggart, 1974). Glenn (2002) provides a description of Kahn that demonstrates his architectural philosophy and appropriateness for the task: "He saw a building as an environment of space and light, and as the personification of the nature and purpose of its use. He was very interested in expressing the inspiration to learn and to question in institutions of learning and of religion."

Although Kahn completed preliminary designs for the new library, he died in 1974 before construction began. San Francisco architects Peters, Clayberg, and Caulfield completed the building in association with Esherick, Homsey, Dodge, and Davis (Helfand, 2002). The construction of the library, however, did not begin without a fight to obtain permits from the city of Berkeley. Some opponents believed the existing 80-year-old structure at the site had historic merit and should not be destroyed. Others charged the library was "an unnecessary expansion" of the union (GTU, 1982, p.14). In addition to these obstacles, funding the building became an additional complication.

To overcome the financing dilemma, a decision was made to build the library in two construction phases. Phase I was completed in 1981 and Phase II was completed in 1987 (Glenn, 2002). The name of the library was changed in May 1987 from its former Common Library title to Flora Lamson Hewlett Library, in recognition of a significant contribution from the Hewlett Foundation (Glenn, 2002). The library occupies the first and second floors of the building and one-third of the basement; the third floor is occupied by the GTU administration, including the offices of the president, dean, business, and institutional advancement (Glenn, personal correspondence, September 26, 2006). The building was one of seven libraries to receive the 1989 Award of Excellence for Library Architecture sponsored by the American Library Association and the American Institute of Architects (DeCandido and Rogers, 1989). This was the same year that the Cerritos Library, another library discussed in this book, received the award. The Hewlett Library is described as a "global village," as well as "the geographic and spiritual heart of the GTU" (GTU, 2006b).

Entrance and Exterior

Helfand (2002) offers a perfect description of the library's exterior as "crisply detailed with wood siding and geometrically patterned windows" (p. 129). The building is surrounded by a terrace that provides striking views of the surrounding UC Berkeley campus, the city of Berkeley, and San Francisco Bay. The main entrance of the library opens to the second floor. The first space visitors experience is a small carpeted foyer with purple, cushioned seating areas to either side.

Second Floor

After passing through the foyer, one is greeted by the circulation desk on the left. To the right are shelves stocked with informational materials on the library and GTU, as well as library research guides on suitable topics for students, including "Early Church History," "American Religion History," and "Medieval and Reformation History." Placing these documents at such a location makes them highly visible to students when they enter or exit the building. Also to the right of the entrance is a new books shelf that is followed by the reference collection that runs much of the length of one side of the floor.

Located in one area of the reference stacks is the archives office. The archival Bede Griffiths Collection allows researchers a view into the life of the Catholic Benedictine monk who was also greatly influenced by Hindu spirituality while living in India. The collection includes published articles, videotapes, audiotapes, and correspondence (GTU, n.d.). Another collection of the Berkeley Free Church documents "an ecumenical venture to serve the needs of the street people and hippie community of the Telegraph Avenue area" (GTU, n.d.) during the years of 1967–1973. In this collection, researchers will discover, among other things, information on the 1960s student movement and Berkeley city issues. The library is home to several other unique archival collections that reflect the ecumenical religious and spiritual nature of GTU.

Across from the reference stacks and archives office is a teaching lab presented in a way unlike instructional rooms found in other academic libraries. The instruction room is surrounded by glass walls, allowing anyone walking by to view the activity of the room. This unusual use of glass walls adds an openness to the interior of the floor, yet it also suggests an interconnectedness between library instruction and the use of materials in the physical library space. Other areas on the second floor include the current periodicals section with a rack of current newspapers at the entrance to the space and the exegesis collection for use in biblical study that is located near the back of the floor.

First Floor

The first floor is accessible from a staircase located near the entrance of the library. This floor contains the circulating books of the library. Shelving is arranged down both sides of the floor. Near the middle of the floor are several

Study carrels line a wall of windows in the Flora Lamson Hewlett Library at the Graduate Theological Union. The windows provide natural light and views of the north Berkeley "Holy Hill" neighborhood.

reading tables. Bound periodicals, two group study rooms, and oversized periodicals are also found here.

Study Spaces

Individual study carrels are arranged around much of the perimeter of the first and second floors. These spaces provide each researcher with a window that offers views of the Berkeley hills and surrounding neighborhood. The abundance of natural light enhances the experience of studying at a carrel. This use of light is in spirit with the philosophy of Kahn. According to Tyng (1984), Kahn's daughter, "Natural light, to Kahn, was the only true light. He considered the window the most significant part of the room, the part that gave character and vitality to the space" (p. 130). In addition to the individual carrels, along one wall of the first floor are locked and reserved study spaces. These spaces are used by visiting scholars who often have personal use of the space for one year (C. Woulfe, personal correspondence, July 24, 2006). Cushioned window seating for reading and contemplation is also available in some corners of the building.

Atrium Skylight

One of the most stunning aspects of the library interior that truly puts a finishing touch on the overall sense of place is a central atrium skylight that illuminates the heart of the building with natural light. On the second floor, noticeable almost immediately upon entry into the building, is a circular exhibit area that lines the circumference of the atrium. The exhibit area consists of a structure of several connected cases that are formed into a large round pattern. Framed in wood, the cases have glass tops and backs, which even allows those on the first floor to look up and see the materials on display at a distance. These cases provide for a variety of exhibits. During the summer of 2005, for example, a collection of artist Patsy Krebs' work was on display, including many watercolors. Viewers of the exhibit may walk the circumference of the atrium to peer inside each exhibit case. Those enjoying the exhibit may also look up to the skylight or look down to the activity of the first floor. While standing at the atrium, the unity of the building and the overarching symmetry of its various unique spaces are fully realized.

References

DeCandido, G. A., and M. Rogers. "Seven Libraries Win 1989 ALA/AIA Architectural Awards." *Library Journal* 114, no. 11 (1989): 14.

Glenn, L. "The Library of the Graduate Theological Union." Berkeley, CA: Graduate Theological Union, 2002. http://library.gtu.edu/archives/history.html (retrieved September 12, 2006).

Graduate Theological Union (GTU). "About the GTU." 2006a. www.gtu.edu (retrieved September 18, 2006).

———. *The First Twenty Years: The Graduate Theological Union 1962–1982.* Berkeley, CA: Graduate Theological Union, 1982.

———. *Graduate Theological Union Archives.* Brochure of selected collections, n.d. (Available at the Flora Lamson Hewlett Library.)

———. "GTU Library." 2006b. www.gtu.edu/library-1 (retrieved September 12, 2006).

Helfand, H. *The Campus Guide: University of California, Berkeley; An Architectural Tour and Photographs.* New York: Princeton Architectural Press, 2002.

McTaggart, J. B. *The Evolution and Continuing Program of the Graduate Theological Union Library.* 1974. Unpublished paper.

Tyng, A. *Beginnings: Louis I. Kahn's Philosophy of Architecture.* New York: Wiley, 1984.

30

Main Library of the San Francisco Public Library

Library Data

Address: 100 Larkin Street, San Francisco, CA 94102
Phone: (415) 557-4400
Web site: www.sfpl.org
Square Feet: 376,000
Circulation: 2,169,770 (2005/2006)
Collection: 1,309,788* (2004/2005)
*This number includes cataloged items only; special collections and government documents are not included.
Sources for above: http://sfpl.lib.ca.us/librarylocations/main/buildmain.htm, and K. Strauss, personal correspondence, July 20, 2006

A small volume titled *My San Francisco* by Joseph Henry Jackson appeared in 1953. In this slim book, Jackson wrote: "The true lover of San Francisco can list a thousand sights, sounds, and smells that his mind holds in readiness to spring as a quick stabbing reminder to him, wherever he is, that San Francisco is his own city" (p. 39). The passion Jackson expressed for his city has appeared countless times in the poetry, music, art, and prose of many.

Known for its liberal atmosphere and beauty, San Francisco has long appealed to seekers and creative types. Several decades before *My San Francisco*, Dunn (1912) described the city as a place of "romance and destiny." He further proclaimed, "To cross the portals of the Golden Gate is to cross the threshold of Adventure" (p. 3). Busse's (1959) collection of sketches of the city includes the declaration: "San Francisco is both a community and a symbol, a place on the map and a dream in the minds of Americans" (n.p.). The declaration continued, "What San Francisco represents is perhaps a dream of a life that consists of more than business, a way of living that satisfies man's hunger for beauty, grace, culture, and civility" (n.p.). In *The San Francisco I Love*, Peterson (1970) found San Francisco to be "a shining, breathtaking and very self-conscious beauty of a city, sitting grandly on its splendid hills, swept clean by fog and wind, torn by love of its brief but heady past and the steady inroads of the twentieth century" (p. 13). What these excerpts reveal is that one will never be at a loss to find protestations of admiration for the city.

One of San Francisco's most palpable qualities is its diversity. There is diversity in the character of the many neighborhoods and in its citizenry. Many would agree that San Francisco is one of the best locations to participate in the art of people-watching.

The open expression, free spirit, and diversity of the city are not elements that can or should be contained, yet one place gives daily homage to the fascinating city: the Main Library of the San Francisco Public Library. The library mirrors the community it serves through a shared space that celebrates the city's rich cultural makeup. In the foreword to *A Free Library in This City: The Illustrated History of the San Francisco Public Library*, writer Isabel Allende (1996) describes the library as a place "full of presences" where "the air vibrates with memories, secret voices, and stories" (p. 8). She continues:

> Everything that has ever happened, is happening, or will happen in this city and its surroundings is contained between those walls, as if the library was a vault where the essence of San Francisco is preserved forever from the erosion of time and the dust of oblivion [p. 8].

It was in the final quarter of the 19th century that the library was born.

Library History

In 1877, residents of San Francisco met to discuss the establishment and funding of a public library. In 1879, the first library opened on the second floor of Pacific Hall on Bush Street. The library did not have borrowing privileges for several years, since there were so few books. Although the collection was small, however, the first library outgrew its space in a relatively short time. Nine years later in 1888, the library moved to Larkin Street where it was housed in a wing of City Hall (Wiley, 1996). In 1893, the library relocated to another wing of City Hall on McAllister Street. The devastating earthquake and fire of 1906 destroyed the library and its collection. By this point in the library's history, six branch libraries had opened. The earthquake also destroyed two branches. After the destruction, the library was housed in temporary quarters at Hayes and Franklin streets. Within seven years, the library reached its capacity and needed a new space. A new main library opened in 1917. By 1943, this building had also reached capacity. It was shortly after this date that several library advocacy groups formed and continued to appear throughout the decades (Wiley, 1996).

In 1949, concerned citizens formed the Friends of the San Francisco Library, which was a short-lived group. The Committee of Fifty, a group that included various cultural and business leaders was created by Mayor Christopher in 1959 to foster library support. This group was followed in 1960 by another citizens' group: San Franciscans for a Better Library and 1961 saw the founding of the citizens' San Francisco Library League (Wiley, 1996). In 1962, the San Francisco Library League, the Committee of Fifty, and San Franciscans for a Better Library joined together to form the new Friends of the San Francisco Public Library. Another group, Keep Libraries Alive!, was established in 1972 as a protest group to take on issues such as the closure of branch libraries. In 1974 the Library Commission, Keep Libraries Alive!, the Friends of the San Francisco Library, and other citizen groups fought to secure a new site for the library that had exceeded its capacity decades before. In 1986 another group, the Library Foundation of San Francisco, was established to also build support for a new building.

To secure funding for a new library, Proposition A was put on the ballot in 1988 to provide, if passed, $109.5 million to build a new main library and renovate branch libraries. An astounding 78 percent voted in favor of the proposition, allowing construction of the new library to begin within a few years. In 1992 a ground-breaking ceremony was held. The new library opened in 1996 (Wiley, 1996). Pei Cobb Freed & Partners of New York and Simon Martin-Vegue Winkelstein Moris of San Francisco were chosen as the architects. James Ingo Freed, who designed the library, also designed the Holocaust Museum in Washington, D.C. (Wiley, 2000). The old 1917 building was eventually transformed and reconfigured into the Asian Art Museum (Littlejohn, 2003).

A brief history of the library is included in Richards' (2002) *Historic Walks in San Francisco: 18 Trails through the City's Past*. Richards writes, "The main façade, with its silver stainless steel recessed columns and understated ornament, makes for a kind of postmodern updating of Classicism that blends well with its much older neighbors" (p. 51). Commenting on the interior, Wiley (1996) states, "Freed was encouraged to design a grand building, and indeed the building features a large central atrium and several multistory reading rooms wonderfully illuminated with natural light" (p. 215–16). Richards describes the opening of the library in 1996 as the event that brought "to completion the grand plan for the Civic Center" (p. 51) that was envisioned many decades before. On June 8, 2004, the library celebrated its 125th anniversary with a festival that included Chinese lion dancers, a high school jazz band, dancing acrobats, and, of course, a birthday cake (Zinko, 2004).

In order to create a library that reflected its users, several focus groups were established in late 1989 with members from the library staff and community. It is obvious from the interior spaces and collections of the library that the focus groups, 17 in all, were taken seriously. Wiley (1996) affirms that collections, including the Chinese and African American, "give the library its unique character." He continues, "These collections, more than any others, are a true guide to the singularities of the San Francisco community" (p. 213). Adding the various spaces within the library to the mix, the interior of the building is a place where one may get happily lost exploring for days or weeks.

BROWSING AREA, BOOKSTORE, AND CAFE

There are three areas in the library that will particularly appeal to those who like to linger. The first floor offers a browsing collection with science fiction, romance, fiction, audio books, compact discs, biographies, nonfiction, and videos. Within the space are express Internet stations and viewing/listening stations. The browsing collection is close to the Book Bay at the Main, a bookstore run by the Friends of the San Francisco Library. The store, which is located immediately after the Grove Street entrance, sells used and new books with many titles arranged by category. Sample categories include African American studies; women's studies; Asian studies; gay, lesbian, and transgender studies; history; and literature.

On the lower level, along with the Koret Auditorium, Jewett Gallery, and Latino/Hispanic Community Meeting Room is the Library Café. Similar to, but not quite as extensive as, the area at the Los Angeles County Main Library, the cafe serves not only snacks, coffee and other drinks, salads, and sandwiches, but hot meals, such as lasagna and burritos. Art is also present in the cafe. In the summer of 2006, a wall display case featured Remembering Persia, an exhibit of images of

The Main Library of the San Francisco Public Library offers several galleries and other exhibition areas, a cafe and bookstore, and diverse spaces that reflect the community it serves.

women and flowers. Following this exhibit, the cafe case featured the work of local artist Lea Rude under the title Seam. It is important to also note that the cafe is adjacent to the much larger Jewett Gallery, which is one of just many other places in the library that often features exhibits that reflect the history of San Francisco and the ethnic communities the library serves.

Galleries and Exhibition Areas

Exhibitions at the library are so rich in their diversity, display, and abundance that several books could be written just on the content of the past exhibitions. Titles of recent exhibitions illustrate the depth and a far-reaching scope: The Migrant Project: Contemporary California Farm Workers; Homage to Lulu: 100 Years of Louise Brooks, a celebration of the silent film star; The 40th Anniversary of the Polish Arts and Cultural Foundation Celebrating Polish Contributions to California History; and The World of Plant Patents.

One of the major exhibit areas is the Skylight Gallery on the uppermost sixth floor where it shares the floor with the library's administration, the Koshland San Francisco History Center, and the Stern Book Arts and Special Collections Center. The attractive display area is more than 2,200 square feet and can be reached via elevators or the interior grand staircase.

Another significant area is the 1,500 square foot Jewett Gallery located on the lower floor. This space is enclosed and "environmentally controlled for temperature and humidity to safeguard rare and valuable artwork and artifacts from the library's own collections, as well as those on loan from other institutions" (SFPL, 2006a). The gallery also holds exhibitions that accompany events taking place in the Koret Auditorium, which is close by on the same floor. Special presentations at the auditorium include poetry readings, author lectures, film screenings, and other events.

Hormel Center

The James C. Hormel Gay and Lesbian Center is a circular space located on the third floor. Hormel has a history of significant philanthropy, including a $600,000 donation to the American Civil Liberties Union and a $1.5 million donation to the School of Social Justice at Swathmore College. He made a $500,000 challenge grant to the Gay and Lesbian Center at the Library. Upon completion, the center was named for him. Hormel is the former dean at the University of Chicago Law School (SFPL, 2006d). He is also the first openly gay man to have served as a U.S. ambassador. In 1999, President Clinton used a rare executive privilege to appoint Hormel ambassador to Luxembourg (Seelye, 1999).

The center has been described as a "ceremonial space" (SFPL, 2005). It

The interior lines and patterns of the Main Library of the San Francisco Public Library give the library its unique sense of place.

provides archival collections, pulp paperbacks, magazines, newspapers, books, and other materials. The room features a circular ceiling mural created by Mark Evans and Charley Brown titled *Into the Light*. The artists used various techniques with rags, hands, and Q-tips to create the effects. The mural is described as "an allegorical construction site in which men, women, and children are working together to move from the darkness of ignorance into the light of knowledge" (SFPL, 2006b). The work includes names of prominent individuals throughout the ages who are known to have had same-sex relationships, including authors Colette, Gertrude Stein, Walt Whitman, Oscar Wilde, and Marcel Proust and various artists and philosophers, such as Frida Kahlo, Correggio, and Caravaggio. Evans and Brown selected the names from lists compiled by the Gay, Lesbian, Bisexual, and Transgendered Round Table of the American Library Association (formerly the Gay, Lesbian, and Bisexual Task Force) (SFPL, 2006b).

In early 2004, the center presented Reversing Vandalism, the largest exhibition to date by the library (SFPL, 2005). The exhibition was of vandalized books that librarians started to find within the stacks in early 2001 (Meyer, 2005). In all, 607 books were slashed by an individual who was eventually caught by a librarian and charged with felony vandalism and a hate crime (Van Derbeken,

2002). "Almost all of the slashed books focused on lesbian and gay culture, the AIDS crisis, or women's sexuality and self-representation" (Meyer, 2005, p. 33). Although nearly all of the books were vandalized beyond repair and had to be withdrawn from the collection, librarian Jim Van Buskirk and San Francisco book artist Sandra Ortiz-Taylor did not want the books to simply be destroyed, so they "put out a public call to artists and library employees to create works of art from the remains of the slashed books" (Meyer, 2005, p. 33). The project, which was conceived as a Bay Area response, ended up involving "almost one thousand amateur and professional artists from the United States, Europe, and Asia" (Meyer, 2005, p. 33), demonstrating how a public library can build a community far beyond its neighborhood.

Nearly 12,000 visitors came to see the exhibit which spanned beyond the Hormel Center's space (SFPL, 2005). Those involved created unique, inspiring, and thought-provoking work, turning the vandalized books into art. Artist Harmony Hammond created *Represent Women: A Primer* "in response to the damaged copy of Linda Nochlin's book *Representing Women*, a Marxist analysis of the representation of women in 19th-century French painting" (Hammond, 2006). She explains, "The back half of the book was missing—sliced off at the spine after page 160. It felt so violent. I felt I needed to reconstitute the book whole, to (re)present women and women's bodies whole again" (p. 19). Other pieces were Sherry Karver's birdlike *Blackbird Singing*, created from the vandalized book *Fighting Words, Personal Essays by Black Gay Men*, and F. Allen Sawyer's untitled work utilizing the vandalized copy of *Two Teenagers in Twenty: Writings by Gay and Lesbian Youth* that retained the S.F. Public Library stamp and call number (SFPL, 2005).

INTERNATIONAL CENTER

Another community space on the third floor is the Kresge Foundation International Center that provides materials in 40 languages (SFPL, 2006c). The center includes the Chinese Center and Filipino American Center. Writing in 1999, Manila stated, "As the new Main Library evolved to include centers representing the region's diverse ethnic and cultural groups, the Filipino American Community took the lead in building community-wide support to create a Filipino American Center" (p. 7). The International Center also provides yet more space for exhibitions, such as the recent photographic displays Life Around the Town of Pakil, Laguna, Philippines and China: The Soul of a Country, as well as exhibits featuring other cultures, including Sacred Walls: Paintings by the Women Artists of Mithila, India.

Fisher Children's Center

A quick tour around the children's area reveals another culturally diverse space. Located on the second floor, the area includes an international language section with books in Armenian, Chinese, Arabic, Bengali, Czech, Farsi, Croatian, and a number of other languages. On display in one area of the children's center during the summer of 2006 was a large collection of Harry Potter books in different languages. There is also a book display featuring staff favorites.

Other Spaces

This chapter would not be complete without mentioning some other unique spaces within the library. The fifth floor, which houses a periodical reading room also contains the Government Information Center and the Wallace Stegner Environmental Center, named after the Pulitzer Prize winner. In addition to the Skylight Gallery located on the sixth floor, the Stern Book Arts and Special Collections Center and Koshland San Francisco History Center are also found here. The Stern Collection includes such wonders as the 250 volume Sherlock Holmes Collection, the 1,500 volume James D. Phelan California Authors Collection, the Robert Frost Collection, and numerous others. The Koshland Center has many unique manuscript and archival collections, including the Hippies Collection, Italian American Collection, and others. Located on the third floor, the same floor as the International Center, is the African American Center. As with the other culturally focused spaces, visitors will find both materials and exhibitions. Demonstrating further the plethora of unique items, the African American Center, at the time of this writing, featured the following exhibitions: G.O.A.T.—Greatest of All Time: A Tribute to Muhammad Ali and Following the North Star: African American Quilts, a display of ten handmade quilts. When making plans to visit the Main Library of the San Francisco Public Library for the first time, one would be wise to devote at least an entire day.

References

Allende, I. Foreword to *A Free Library in This City: The Illustrated History of the San Francisco Public Library* by P. B. Wiley. San Francisco: Weldon Owen, 1996.
Busse, F. *San Francisco, City at the Golden Gate.* New York: Arts, 1959.
Dunn, A. *Care-free San Francisco.* San Francisco: Sunset Publishing House, 1912.
Hammond, H. "How to Change Vandalism into Art." *Gay and Lesbian Review* 13, no. 3 (2006): 19.
Jackson, J. H. *My San Francisco.* New York: Thomas Y. Crowell, 1953.
Littlejohn, D. "The Gallery: The Bay Area's Asian Art Checks into the Local Library." *Wall Street Journal,* May 1, 2003.

Manila, E. "The Filipino American Center." *Heritage* 13, no. 3 (1999): 7.
Meyer, R. "Slasher Story." *Art Journal* 64 (2005): 32–41.
Peterson, J. *The San Francisco I Love.* New York: Tudor, 1970.
Richards, R. *Historic Walks in San Francisco: 18 Trails through the City's Past.* San Francisco: Heritage House, 2002
San Francisco Public Library (SFPL). *Out at the Library: Celebrating the James C. Hormel Gay and Lesbian Center.* 2005.
_____. "Gallery, Jewett — Lower Level." 2006a. www.sfpl.org/librarylocations/main/jewett.htm (retrieved December 15, 2006).
_____. "Gay and Lesbian Center Mural." 2006b. www.sfpl.org/librarylocations/main/glc/glcmural.htm (retrieved December 5, 2006).
_____. "International Center." 2006c. www.sfpl.org/librarylocations/main/ic.htm (retrieved December 15, 2006).
_____. "James C. Hormel." 2006d. www.sfpl.org/librarylocations/main/glc/hormel.htm (retrieved December 5, 2006).
Seelye, K. Q. "Clinton Appoints Gay Man as Ambassador as Congress Is Away." *New York Times*, June 5, 1999.
Van Derbeken, J. "S.F. Gay-Book Slasher Put on Probation: Vandalism Charge also a Hate Crime." *San Francisco Chronicle*, September 19, 2002.
Wiley, P. B. *A Free Library in This City: The Illustrated History of the San Francisco Public Library.* San Francisco: Weldon Owen, 1996.
_____. *National Trust Guide: San Francisco: America's Guide for Architecture and History Travelers.* New York: Wiley, 2000.
Zinko, C. "Proclamations and Performances Mingle as Public Library Turns 125: A Lively Celebration at the Main Branch — Not Too Bookish. *San Francisco Chronicle*, June 8, 2004.

Part VIII
Northern California Coast

31

Mendocino Community Library

Library Data

Address: 10591 William Street, Mendocino, CA 95460
Phone: (707) 937-5773
Web site: This small community library does not have a Web site.
Square Feet: approximately 1,000
Circulation: 15,772 (estimated annual circulation figure based on circulation for a six-month period from March 2006 to August 2006)
Collection: 12,700 total cataloged items, not including audio books, puzzles, and other uncatalogued materials (October 2006)
Source for above: D. Driver, personal correspondence, October 16, 2006

The California Highway 1 Book (Adams and McCorkle, 1985) describes the main pathway along California's coast as a highway with a "make-believe character" and one "that distinguishes itself from other roads as romance divides from reality" (p. 12). The description continues with the dramatic statement that there is "always ... the air of the miraculous." One could argue that the miraculous, make-believe, and romantic character of Highway 1 reaches its pinnacle in the town of Mendocino. Not only is the drive up the coast to Mendocino from San Francisco astonishingly beautiful, but those who elect to reach Mendocino via Highway 128 will also find themselves on a magical journey down a two-lane road that passes through the vineyards of Anderson Valley and into the domain of majestic redwoods before arriving at the Pacific Ocean.

What traveling to Mendocino ultimately reveals is that all roads leading to it are wondrous. The city is equally impressive with numerous historic structures, a thriving artist colony, and narrow streets that lead to the beach. The Mendocino Community Library sits in the heart of the city. Similar to the journey to visit the Henry Miller Memorial Library at Big Sur, traveling to the Mendocino library is not an easy task for those with minimal experience driving on twisting, narrow roads, but the library is well worth the expedition.

Mendocino

The town of Mendocino is located in Mendocino County in between Fort Bragg to the north and Point Arena to the south. Mendocino was listed as a post office in 1858. "The houses and commercial buildings that make Mendocino of historic interest today were mostly designed by New Englanders" (Bear and Stebbins, 2000, p. 7). The Presbyterian Church of Mendocino (1868), the MacCallum house (1882), the Kelly House (1861), and the Elisha W. Blair house (1888) are just a few of the historic structures that line the streets and give Mendocino its distinctive appearance. No single architectural style was followed, but "inventiveness and experimentation were encouraged" (Bear and Stebbins, 1986, p. 20). Considering the town's beauty and unique character, it is no wonder that it has been a favorite of filmmakers.

More than 15 major movies have been filmed in Mendocino. Oscar winners filmed in the town include *Frenchman's Creek* (1943), *Johnny Belinda* (1947), *East of Eden* (1954), *The Russians Are Coming* (1965), and *The Summer of '42* (1970) (Adams and McCorkle, 1985). The fictional town of Cabot Cove from the television series *Murder, She Wrote* is actually Mendocino. The historic Blair House, that served as Jessica Fletcher's residence in the series, is a short walk down the street from the Mendocino Community Library.

Mendocino is also a town with a thriving art culture. A free publication, *Mendocino Arts*, that presents the artistic nature of the area through gallery listings and features on artists is available at many locations along the coastline. The publication is made available by the Mendocino Art Center, "an educational, exhibition, and resource center for the visual and performing arts" that was established in 1959 (Mendocino Art Center, n.d.). Similar to the historic Blair House, the art center is also located just a short stroll down the street from the library, illustrating the splendid neighborhood where the library is found.

Library History

What is now the Mendocino Community Library was started in 1947 by members of a local women's studies club. Helen F. Thomsen was the librarian for many years. Over the decades, the library went through various incarnations until it became a nonprofit organization in the mid–1980s. It has been run solely by generous community volunteers since its establishment nearly 60 years ago. Volunteers, who currently number approximately 65, normally work two three-hour shifts per month (D. Driver, personal correspondence, October 16, 2006).

The library is not a free public service, but one that offers memberships for families, individuals, and students at the corresponding annual rates of $15.00, $8.00, and $2.00. Since the library receives no government funding, it is supported by memberships, book sales, donations, and gifts. As of October 16,

The Mendocino Community Library is located along the northern coast in Mendocino, a town with a thriving art culture. Since its establishment nearly 60 years ago, the library has been operated solely by volunteers.

2006, the library had 550 members from Mendocino and the surrounding communities of Point Arena, Westport, Boonville, and others (D. Driver, personal correspondence, October 16, 2006).

The structure that now houses the library is a converted yellow house that was donated to the library by a former volunteer approximately 15 years ago. Those unfamiliar with the library may drive or walk by and assume they are passing a residence, unless they notice the small sign designating the building as a library. The building shares in the city's film industry history; an exterior shot of the supposed bordello in *East of Eden* is actually the library when it was still a home (D. Driver, personal correspondence, October 16, 2006). The nooks and crannies of the interior of the former residence add to the character of the library.

ENTRANCE AND CIRCULATION DESK

A few steps lead to the library's front door. Immediately inside the entrance is a small room that opens in several directions to other areas of the library. It is possible that this space may have been a foyer in the original residence. The circulation desk is located immediately to the left of the entrance and an administrative area for volunteers is to the right. This small room has shelves full of the library's video collection and new fiction and nonfiction books. Videos also line the shelves behind the circulation desk, demonstrating how nearly every bit of space in the room is used for displaying the library collection.

FICTION AND NONFICTION ROOMS AND HALLWAY

To the left of the small entrance room is a fiction room that also has the one computer available for visitors to search the library catalog. This room also leads to a small, narrow nook that continues the fiction collection. Immediately in front of the entrance room is the Helen F. Thomsen Room of nonfiction and reference. In the center of the room is a round table with six chairs. During my visit to the library in October 2006, several local periodicals were spread out on the table for one's perusal. A small reference nook is located on one side of the room. The nonfiction collection continues down a slim hallway and into another room. This second room of nonfiction also includes an assortment of free magazines.

STUDY CLUB ROOM

Another narrow hallway joins the second nonfiction room to the final space in the library: the Study Club Room. This hallway has shelves with juvenile books on one side and jigsaw puzzles on the other. Offering a puzzle collection is quite

31. Mendocino Community Library

The Mendocino Community Library is located in a converted yellow house that was donated to the library by a former volunteer.

unique. Although the puzzles do not circulate as much as other materials, 180 were checked out during the latest 12 month period.

The Study Club Room, or the back room, is the largest space in the library. It was not part of the original house, but was added on by the library (D. Driver, personal correspondence, October 16, 2006). The walls of the room are lined with bookshelves. The first area is a children's space with a child-size round table and chairs. Another table in the children's area has books organized on top of it. A shelf divides the children's area from the larger part of the room. In the larger space is a conference table where meetings are held. A door along one wall leads to a closet that serves as a tiny mending workroom. The bookshelves are primarily taken up by mysteries and westerns. There is also a small rack of paperbacks for sale, as well as one area of the shelves reserved for sale items. Books on tape and periodicals are located on the far wall.

Unless one was permitted to walk through the administrative area of the library after completing a visit to the back room, one would need to continue the path back to the front through the two narrow hallways and other rooms to reach the exit and circulation area. Although the interior of the building is clearly a library, the experience of walking around within it does feel like being inside a home. The Mendocino Community Library is a labyrinth of welcoming spaces.

REFERENCES

Adams, R., and L. McCorkle. *The California Highway 1 Book: An Odology of America's Most Romantic Road.* New York: Ballantine, 1985.
Bear, D., and B. Stebbins. *Mendocino.* Mendocino, CA: Mendocino Historical Research, 1986.
_____. *A Tour of Mendocino: Thirty-Two Historic Buildings along the Streets of Mendocino.* Mendocino, CA: Bored Feet Press, 1991.
Mendocino Art Center. "About the Mendocino Art Center." n.d. www.mendocinoartcenter.org/level2/about.lasso (retrieved October 23, 2006).

32

Coast Community Library

LIBRARY DATA

Address: 225 Main Street, Point Arena, CA 95468
Phone: (707) 882-3114
Web site: www.co.mendocino.ca.us/library/coast.htm
Square Feet: 5,800
Circulation: not available at time of inquiry
Collection: 17,130 total materials (July 2006)
Source: T. Black, personal correspondence, July 6, 2006

One can walk the length of the downtown area of Point Arena in a matter of minutes. The 130-mile journey to this small city from San Francisco may take well over three hours, due to hairpin turns and cliffhanging views along Highway 1. Once one is an hour outside of San Francisco, the terrain of the highway becomes a mixture of long, inhabited stretches on a two-lane road, spectacular ocean views, and occasional small towns, often with populations in the low hundreds or less. So small are some of the towns that drivers may quickly come upon them and pass on within a few seconds. This rugged area of the coast is prime territory for nature lovers, artists, and those who seek a California that is far removed from the busy cities to the South.

A destination spot for some travelers in this region is the Point Arena Lighthouse. Many sections of the rugged northern California coast have a history of shipwrecks. Point Arena is no exception. In their book, *The Early Days of Point Arena*, Oliff and Carlstedt (2005) provide a list of the many marine disasters to hit the Mendocino Coast between 1854 and 1956, including a wreck north of Point Arena in 1915 where nine lives were lost. Due to the number of shipwrecks, the federal government issued an executive order on June 8, 1866, to construct a lighthouse at Point Arena. The devastating 1906 San Francisco earthquake caused damage to Point Arena, including considerable damage to the lighthouse that required the structure be demolished and rebuilt. The second lighthouse that was completed in 1908 still stands today.

The Point Arena Lighthouse is not the only reason, however, to visit the small city. Unlike some of the shopping districts and rich-looking residences found in other

California coastal towns, Point Arena has a character that is equally down-to-earth, simple, and free-spirited. The city is home to such individuals as Lauren Sinnot, a painter, seamstress, and creator of the company ArtGoddess. A brightly painted car with a personalized "GODDESS" license plate can be found parked along Main Street in front of ArtGoddess. Point Arena is the home of *SageWoman* magazine, a periodical devoted to "celebrating the goddess in every woman." Point Arena is also a community of people who have displayed love and dedication to their library.

The Coast Community Library shares the block with Think Visual Gallery, the Arena Pharmacy, Franny's Cup and Saucer Bakery, and Everything Under the Sun, a store selling third world and local crafts. Point Arena City Art Gallery and a movie theater are located across the street. The theater, complete with an Art Deco façade and old-fashioned ticket kiosk, screens two movies most nights (McHugh, 2005). The library, appropriately located in the heart of the small city, is a reflection of its community.

Library History

The need for a public library in Point Arena was first brought to the community's attention by a group of individuals during the annual Fourth of July parade in 1989. Shortly after, on July 21, 1989, nine citizens met at St. Paul's Methodist Church and founded the Friends of Coast Community Library (Presentation, 2006). The library was first housed at the Methodist church. Opening on November 5, 1989, the collection consisted of three boxes of donated books. In less than two years, the library moved to a small building at 280 Main Street (Presentation, 2006). A myriad of fundraising events were hosted by the Friends over the years, including golf tournaments, bake and book sales, garden tours, and murder mystery theater dinners.

Geniella (2003) reports that the group collected hundreds of thousands of dollars, enabling the library to relocate into larger quarters. In May 2003, the Friends purchased the historic Gillmore Store at 225 Main Street that had closed for business. When it was operational, the store sold a wide array of products from groceries to farming equipment. The building was beautifully renovated under the direction of architect Richard Perkins (Presentation, 2006). Volunteers, including the local Rotary Club, worked on the year-long project. In addition to countless hours donated by community members, a single donor provided the new library with $45,000 of furniture.

A clear demonstration of the residents' support of the library occurred before opening day with the formation of a "book worm." Beginning at the old library building, people formed a human chain down and across the street to move the books, hand-by-hand and side-by-side, to the new location. On November 5, 2004, the new library opened.

Volunteers remain an instrumental part of the library's operation. Not only do they donate their time, but they manage and run various services and develop programs. The library also has a quarterly newsletter, the handsome and well-written *Redwood Coast Review*, which is published in cooperation with the *Independent Coast Observer* of nearby Gualala. The newsletter features essays, reviews, fiction, and poetry, as well as "Book Box," a listing of recent arrivals at the library.

Main Room

The entrance to the Coast Community Library leads to the main space of the library where the majority of the collection is held and most activity takes place. Although the library is relatively small, the interior of the room is designed so well that it feels spacious. Significant room is available in and around the furniture, including two generous pathways that run up and down in the middle of the room. A ceiling with four vaulted skylights adds greatly to the feeling of expanse.

Immediately inside the door is a centrally located circulation desk. Behind the desk is an original wood and glass case that was part of the former mercantile store. Several items are on display in the case, including a historic ledger from the store.

Books and audio-visual materials run the length of nearly an entire side of the library. New additions are arranged first and followed in order by nonfiction, audio-visual items, biography, and fiction. Young adult, Spanish, and oversize books are found across the room on the other side near a bank of computers. A $25,000 grant from a local software company, XIDAK, provided the library with six public access computers (Presentation, 2006).

Several areas for individuals or groups to sit are found down the center of the library. A round table with a chess and checkers board is located behind the circulation desk. This table is followed by a rectangular table situated next to a display of books and magazines for sale. A similar table is on the other side of the sale display. Near the back of the library, one will find a reading space next to the periodicals. Located here are several gray, cushioned chairs. Each chair has a red pillow with white trim. A final place to sit, another round table, is located in the adjacent reference area in one of the library's far corners. These ample seating options should satisfy almost any visitor's desires.

Children's Room

To the left upon entry to the library is the children's room. Furniture in the space includes two tables, pillows, a rocking chair, and a cushioned chair. The room is decorated by a large mural created by several artists and titled "Oh the Places You'll Go." The mural, sponsored by the Rural Murals Project, an after-school program for Mendocino County youth, and other groups, was dedicated on June 24, 2004. In the center is a figure of a boy reading. Around the

The interior of the small Coast Community Library in Point Arena is designed so well that it feels spacious.

boy, displayed in vibrant colors, are animals and magical creatures from children's books. The mural runs nearly the entire length of the wall.

Community Room

Across from the children's room and to the right upon entry to the library is the community room. Found here is a conference table, podium, small sink, and cabinet. In addition to chairs around the table, some chairs also line the perimeter of the room. Any nonprofit group can use the community room by making a deposit of $25.00. In addition to group-related events, book sales are held in the room (A. Woodward, personal correspondence, October 16, 2006).

Ties to Building History

The library has retained several items from the old mercantile store. Many objects are displayed on the top of the bookshelves, including cans, crates, and baskets that once held Ghirardelli Chocolate. The reading area near the periodicals has two unique features from the days of the general store: a large pot-bellied stove and an old safe. These objects not only add character to the space but they also tie the library building to its historical roots.

REFERENCES

Geniella, M. "Library Dream Nears Reality: Point Arena Volunteers Raised $300,000 to Buy, Convert Abandoned Store." *Press Democrat*, June 19, 2003.

McHugh, P. "The North Coast: A Kayak Adventure, Self-Reliant Hamlet." *San Francisco Chronicle*, October 5, 2005.

Presentation to the Mendocino County Board of Supervisors. June 18, 2006. Document provided by Coast Community Library.

Oliff, S., and C. Carlstedt. *The Early Days of Point Arena*. Point Arena, CA: Olyoptics, 2005.

Index

A.K. Smiley Public Library 17–24; children's room 21–22; history 18–19; interior spaces 20–23; lawn and entrance 19–20
Allende, Isabel 231
art in libraries 54, 62–63, 94–96, 126–128, 131–132, 153, 162–163, 177, 185–186, 204, 220, 233–237
Austin, Mary 200, 205

Bachelard, Gaston 8
Bassett Memorial Library 174–179; art 177; history 175–176; interior spaces 176–177, 179; outdoor deck 179
Beale Memorial Library 157–163; art 162–163; atrium 161–162; children's room 161; history 158–159; interior spaces 159–163; maps 162; special collections 162
Beauvoir, Simone de 216
Bede Griffiths Collection 226
Berkeley, city of 215–217
Big Sur, city of 191–192
bookstores and book sales in libraries 33, 85–86, 171–172, 233
Bradbury, Ray 5–6
Brand Library & Art Center 91–96; art 94–96; history 92–93; interior spaces 93–96; music collection 94; programs 96

cafes in libraries 61, 108, 123, 183, 233–234
California State University, Fullerton: history 79–80
Campbell, Joseph 145–148
Campbell, Robert 202–203
Cardiff-by-the-Sea, city of 31
Cardiff-by-the-Sea Public Library 31–35; bookstore 33; children's room 33–34; displays 34; history 32; interior spaces 33–34; programs 32–33
Carmel, city of 199–200
Carnegie buildings 151, 165, 208–209

Central Valley region 157–158
Cerritos Library 97–105; children's room 101; computers 101–102; displays 104–105; history 98–99; interior spaces 100–105; reading room 100; young adult room 100–101
Chapman University: history of 58
Charles Franklin Doe Memorial Library and Gardner Stacks, University of California, Berkeley 1, 5, 215–222; art 220; displays 220–221; history 217–218; reading rooms 218–219; stacks 219
children's rooms 21–22, 28, 33–34, 40, 101, 161, 171–172, 204, 210, 237, 246, 249–250
Claremont, city of 134–135
Coast Community Library 247–251; children's room 249–250; community room 250; history 248–249; interior spaces 249–251
Corona del Mar, city of 49

Daisaku and Kaneko Ikeda Library, Soka University 66–71; history 67–68; interior spaces 68–70; outdoor spaces 70; reading room 70
Del Mar, city of 25
Del Mar Public Library 25–30; children's room 28; entrance 28; history 25–26; interior spaces 28–29; library wall 27; terrace reading room 28
Didion, Joan 157
displays in libraries 34, 44–45, 52, 81, 104–105, 115, 170–171, 220–221, 228

events *see* programs in libraries
exhibits *see* displays in libraries

Fisher, Muriel 45
Flora Lamson Hewlett Library, Graduate Theological Union 223–229; archives 226; displays 228; history 224–225; interior spaces 226–228; study spaces 228
Freed, James Ingo 232
Freeman, Jo 216–217
Fullerton, city of 78–79
Fullerton Public Library 1

Genthe, Arnold 200
Gimbutas, Marija 146–148
Ginsberg, Allen 216–217
Golden Hill (San Diego) 42
Graduate Theological Union, history of 223–224

Hall, Manly P. 129, 132
Harrison Memorial Library 199–206; art 204; balcony 202; garden 201; history 200–201; reading room 202; reference room 202
Helen Hawkins Memorial Library and Research Archive, Women's History Museum and Educational Center 42–46; displays 44–45; entrance 43; gift shop 44; history 43; interior spaces 44–46
Henry Miller Memorial Library 5, 191–198; archives 198; history 192, 194; interior spaces 197; outdoor spaces 195–197; programs 195; visitors 194
Hillman, James 147
Hormel, James C. 234–235
Howard, John Galen 217–218

Jeffers, Robinson 192, 199–200
Johnson, David 186
Joseph Campbell & Marija Gimbutas Library, Pacifica Graduate Institute 143–149; collections 145–147; garden 147; interior spaces 148–149
Julian, city of 36–37
Julian Public Library 5, 36–41; children's room 40; entrance 39; history 37, 39; interior spaces 39–40; programs 40–41; young adult room 40

253

Index

Kahn, Louis I. 225, 228
Kerouac, Jack 192, 216
Kingston, Maxine Hong 157, 215

Leatherby Libraries, Chapman University 8, 57–65; art 62–63; exterior spaces 60; history 58, 60; interior spaces 61–65; rotunda 61
Levine, Philip 157
Lincoln Shrine 23
local history rooms 204–205
Los Angeles Public Library, Central Library of the 119–128; art 126–128; cafe 123; gardens 122–123; history 120, 122; interior spaces 123–128; library store 123; programs 125–126; young adult room 124

Mariposa County 168–169
Mariposa County Library 168–173; book sale 169–170; children's room 171–172; displays 170–171; entrance 169; history 169; interior spaces 170–172; patio 172
Maybeck, Bernard 200, 202
Mendocino, city of 242
Mendocino Community Library 241–246; children's room 246; history 242, 244; interior spaces 244–246
Miller, Henry 192, 194, 205
Moore, Thomas 9
Muir, John 158, 165, 174–175

Neruda, Pablo 8
Nin, Anaïs 194

Oldenburg, Ray 10–11
Orange, city of 57–58

Pacific Grove, city of 207
Pacific Grove Public Library 207–211; children's room 210–211; history 208; interior spaces 209
Pacifica Graduate Institute 143, 145
Park Branch Library 199–201, 204–206; children's room 204; history 201; local history room 204–205

Pasadena, city of 106–107
Pasadena Public Library, Central Library of 106–112; history 107–108; interior spaces 109–112; outdoor spaces 108–109
Paulina June and George Pollak Library, California State University, Fullerton 78–87; archives 84–85; book sale 85–86; displays 81; history 80–81; interior spaces 81–86
Philosophical Research Society 129–130
Philosophical Research Society Library 129–133; art 131–132; entrance 131; history 130–131; interior spaces 131–133; reading room 131–132
Point Arena, city of 247–248
Point Arena Lighthouse 247
programs in libraries 32, 40–41, 55, 96, 125–126, 138–139, 185, 195

Rancho Santa Ana Botanic Garden Research Library 134–139; garden 135–137; interior spaces 137–138; programs 138–139
reading rooms 28, 53–54, 70, 100, 131–132, 153, 183–184, 202, 218–219
Redlands, city of 17–18
Reed, Ishmael 215

San Francisco, city of 230–231
San Francisco Public Library, Main Library of the 230–238; art 233–237; bookstore 233; cafe 233–234; children's room 237; history 231–232; International Center 236; James C. Hormel Gay and Lesbian Center 234–235
Santa Barbara, city of 150–151
Santa Barbara Public Library, Central Library of the 150–154; art 153; entrance 151; history 151; interior spaces 151–154; reading rooms 153
Sherman Library & Gardens 49–56; archives 54–55; art 54; displays 52; entrance 52; gardens 50, 51; history 49–50;
interior spaces 52; maps 55; programs 55; reading room 53–54
Silverado Canyon 72–74
Silverado Library 72–77; history 74; interior spaces 75; library cat 75–77
Soka University, history of 66–67
Soto, Gary 166
Spicer, Jack 216
Steinbeck, John 157, 207
Sterling, George 200
sustainable library buildings 32, 182

teen rooms *see* young adult rooms
"third places" 10–11

University of California, Berkeley, history of 217
University of California, Merced, history of 181–183
UC Merced Library 180–187; art 185–186; cafe 183; history 183; programs 185; reading rooms 183–184; technology 184–185

Visalia, city of 164–165
Visalia City Library 164–167; history 165; interior spaces 166–167; local history room 166–167

Watkins, Carleton 162–163
Watts, Allen 148
Wawona (Yosemite National Park) 174 175
Wheelwright, Jane Hollister 147
Wheelwright, Joseph 147
Whitman, Walt 9
Writers Guild Foundation Shavelson-Webb Library 113–118; displays 115; interior spaces 115–118; mission 114–115
Writers Guild of America, West 113–114

Yosemite National Park 168–169, 171, 174–175, 177–179
young adult rooms 40, 100–101, 124